Also by Elizabeth Letts

Family Planning

Quality of Care

The Eighty-Dollar Champion

Ballantine Books | New York

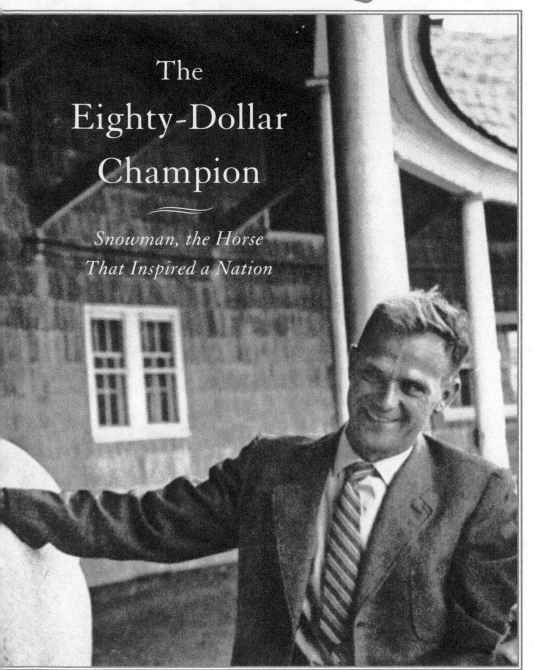

The Eighty-Dollar Champion

*Snowman, the Horse
That Inspired a Nation*

ELIZABETH LETTS

Copyright © 2011 by Elizabeth Letts

Published in the United States by Ballantine Books,
an imprint of The Random House Publishing Group,
a division of Random House, Inc., New York.

BALLANTINE and colophon are registered trademarks
of Random House, Inc.

The illustration credits are located on pages 327–329.

Library of Congress Cataloging-in-Publication Data
Letts, Elizabeth.
The Eighty-Dollar Champion : Snowman, the horse that inspired
a nation / Elizabeth Letts.
p.   cm.
Summary: "The Eighty-Dollar Champion tells the dramatic
odyssey of a horse called Snowman, saved from the
slaughterhouse by a young Dutch farmer named Harry.
Together, Harry and Snowman went on to become America's
show-jumping champions, winning first prize in Madison Square
Garden. Set in the mid to late 1950s, this book captures the
can-do spirit of a Cold War immigrant who believed—
and triumphed"—Provided by publisher.
Includes bibliographical references and index.
ISBN 978-0-345-52108-8
eBook ISBN 978-0-345-52110-1
1. Snowman (Horse)   2. Show jumpers (Horses)—United
States—Biography.   3. Show horses—United States—
Biography.   I. Title.
SF295.565.S66L48 2011
798.2'5079—dc22   2010050993

Printed in the United States of America on acid-free paper

www.ballantinebooks.com

6 8 9 7 5

Book design by Virginia Norey

This book is dedicated to Harry and his family

and to the memory of the gallant horse Snowman

So many of our dreams at first seem impossible,

then they seem improbable, and then, when we

summon the will, they soon become inevitable.

—CHRISTOPHER REEVE

Contents

Prologue

A Night in the Spotlight

Madison Square Garden, New York, November 1958

The horse vans parked along Seventh Avenue came loaded up with dreams. As each ramp banged to the ground, a groom held tight to a high-strung horse whose nostrils flared at the unexpected scents of midtown Manhattan. Hooves clattered down onto hard asphalt. Steam rose from beneath thick woolen blankets. Photographers' cameras flashed. Anxious tweed-clad owners called instructions from a distance while grooms murmured into their four-legged charges' ears. Police in brass-buttoned coats lined up abreast to hold back gawkers. Grays and chestnuts, palominos and bays—the most pampered show horses in the world—were gathered here for the premier equestrian event of the year: the National Horse Show at Madison Square Garden.

A compact, sandy-haired man stood in the crowd of horse handlers, holding a slack lead rope. His horse, a big gray gelding, looked like a workaday police horse or a Central Park hack. Nervous thoroughbreds and finicky hackney ponies scrambled up the walkway to the stables, spooked by the unfamiliar clatter of their footsteps on the ramp. But when the big gray's turn came, he walked up willingly, ears forward, perfectly calm. Above the simple canvas blanket that covered his body, his head and neck glowed in the murky Manhattan light.

Inside the basement stables, grooms blacked boots and rubbed French leather bridles to a shine. Horses pawed and stamped. The riders, nowhere in sight, were back at their hotels primping for the parties and balls. Down at the end of a row, past much fancier stables, the gray's owner, Harry de Leyer, held a four-tined pitchfork; he was spreading fresh straw in the stall, settling in his one-horse stable for the night. Tacked on the stall door was a sign hand-lettered by his children: SNOWMAN.

Madison Square Garden, the largest indoor venue in the country, would fill to the rafters for eight consecutive nights. Down at ring-side, swells in top hats and tails would pop champagne corks. Up in the cheap seats, near the smoke-filled ceiling, families would strain to catch glimpses of the gleaming horses and their elegant owners. In the lobby, reporters from *Vogue*, the *New Yorker*, the *Herald Tribune*, and the *World American* would mill about, flashbulbs popping as they caught sight of dignitaries in the crowd. Outside of Hollywood, it was hard to find this much glamour under one roof.

Once, a ragtag band of competitors had traveled the show circuit with just one or two horses—farmers and old cowboys who cobbled to-gether a living from prize money and odd jobs, such as leather repair or horseshoeing. But by 1958, big money had entered the arena and those old-timers were a dying breed. Now expensive horses and the best train-ers vied for the crown jewel, the open jumper championships, in argu-ably the most rarefied atmosphere in the country. How could Harry and his eighty-dollar former plow horse hope to compete? It was the lon-gest of long shots, but Harry—who had fled ravaged postwar Europe with only a few simple possessions—had never been afraid to dream big dreams.

The Eighty-Dollar Champion

I

The Kills

New Holland, Pennsylvania, 1956

The largest horse auction east of the Mississippi was held every Monday deep in Pennsylvania Amish Country. Anyone with the time to drive out to Lancaster County, Pennsylvania, and a good eye for a horse could find a decent mount at a reasonable price, especially if he arrived early.

The New Holland auction was founded in 1900 and hadn't changed much since. Farmers and their families drove to the auction in their buggies. Wives gossiped while children played and enjoyed the festive atmosphere. Vendors sold hot pretzels and sugared *fasnacht* doughnuts. Farmers gathered on benches around the sides of the big covered arena while the auctioneer called out the merits of the horses. Each prospective purchase trotted across the ring just once. The auctioneer had a habit of saying, "*Yessiree,* this horse is sound."

Horses arrived at the auction from near and far—the racetracks at Pimlico and Delaware Park unloaded thoroughbreds that were too slow to race. Trainers with sharp eyes and generous budgets scouted them out as show prospects. Farmers brought plow horses that could no longer plow; riding stable owners sold decent horses to raise quick cash. Sadly, many of the horses for sale arrived here only after having exchanged hands one too many times: they were good enough, but past their prime—tired hunters, outgrown ponies, shopworn show horses.

Among these sturdy, well-trained hacks, Harry hoped to find a quiet lesson horse for his riding pupils at the Knox School.

For all of their size and strength, horses are surprisingly fragile creatures. Bearing tremendous weight on their slender legs, they are subject to all manner of lameness—bone spavins, pricked feet, broken knees, corns. Some have faults of confirmation that put unnecessary strain on their legs. Some have been ill used—jumped too much or ridden too hard.

A smart salesman knows how to camouflage some of these faults; he can hold a lead rope tight to hide the bobbing head of a lame horse. He can bandage to reduce swelling or mix a painkiller into the horse's bran mash. Most common of all, he can hope that in the blur of a fast trot across an auction ring, a potential buyer will be swayed by flashy coloring or a nicely set head, and overlook any flaws.

But Harry knew horses. He had confidence in his judgment. With a budget of only eighty dollars, he knew the thoroughbreds would be out of his reach. Even the slow ones sold in the hundreds, if not the thousands. But with his keen eye, Harry believed he could spot an older horse who was well trained and reasonably priced.

On a typical day outside the auction grounds, teams of horses still hitched to their buggies would be tied up alongside cars with out-of-state license plates. Big racetrack vans flanked two-horse trailers owned by hopeful backyard buyers.

By the end of the auction, two to three hundred horses would have been trotted through the arena, looked over, bid upon, and sold. For some horses, the transaction would be their salvation—a dud on the racetrack snatched up to be groomed as a horse show star. For others, it was a step down—a retired show horse might be sold as a lesson horse. At the end of every auction, there were always a few that found no buyers: the ones whose lameness couldn't be masked, the sour-tempered ones who lashed out with hooves and teeth, the broken-down ones who stumbled their way into the ring.

But no horse left New Holland unsold.

The same man always made the final bid: the kill buyer. He purchased horses for the slaughterhouse so that their carcasses could be ground up for dog food and their hooves boiled down into glue.

The auction lasted only three or four hours, a testament to how quickly the horseflesh would move through the arena. At the end of the morning the Amish farmers would clamber back into their buggies, the race vans would head back to the track, and the new horse owners would coax their horses into trailers and go home.

No one would be left on the grounds but the kill buyer, loading up the last of the horses to take to the slaughterhouse.

That Monday, in February 1956, Harry de Leyer was running late. The headlights didn't work on his beat-up old station wagon—not surprising, since he'd paid only twenty-five dollars for it. A new car, for close to fifteen hundred dollars, would have been far beyond the Dutch immigrant's modest budget. Although he had arisen long before dawn on this wintry morning, the snow and a flat tire had set him back.

By the time Harry finally arrived at the auction, the grounds were deserted and there were no horses to be seen. After the long drive down from New York, now he'd have nothing to show for it.

Only one vehicle remained, a battered old truck with slatted sides, more cattle car than horse van. A bunch of horses, fifteen or so, were crowded in its back. A rough man dressed in a barn jacket and dungarees was just closing up the ramp.

Unwilling to give up after his long drive, Harry leaned out his car window and called to him.

The man seemed as though he didn't want to be bothered. "Nothing left but the kills," he said.

Harry got out of his car, walked over, and peered through the vehicle's slatted sides. It was a cold day, and the horses' breath made steam rise up in the air. Anyone who has ever had the misfortune of seeing a horse bound for slaughter will attest that the animals seem to sense when they are hitting the end of the road. Sometimes, horses react with fear, feet scrambling for purchase on bare wooden floors, metal shoes clanging against the van's sides. Other times, they just look haunted, as if they know where they are headed.

A pit formed in Harry's stomach. He would never be able to think of a horse as a collection of body parts to be turned into horsehide, dog food, and glue. Back in Holland, old horses past their prime were put out to pasture. His father had taught him that a horse who had served man deserved to live out his days in peace.

Could none of these horses still serve some useful purpose? He peered into the truck's gloomy interior. In a proper horse van, horses travel in padded stalls, their legs bandaged in thick cotton batting, with fresh hay suspended within reach. But this van offered nothing like that. More than a dozen horses were packed together on the bare metal floor, fenced in by rough slats that did nothing to protect them from the elements or from one another. Harry could smell fear rising up from them; the sound of hooves striking metal was almost deafening, and in the shadowy interior he saw flashes of white in their eyes.

But one of the horses stood quietly, crammed up against the truck's side, seeming to pay no mind to the chaos around him. Between the slats, Harry saw large brown eyes. When he reached out his palm, the horse stuck his nose toward him. Harry saw one eye looking at him. Asking.

"What about that one?" Harry asked.

The man was already loaded up and ready to drive away. "You don't want that one. He's missing a shoe and his front is all cut up from pulling a harness."

"I just want to take a look," Harry said.

Knackers generally paid sixty dollars a head. Was Harry prepared to pay more than that?

Harry hesitated, then nodded. The horse was still watching him.

Grudgingly, the man backed him out of the trailer. Scrambling down the steep ramp, the horse almost fell, but then righted himself.

Once the animal was off the trailer, Harry got a better picture, and it wasn't a pretty one.

The big horse was male, a gelding, as Harry had expected. His coat, the dull white color that horsemen call gray, was matted and caked with mud. Open wounds marred both knees. His hooves were grown out and cracked, and a shoe was missing. The horse was thin, but not completely undernourished—not as bad off as the horses normally seen on a killer van. The marks across his chest showed that he'd pulled a heavy harness. He had a deep chest; Harry noticed the strong gaskins and well-muscled shoulders, probably developed by pulling a plow. The man dropped the rope on the ground, but the horse made no move to run.

His teeth showed that he was "aged"—not younger than eight years old, and quite possibly older. Harry scanned his legs—pasterns, fet-locks, cannons, hocks—and found no obvious flaws. The auction roster sometimes read like an illustrated veterinary primer: bowed tendons, bone spavins, strangles, laminitis, swaybacks, broken wind—a compendium of ways that a horse can be lame, contagious, or otherwise unfit. But this horse had no such ailments: he was just undernourished, beat up, and broken down, an ordinary horse who had hit hard times.

The unfamiliar setting of an auction made most horses jittery, but this one seemed calm. He followed Harry with his eyes, and when Harry spoke a few words to him, he pricked his ears forward: they were small and well formed, curving inward at the tips.

Purebred horses are bred for looks and certain characteristics—thoroughbreds for speed, Arabians for their dished faces and high-set tails, Tennessee walking horses for a gait so smooth that a rider can carry a wine glass without spilling a drop. A horse's ears are an indicator of refinement. Harry took a harder look at the horse underneath the caked-up dirt.

This gelding, even cleaned up and well fed, would never be beautiful. He was as plain-faced and friendly as a favorite mutt—wide-eyed and eager to please, a man's-best-friend kind of horse.

The horse stretched out his neck and blew a soft greeting.

Harry reached out, sorry that he had nothing to offer but the palm of his hand.

Despite his sorry condition, a spark of life lit up the gray's eyes. He had a strong body that would fill out with proper care. Any horseman can recognize an animal whose spirit has been broken, from the listless head and dull eyes, the slack lips and shuffling gait. But this horse was not broken—he had an air of self-possession. All he needed was someone to care for him. Harry was sure that if he was given affection, this horse would return it in abundance.

But Harry knew he couldn't be that person. The de Leyers counted every penny. There was no room in his life for whims.

"You want him or not?"

Making it in the equestrian business meant being hard-hearted. For every prospect that might become a riding horse, a dozen nags were too old, too lame, or too ornery to stand a chance. Common sense told

Harry he should cut his losses, keep his cash in his pocket, and head home.

The slaughter truck yawned open behind them. The horses were scrambling against each other; a few more minutes and a fight might break out. One sign from Harry and the truck driver would lead the big gray back up that ramp. The story would end quickly. First, a cold, crowded, terrifying ride. Then the short, brutal end: a captive bolt through his head. The thought made Harry flinch.

Back in Harry's village in Holland, the day when the Nazi soldiers had led the horses away, the villagers had stood with their hands clenched at their sides, trying to hide the tears in their eyes.

Harry knew what it felt like to be powerless.

Beat up or not, this horse seemed brave: Harry noted the quiet way he stood there, the gaze that said he was ready to trust. Horses are herd animals. They smell fear, and sense danger. But this horse held out hope; he seemed to put his trust in a strange man, even though it was clear that, thus far, men had treated him poorly.

The horse stood motionless, square on all four, looking straight at Harry.

"How much you want for him?" Harry asked.

The man said again that he would bring sixty dollars for dog food. Harry felt his resolve melting under the horse's steady gaze.

He repeated his question. "How much you want for him?"

The man grinned broadly, probably thinking he stood a chance to make a buck on this guy. "You can have him for eighty."

Harry averted his eyes, fingering the rolled-up bills in his pocket. He could buy a lot of meals for his family for eighty dollars, a lot of bales of hay and sacks of grain for the horses. It was hard to imagine facing his wife with his money spent and nothing but this broken-down ex–plow horse to show for it.

Hadn't Harry gotten over being a sucker for horses?

But there was something about this horse. Harry turned back and the horse was still watching him intently: he was wise, an old soul, a horse whose steady demeanor seemed to cover hidden depths.

Man or beast, Harry did not like to see a proud soul held in captivity.

"Might make a lesson horse, if we can fatten him up," Harry said.

He handed over the eighty dollars and never looked back.

2

On the Way Home

St. James, Long Island, 1956

E ighty dollars poorer, Harry had made a deal. Now it was time to hit the long road home. The truck driver was heading back to New York anyway—to the rendering plant up in Northport, not far from St. James. The eighty-dollar price tag included ten dollars to drop the horse at Harry's barn. Ten dollars in the pocket for the butcher's driver was enough incentive to spare the horse's life. Nothing left for Harry but the long drive back through the snow in his beat-up Ford. On the front seat of the car lay the flashlight he used when the headlights went on the blink. Maybe he could make good time and get home to his family before nightfall.

As he drove, Harry pondered his purchase. A horse for sale is more than a flesh-and-blood animal; he is also an embodiment of a promise. Along with his physical attributes—coat color, four legs, a strong back, a facial expression—he also carries hope: that he will be strong and brave, faithful and true. For a man in the horse business, a horse is a financial transaction as well. A good buy made a safe lesson horse; a better one made a profitable resale. Harry fell in love from time to time along the way—an occupational hazard. He considered himself sensible, though he also had to admit that he seldom met a horse he did not like.

Leaving New Holland, Harry navigated his way around black carriages pulled by Amish teams that reminded him of home; the simple farms, the horse-drawn wagons harked back to St. Oedenrode, the village he had grown up in, before it had been ravaged by the Second World War. His route back to Long Island took him along the Philadelphia and Lancaster Turnpike. Now a modern highway, the turnpike was first built for heavy six-horse coaches pulled by sturdy Pennsylvania Conestoga horses. In horse-and-wagon days, New York City and its suburbs had one of the highest equine populations in the country, and eastern Pennsylvania was home to the farms where these workhorses were bred. Harry was only the latest in a long succession of men who had taken this route in search of a good horse.

But the farther Harry got from Pennsylvania, the more the world around him changed, as if the road itself mirrored his own journey, just six years earlier, from a small Dutch farm to America. When he and his wife had arrived from their village, Harry possessed little more than a strong back and a gift for horses. Now he lived only fifty miles from New York City, the biggest metropolis on earth.

The smooth asphalt surfaces and long stop-free expanses of the modern New Jersey Turnpike, opened in 1952, had made the trip shorter, but the big American cars, decked out with chrome and fins, zoomed along the new interstate, opening up more and more farmland to housing, bringing along the suburban shopping centers, drive-in movies, supermarkets, and motels, all of which catered to the new driving lifestyles. The cars themselves looked futuristic: studded with portholes that brought to mind rockets and other signs of modernity. Nineteen fifty-six was a catastrophically bad year for the automotive industry. The venerable Packard automobile company merged with Studebaker and then closed its Detroit plant, laying off hundreds of workers. Detroit was poised for the worst recession since the war, and unemployment in the city would soon rise above 20 percent. But it was clear that the age of the automobile was here to stay. The country's economic troubles didn't affect Harry that much. He and Johanna had lived on a strict budget since the day they'd arrived in America. As Harry drove up the new freeway in his beat-up old car, what he saw around him was a land of opportunity.

After making his way through New York City, Harry started the long trek across Long Island, past the subdivisions that seemed to be springing up in every cornfield, each house a matching box on a postage-stamp-sized lot. A couple of hours later, he reached Suffolk

County, where the gray waters of Long Island Sound faded seamlessly into the patchy, sandy soil where farmers grew potatoes. Harry breathed easier as he left behind the noise and confusion of the city and its new suburbs. St. James, where he was headed, was a peaceful hamlet on Long Island's North Shore. The area around St. James had some huge estates: the department store magnate Marshall Field had a home there, as did the Barrymores, the famous film star family; it was a summer retreat for rich New Yorkers. But there were also small farmers and tradesmen who worked on the big estates—and some hardworking immigrants like himself. It was a good place to raise a family.

Harry got home before the horse trailer. It was snowing hard as he pulled into the driveway, but their big three-story farmhouse on Moriches Road was lit up and looked welcoming. Harry's job as a riding instructor at the Knox School had brought the de Leyer family something they could have only dreamed of before: their own home. Sure, it was a converted chicken farm on a modest lot. Harry had single-handedly rebuilt the chicken coop into a stable with six box stalls, twelve standing stalls, and barely enough room for a small paddock. It was too small for a proper horse establishment, but at least he had his own piece of ground. He'd proudly christened it Hollandia Farms, after his homeland. As he turned off the ignition, the car shuddered to a stop. It felt good to have a place to call home. After a moment, Johanna and the children rushed out the door to greet him.

Johanna worried when Harry made these long drives down to Pennsylvania in the winter. It was a five-hour trip, at least, even when the weather was good. Just a few months earlier, Harry had been hauling four horses in the big horse van on the highway when he'd had a freak accident. A man had flicked a lit cigarette out of his car window and it had landed inside Harry's horse van, lighting the straw inside on fire. From the cab of the van, Harry could not see the smoke. Another car drove up next to him, its driver waving frantically. Harry steered the van off the road into a ditch and saw thick black smoke pouring out of the tack compartment of the trailer. Just then, a police car pulled up. The noise of the horses' hooves against the side of the truck was deafening. Harry didn't have a moment to spare. He climbed through the burning truck to untie the safety knots that secured the horses and got them out onto the grassy highway shoulder—not a moment too soon. In a flash, the entire truck ignited in flames. The policeman was impressed by Harry's quick action in the face of danger, but Harry shrugged it off. He had seen burning vehicles before—he had lived through the huge Allied offensive Operation Market-Garden, where charred trucks had littered a road that became known as Hell's Highway. It would take more than a fire in a horse van to shake Harry. The horses were okay, a new van was procured, and they continued on their way. But since then, Johanna had worried even more.

This time, in spite of the snow, Harry made it home with no problems. Later that evening, the knacker's truck pulled into the de Leyer driveway. The driver had stopped at Northport first, unloading the unlucky horses into the cramped pen where they would be held crowded together on this bleak winter night, awaiting their sad fate.

Only one horse remained on the truck, and as it rattled into the driveway that night, the weary beast could have looked through the vehicle's slatted sides at the lights of the house. He would have seen the people come out, in spite of the cold, to greet his arrival. Every sight, every smell, every sound was unfamiliar.

The family stood in the front yard, waiting. The beat-up, nearly empty open truck looked like no place for a horse, especially on a frigid night like this. The burly driver untied the horse's rope and put the ramp down, then tugged on his tail.

The big gray stumbled as he clambered down, then stood blinking in the light glowing from the windows of the house. At first, nobody said a word. Harry had already forgotten what a sorry state this animal was in—scrawny and underfed, covered with sores, his unkempt mane matted. Even at night, he could see the dark stains, the knocked-up knees and harness rubs.

But when the giant creature turned his head and caught Harry's eye, he felt it again—that sense of connection.

Harry's three towheaded children were lined up in a row, bundled up in jackets and boots. Johanna was carrying the youngest, Marty, in her arms. They looked the horse over carefully, saying nothing.

The gray stood still, ears pricked forward, eager as a puppy wanting to be adopted from the pound. Snow drifted down, leaving a dusting across his broad haunches.

The piping voice of Harriet, age four, chimed out through the silence, clear as a bell:

"Look, Daddy, he has snow all over him. He looks just like a snowman."

Yes, the other children agreed, a snowman.

Green stains from sleeping in his own manure marred his coat, making it hard to imagine that he would ever clean up or ever look anything but dingy. But the children did not see the stains or the shaggy mane. They didn't notice the untended hooves or the missing shoe. To them, the horse was a white and gleaming wonder. A snowman. That soon became his official name.

It was a hopeful beginning.

Harry grasped the lead rope and Snowman followed along quietly, as though he knew he was home. The big old knacker's truck rattled out of the driveway and away. Nobody knew if the gelding had any idea of his close brush with death, but he went calmly into a stall and started munching on hay without so much as a skittish look around. Harry had given him one of the box stalls, knowing the horse needed to move and stretch his legs after the long, hard ride in the crowded truck. Now he filled the stall with straw, even adding a little extra to make the bed soft. Before he went back into the house, he slipped off his wooden shoes, leaving them by the door, then turned to look back at the quiet stable. This horse would clean up just fine, and he would be useful. The de Leyer family had just grown by one.

In the de Leyer household, everyone did everything together, so a new horse in the barn was a project for the whole family. The first order of business was to nurse Snowman back to health. It took several sudsings from top to toe to get him clean. The coat that emerged from under the filth was the color horsemen call "flea-bitten" gray: white with small brown flecks. Harry pulled his mane, trimmed his whiskers, and called the farrier to replace his missing shoe. Joseph, whose nickname was Chef, and Harriet were assigned the job of currying him—using a hard comb to bring up dander and get rid of dead hair so that his coat underneath started to shine. The gray was quiet for grooming and his barn manners were excellent, as if he knew that he had come to a place where he would be cared for. He was good-sized, with the strong muscles of a workhorse, and, though thin, he was not completely wasted. With a new diet of fresh hay and plump oats, he filled out quickly, laying down flesh over his ribs and covering his bony hips. He'd never win a beauty contest, but after a short time in the de Leyer barn, Snowman lost the neglected look and started to resemble an animal who was loved.

Harry and Snowman in the field near the stable on a winter day.

After a few days of rest and food, Harry decided it was time to see what the big horse could do. He slipped an old bridle over his ears and a rubber bit into his mouth and started by ground-driving him on a long rein, walking behind him. Snowman's coat still showed rubbed-off places—the traces of a harness collar. As best Harry could tell, he had been used for harrowing and cultivating, but never as a riding horse. Accustomed to driving a straight line, the horse had no idea how to turn, and he wavered like a drunken sailor. Harry persisted, firm but patient. The bit he had chosen, a rubber D-ring snaffle, was soft on the horse's mouth. But Harry, with the wiry body of a lifelong farmer, knew how to put just the right amount of pressure on the reins. Snowman wove and stumbled, confused to find a man behind him instead of a plow, and puzzled when he was asked to turn in a tight arc—pulling a plow requires few sharp moves. Harry, however, sensed right away that this was a horse who wanted to cooperate, so he continued the way he always persisted with his charges: gently but with confidence.

Once the horse seemed to have gotten the hang of steering, Harry put a saddle on his back, carefully settling it on top of a thick folded woolen blanket. He cinched up the girth around the horse's broad barrel. At first, Snowman's sides twitched, bothered by the unfamiliar feeling, and he turned and bit at the saddle flap as though it were a fly settling on him; but, perhaps dulled by years of pulling a heavy burden, he did not put up a fight. Harry placed a hand on the horse's shoulder to steady him, then walked a few steps. There he stopped to tighten the girth again, then moved a few more steps forward. To reward the horse, Harry fished down into a pocket for a stub of carrot and let the gray lip it up from the palm of his hand. Then he reached up and scratched him above his withers. Snowman arched his neck out and curled up his lip, baring his teeth.

"He's laughing," one of the children said. Harry laughed, too. When he scratched the same spot a second time, Snowy laughed again.

The horse was starting to trust him, and Harry knew from experience that once a horse trusted you, he would soon become your ally.

The next challenge was to get on his back. Snowman was docile around people, but an old plow horse might have never carried a rider. For most horses, the first response to a man settling on its back is to try to unseat the rider by any means possible—the same instinct that fuels the rodeo sport of bronco riding. How was a horse to know that the weight of a man on his back was not a mountain lion? In the wild, predators jump onto a horse's back in order to access the jugular vein. A horse defends himself by trying to throw the predator off, then using his greatest asset, his speed, to leave his foe behind.

Harry led Snowman next to a mounting block, then gently leaned his weight over the horse. He waited—five, ten, fifteen seconds—then took his weight away. This old plow plug did not have the energy to put up a protest. But Harry knew that even a quiet horse could be unpredictable when mounted.

It was time to find out.

With the grace of a cat, Harry swung up into the saddle and landed gently in the seat, his body tightly coiled, ready to stick out a bucking fit or, as a last-ditch resort, to bail off and roll away from the path of flailing hooves.

His touch in the saddle was light; he held himself carefully balanced. The horse danced a jig, first to one side, then the other. Harry waited, poised. The initial few moments were always the hardest.

Snowy's back felt tense underneath him. Uncertain. Harry settled his seat bones deeper into the saddle. He clucked, using the command that he had taught the horse meant "go forward." The gray's ear flicked back, listening.

Harry and Snowman out riding. Snowman proved to be a quiet and steady mount.

After a moment's hesitation, Harry felt Snowman's back relax, accepting his presence. He nudged with his heels and the horse started off at a plodding walk, apparently already resigned to bearing another load. Harry responded with an immediate signal of trust. He let the reins slide out between his fingers, almost all the way to the buckle that joined the two pieces. If the gelding startled and took off now, Harry would have no way to stop him. Snowman responded to that trust by stretching his neck out, lowering his head. Harry gave him a pat on the shoulder and spoke a word of praise, and one of Snowy's well-formed ears flicked back again.

Harry relaxed into the saddle. His slaughterhouse reject would make a good pleasure horse for someone—maybe one of his timid riders at the Knox School. Snowman was a nice big horse with a broad back. He could easily carry one of the bigger girls.

Over the next few weeks, as Harry rode Snowman in the ring and around the countryside, the horse proved steady and sure-footed. His preferred pace was the walk, and he had to be coaxed even into a dull trot. Snowman was like an old teddy bear. As he continued to fatten up, filling out his ribs and bony haunches, his soft, broad back was perfect for a child to climb on bareback.

Every morning, as soon as Harry came out to the barn, Snowman blasted out three loud whinnies. Always exactly three. Harry had to chuckle—on the old chicken farm, Snowy had taken on the role of family rooster.

After three weeks, the last of the manure stains had faded from his coat and a nice speckled pattern had emerged. His mane had been detangled and pulled to a reasonable length. His tail was silky. Harry thought he looked respectable enough to fit in at the stable at the Knox School. As a trial, Harry put one of his own kids up on the horse's back. The gray plodded gently around the ring, the rein out to the buckle while Harry walked alongside.

With so little money to spend on horses, Harry tended to get hotheads that were touchy and difficult to handle, racetrack refugees and skittish beauties that needed a calming hand. But the big gray horse was more like an old mutt. Harry thought about keeping Snowman around for his kids, but he had paid good money for this horse, and now Snowy needed to start earning his keep.

By the beginning of March, Harry knew the horse was ready to move to the school. He was as nervous as a proud father taking his son to football practice. He wanted Snowman to make a good first impression.

3

Land of Clover

C lean, trimmed, and with his mane and tail glossy, Snowman may not have looked quite like a gentleman, but at least now he resembled a presentable tradesman. His wounds had healed, his ribs had filled out, and his coat glowed from constant currying.

Harry hacked the five miles from the de Leyer farm down to the school, guiding Snowy at a pleasant pace across open fields and skirting the Ryan estate, enjoying the gray's steady manner in open country. The land around St. James was hilly and wooded. Up near Harry's farm, there were other small farms and modest houses, many of them owned by immigrants. He passed the St. James General Store, an old wooden building that sold candy and sundries. As the trails led closer to the water, the atmosphere changed. Here, big stone gateways led to huge estates. The country lanes were quiet, but if a car passed, it was likely to be a Bentley with someone's chauffeur at the wheel. Before long, Harry caught sight of the gates that marked the entrance to the school. Seagulls swooped overhead, and the shingled water tower stood out against the blue sky.

Harry led the horse through the arched entrance into the school's grand stable, which was prominently set just inside the front gates. Knox did not even look like a school. Tucked onto a spit of land between Stony Brook Harbor and Long Island Sound, its huge brick Georgian house, stables, and grounds resembled a wealthy tycoon's country manor.

Ja, Harry remembered how he had felt the first time he set foot on the grounds of Knox, strangled by the unfamiliar necktie and bashful about his broken English. Maybe blazing bullets in wartime and Nazi troopers stomping through his village had taught Harry to be brave, but his interview at the Knox School—*that* had been a nerve-racking experience.

Inside the stable courtyard, Harry gave Snowman a pat on the neck and fished down into his pocket for a carrot. He could understand how the big horse must feel.

It is hard to imagine a place more serene than the setting of the Knox School. Gentle meadows ringed by dogwood trees flowed into wooded countryside crisscrossed by sandy trails. Off in the distance, down a peb-bled lane, the mullioned windows of the manor house glittered as light glinted up off the water that lapped the campus's edge. Here and there, girls in uniforms walked back and forth in twos and threes—lucky girls who were being educated in a manner befitting their backgrounds. It was a scene of entitled privilege.

Built for a United States senator, the estate was named Land of Clover, its manor house constructed of weathered brick imported from Virginia and its outbuildings including a grooms' cottage, a trainer's cottage, a henhouse, a caretaker's house, and a piggery. But the senator's family had fallen on hard times during the Great Depression and run out of money, finally putting the whole place up for sale in the late 1930s. Even in an economy still crippled by unemployment, the property sold for the astronomical sum of $100,000 to the La Rosa family, Italian-Americans who had made their fortune selling spaghetti with a pink rose on the box, made famous by radio pitchman Arthur Godfrey.

The gray-shingled stable was shaped like a horseshoe, its courtyard wide enough to accommodate the large carriages that had once graced the estate. Around the perimeter, stalls with green-and-white double Dutch doors faced inward onto a covered track. When the school had still been a private manor, Mr. La Rosa used to stand in the center with a long bullwhip and watch his fine hackney ponies go around him in a circle. When he cracked the whip, the ponies would stop on a dime, then turn around and circle the other way. The horseshoe-shaped stable

Riding lessons in the courtyard of the horseshoe-shaped stable at Knox.

at Land of Clover would eventually be declared a historic landmark, but now, in 1956, it was the gray plow horse's new home.

Harry settled Snowman into one of the empty stalls, loaded up with fresh straw. The horse would like this stable—with its semicircular shape, the animals could see one another, as well as any activity in the courtyard, from any of the stalls. Snowman was a social animal; he liked to be around people and other horses. The girls of the Knox School might be to the manner born, but out at the stable, around the horses, they relaxed and turned friendly and happy, just like other kids. Harry thought the old teddy bear would like his new home.

The former Land of Clover was not the only large estate in the area. St. James's gingerbread train depot had been one of the first stops built on the Long Island Rail Road, giving the area easy proximity to New York City. Around the turn of the twentieth century, prominent and wealthy New Yorkers had built grand estates ringing Long Island Sound. The famed society architect Stanford White, of the architectural firm McKim, Mead and White, had built a house for himself there, then designed a number of other large mansions surrounded by elaborate gardens and grounds. With their demand for servants, groundskeepers, and farms to supply them, the estates drove the local economy.

Constructed during boom times, these wedding-cake constructions that lined the North Shore encompassed libraries, grand ballrooms, and dining rooms that could seat scores at formal dinners—but by the 1950s, the old WASP fortunes, built around shipping and mercantilism, were fading. Estates once kept running by a cadre of servants had become too large to be maintained by a single family. Many were being shuttered, the properties broken up and sold for development.

Land of Clover had the good fortune to be spared intact when the mansion and grounds were purchased for use as a school for girls. Laced with scenic trails winding through piney woods that opened to reveal the gray waters of the sound, it was the ideal site for young girls who liked to ride horses. In this remote and sheltered place, the girls were educated in a splendid isolation, their lesson horses housed in a stable designed for rich people's leisure.

In his eight years on earth, Snowman had pulled a plow, suffered neglect, and been given up for dog meat, then adopted by the de Leyers, nursed back to health, and turned into a riding horse. As he gazed out over the courtyard from his new digs, a roomy box stall in the grand stable of Land of Clover, the horse must have been struck by a sense of improbable wonder at his good fortune.

4

An Ordinary Farm Chunk

Lancaster County, Pennsylvania, 1947 or 1948

I n 1950, there were still six million horses in America, or one for every
twenty-five people. By 1960, that number had declined by half. During that decade, the last family farms were mechanized, tractors replac-
ing the plows that until then had tilled the smaller fields. The reduction
of the equine population, which had begun in the 1920s, accelerated
rapidly after World War II, declining from east to west, with the numbers dropping fastest along the eastern seaboard, except in specialized
pockets, such as Amish Country, where horses were used because of
religious and cultural preference. Some of the decline came by natural
attrition—by the 1950s, the horse population was aging, with many old
workhorses retired. Breeding of workhorses had also declined significantly, and along with it, the veterinary profession was shrinking so rapidly as to be in crisis: programs in veterinary medicine were closing their
doors, and some journalists even predicted the demise of the entire profession. Farmland that had once been used to grow horse feed was being
converted to other crops, creating surpluses that were one of the underlying elements in the severe drop in farm prices during the Depression,
and again after World War II. As demand for horses dropped, farmers
also lost income from breeding them, which had once provided a good
source of additional cash. But even with reduced breeding and an aging
population, by midcentury there was still an excess of horses—unwanted
animals that were expensive to keep and care for.

In 1900, the value of all the horses and mules in the country exceeded that of all the cattle, sheep, goats, and hogs put together. States in the Mississippi Valley and the East tended to import horses—they produced only a small number of the horses that they needed. The rest were bred in the West, then shipped eastward through established distribution points. Starting after the Civil War, St. Louis, Kansas City, Chicago, and Memphis had developed large horse markets. Different regions were known for different kinds of horses: draft horses were typically bred in the Midwest and the Northwest; most lighter-boned saddle horses were bred in the Southwest, as were the mules that powered the cotton economy of the Deep South. Horse dealers frequented auctions specializing in different categories. Some handled the massive and valuable draft horses. Others sold general "farm chunks," all-around horses that could be used to pull lighter loads, such as smaller plows and wagons. Still others made their fortunes in the carriage trade, selling fine saddle or carriage horses that were kept for personal use and pleasure riding.

By the middle of the twentieth century, there were many more sellers than buyers. Ben K. Green, in his reminiscence *Horse Tradin'*, talks about tractor dealers in the late 1940s whose backlots contained pens for the horses and mules the tractor dealers had taken in on trade. "Great big broad-hipped, good kind of sound, beautiful-headed, heavy-bodied Percheron and other draft-type horses weren't much in demand," Green writes. "Every tractor trader had a penful of them somewhere around the edge of every little town, and they were hard to sell." There were too many horses. The big auctions served as a whittling-down point. Camps, dude ranches, and riding academies bought some of these horses for the summer, then off-loaded them at season's end. A 1956 article in *Horse Magazine* described the fate of these horses: "In the fall, many of these unfortunate creatures, cow-hipped and sore-backed, are trucked off by the killers." Tens of thousands of horses, many of whom might have been perfectly useful if given proper care, found no buyers and ended up at the slaughterhouse.

While the precise number of horses who were slaughtered in the 1950s is not known, the fact that three million horses disappeared from the American landscape at midcentury is well documented. In the 1970s, the horse population rebounded to about seven million, where it has stayed steady since. However, virtually all of those horses are now pleasure horses, many of them specialty breeds. The draft horse and the fine carriage horse have also lived on in the hobby markets. It is the general "farm chunk," the average horse—the crossbred, lighter-boned grade horse—that has all but disappeared. Some died of old age, some were retired to pastures, and many undoubtedly ended up in a dog food can on a supermarket shelf.

The horses in the killer pen were mostly anonymous. A few might be marked with a brand, showing that they had started life on a western ranch. Every registered thoroughbred had its unique number tattooed on the inside of its lip. But most horses were ordinary, and the marks and traces they bore were those of hardship—scarred hides, rheumy eyes, cracked and curling unshod hooves.

Snowman brought no story except the one inscribed on his body: the cups in his back molars told that he was nearing nine; the cuts on his knees signaled some kind of accident. Across his broad chest, the hair was rubbed away—signs of being yoked to a burden. The green manure stains, the matted tail, and the unclipped legs and muzzle indicated ne-glect. The missing shoe and thin frame hinted toward an owner who'd refused to invest money in an unwanted horse.

But beneath all of these superficial marks, this horse still carried the story of his bloodlines, the broad chest and strong cannons perhaps originating in the elegant Percherons of France. Even better hidden, in his small, well-set ears and the proud look—often described as "the look of eagles"—in his eyes, he carried the mark of a thoroughbred, and bloodlines that could be traced all the way back through England to the Godolphin Arabian and the desert sands of Morocco.

By best guess, Snowman had been born in 1948—a grand year for the American thoroughbred. In horse racing, Citation triumphed as the eighth winner of the Triple Crown, thrilling a country that was newly cheerful after the war's end.

That year also marked the return of the summer Olympic Games, after a hiatus during the conflict. On opening day in London's Wembley Stadium, the British track star Lord Burghley said the London games represented a "warm flame of hope for a better understanding in the world which has burned so low." After 1948, the equestrian competition would no longer be an all-military sport; that year's team may have been the best one the United States had ever fielded. America's Major Earl Thompson won an individual gold medal, and the United States brought home the team silver in dressage, the demanding equestrian sport sometimes called "horse dancing," which was normally ruled by the Europeans.

After the war, hundreds of German-bred broodmares and stallions had been brought to America as spoils of war. Europe and, especially, Germany had dominated equestrian competitions for most of the twentieth century. Their horses were perhaps the finest in the world. But the American Jockey Club refused to certify German stallions as "thoroughbreds," reluctant to incorporate the horses into the American line, even though their ancestry had been meticulously documented by the Germans. The Jockey Club's officers' justification for this refusal was that they would have to take assurance of the horses' bloodlines from "the enemy." The American thoroughbred horse, proud and noble, beautiful and homebred, had become a symbol of the country's new postwar pride.

At that time, most thoroughbred stallions were kept on manicured stud farms, primarily located in the bluegrass region of Kentucky. The stud fees were high, and the horses were part of the horse-racing pipeline, the bloodlines carefully watched over to produce superior racing stock. Some small and very specialized breeding operations bred saddle horses for hunter and jumper competitions—these tended to be small-scale operations owned by wealthy private breeders who kept one or two horses at stud.

Despite the declining use for workhorses in the twentieth century, historically the United States had long been proud of its equine product. The rangeland of the western states had always been an excellent environment in which to breed horses. Through the late nineteenth century, domestic horse production had been so high that in addition to supplying workhorses for the large eastern cities and remounts for the U.S. cavalry, the western states had been the world's top producer of military horses, eventually becoming the breeding ground for horses used in European wars. Prior to the First World War, most of the countries in Europe imported horses. For example, in 1899, the United States exported nearly 100,000 mounts to the United Kingdom for use in the Boer War. But with the advent of the motorcar, after 1910 the horse population in the United States began dwindling rapidly, provoking widespread concern that the army would not find enough horses to muster in time of war.

Horse scarcity was a genuine national security concern. Wartime consumption of horses was astronomical: it's approximated that more than 1.3 million horses were pressed into service by Allied forces between 1914 and 1918. Of these, many were fatally injured in battle, and even more were lost to equine infectious diseases, which ran rampant as horses were transported via ship and train in difficult conditions. In wartime, horses were so expendable that the demand was insatiable and the supply difficult to maintain.

To address the concern about the declining horse population, in 1912 the U.S. Army established the Remount Program, a systematic horse-breeding operation for the cavalry. Its goal was to improve the general stock of American horses for use in war. (The term "remount," used to describe a cavalry horse, actually stems from the need to re-supply soldiers with *fresh* horses.) The program selected stallions that were considered the best type of the American horse, sometimes described as a "usin' kind of horse." Appropriate for riding, the horses were bred to be well balanced, with well-sprung ribs and a deep heart girth to provide plenty of lung capacity, a well-developed set of withers to hold the saddle in place, legs of sufficient bone to stay sound, and a foot large enough to provide a solid foundation. In addition, the horses' temperament was a factor, with emphasis given to "a gentle disposition and a willing mind." These excellent stallions "would be made available at a nominal fee" to improve the quality of American stock. The United States cavalry, the mounted force of the U.S. Army, needed a supply of quality horses to be ready during times of war.

In the 1920s, '30s, and '40s, as mechanization increased, domestic consumption of horses continued to plummet. The number of civilian buyers declined, so that by 1940 the U.S. Army became the largest single purchaser of horses. At that time, the army paid about two hundred dollars for a well-bred gelding, or about one-fifth of the price of a new automobile.

Remount stallions were dispersed throughout the country and bred to "certified mares"—broodmares who had been deemed healthy and suitable to participate in the program. The stud fee was a mere ten dollars and the product of these matings belonged to the owner of the mare, with the understanding that the army would have the first opportunity to bid. As the market for workhorses declined with each progressive decade, large-scale western horse-breeding operations were funded largely by sales to the army.

But the Second World War, the first fully mechanized war, was the end of the line for the army's role in horse breeding. The army procured tens of thousands of horses in 1940 and 1941, stockpiling them in the remount stations. Only times had changed. Battles could now be fought without horses, and by 1942 and 1943 the army was already dismounting its units and selling off the excess horses. After the war, in 1948, the army's Remount Program was disbanded. The remount stallions, bred specifically to be the best of their type, were distributed across the country and put into private hands, their services now available to the casual or backyard breeder.

The general quality of American horses was greatly improved by the Remount Program, but remount stallions were not the only reason for this. Throughout the nineteenth century, while exporting remount horses to Europe, farmers had also been importing the great European draft breeds—Percherons, Belgians, and shires—to develop the American workhorse. The great draft horses were also crossbred, producing offspring that were lighter than their giant forebears, easier to manage, and less expensive to feed and keep. Thus, the typical grade horse—one without a pedigree or a specific breed, the kind that might have shown up at the auction in New Holland in the 1950s—might have had strong and gallant bloodlines hidden beneath its plain exterior. It might have carried the blood of draft horses bred for strength to cultivate fields, of thoroughbreds honed for speed to win at racecourses, and of warrior horses prized for their sturdy physiques and gentle, courageous temperaments.

By the time Harry bought Snowman, in 1956, time had erased the exact details of the horse's birthplace and parentage. No one remembered the big gray gelding with the harness scars and the peaceful look in his eye. No one emerged later to claim credit for him. Most likely, he'd been bred and born and suckled down a country lane somewhere, in a big white Amish barn, on the straw-filled bed of a foaling stall. What happened after that is pure speculation.

On Amish farms as elsewhere, horses stay with their mothers as sucklings until they are about six months old. At that age, a foal is weaned. Separated from their broodmares, weanlings are still small and relatively easy to handle. A weanling learns to be handled by people—first growing accustomed to a person's touch, next to a halter, and, eventually, to a bridle and bit.

Yearlings are generally put out to pasture with other agemates, and spend that second year at freedom and play. But when a horse turns two, his training for a life of work begins. Amish handlers first train a horse to voice commands: *ho* for stop, *easy* for slow down, and *break* to change pace.

Once a horse understands the commands, he is broken to harness— first to the yoke around the neck, then to the bridle and reins, and last to the harness shafts. Each step takes patience, as the handler teaches the horse to accept the equipment without putting up a fight. After that, the training starts in earnest. The farmer follows behind the horse, on a twelve-foot line, practicing simple walking, stopping, and turning. Eventually, the farmer ties a big rubber tractor tire to the end of a rope and lets the horse get used to pulling it behind him. By the time a horse has reached his third year, he should be trained to work, although he does not reach his full potential until age five.

With good care, a modern pleasure horse can often be ridden well into his twenties, and often lives to thirty or forty years old. But this was not true in the era when horses were used as beasts of burden. The traditional American workhorse's useful life was short—averaging five years, from ages five to ten. Up until age five, a horse was fed and nurtured for the prospect of sale. After age ten, its career was finished. Once it could no longer work it was put up for sale or destroyed.

A commodity, bred for its economic usefulness, the horse used to be considered a "living machine" rather than a sentient being. As the horse illustrator C. W. Anderson once said, "Many people have sighed for the 'good old days' and regretted the 'passing of the horse,' but today, when only those who like horses own them, it is a far better time for horses." When horses were seen as primarily a means of locomotion, little sentimentality was attached to them. A horse that could no longer work was a horse that could be—and usually was—discarded.

A variety of ailments could cause that day to come sooner; the most common was lameness, followed by equine infectious diseases and accidents. Horses collided with other horse-drawn conveyances and with motor vehicles; they slipped on ice; they spooked and shied and ran away, entangling themselves in their harnesses, farm equipment, or the horses with which they were yoked together.

Horses were generally sold in teams. Most people preferred horses of the same color, wrongly believing that color reflected a level of underlying similarity. A team also needed to be matched in size, strength, and temperament. As herd animals, horses developed strong preferences. Used to being hitched with a stablemate, a horse might become balky or nervous if asked to go out with an unfamiliar partner. Any horse that was part of a team would lose most of its value if something happened to the teammate. But every horse, even a dead horse, had value.

In the nineteenth century, when a horse died on the street it was simply left where it fell until an enterprising butcher came to cart the carcass away. Photographs of urban street scenes from the nineteenth and early twentieth centuries show children playing in the street, seemingly oblivious to the nearby hulk of a dead horse.

Horses that did not die in the street were normally euthanized. The rendering plant was a necessary and economically vital part of the horse economy. Horses that were sick, lame, or just too old to work were shipped to the cannery, where they were killed with a bullet or a captive bolt to the head. In a midcentury veterinary manual, above the matter-of-fact caption "Where to shoot a horse," a photograph shows a horse with a white mark on his forehead, indicating the best spot to place the gun. After death, the carcasses of horses were rendered. Due to cultural preferences, horsemeat was not typically consumed in the United States, although during World War II there was an attempt to promote horsemeat consumption to help alleviate wartime shortages of beef. A graphic picture from *Life* magazine in 1943 showed horse carcasses hanging on hooks as butchers stripped their hides; on a facing page, smiling customers purchased government-inspected horsemeat from a butcher shop disconcertingly named the Man o' War. More often, horsemeat was marked with charcoal to tag it as dog food, so that unscrupulous butchers would not try to pass it off as beef. Every part of the horse was used: the horse's long tail hair was prized for violin bows, and the bones and hooves were boiled down and turned into glue.

Before the advent of the internal combustion engine, the horse was an essential helpmate, pressed into service to clear and till the fields, fight the battles, and pull the heavy loads of the great industrial cities. But the horse remained anonymous, invisible, and routinely subject to overwork and abuse. When English author Anna Sewell wrote *Black Beauty*, in the late nineteenth century, she said that her aim was to "induce kindness, sympathy, and an understanding treatment of horses." Though now considered a children's classic, the book was originally intended for an adult audience. Narrated from the horse's point of view, the novel describes Black Beauty's life, from his earliest memory, of "a large pleasant meadow with a pond of clear water in it" to his wretched existence pulling a heavy load for a cruel peddler. The sentimental and emotionally wrenching book was wildly popular, quickly becoming a bestseller first in England and then in the United States, where it became a favorite of the progressive movement. Sewell's book was the first to popularize interest in the plight of the horse and to generate widespread concern about the beast of burden's treatment.

This point of view dovetailed nicely with the views of the urban reformers of the late nineteenth century. By this period, the conditions in large cities were cause for dismay: urban environments, crowded with tenements built to accommodate waves of new immigrants, were considered filthy and dangerous and, from the nineteenth-century point of view, centers of moral decay. Progressives wanted to clean up cities by promoting a cleaner and more orderly environment, and horses were at the center of their reform projects. The new steam, electric, and internal combustion engines were seen as the wave of the future, while horses were considered dirty and prone to accidents, and their manure was a major contributor to urban filth and an important cause of disease. In addition, the culture of the teamsters, the men who drove the horses, and the livery stables they frequented were seen as centers of immoral behavior—teamsters, in the popular mind, were associated with public drunkenness and foul language. The sight of teamsters beating their horses in public was a frequent urban spectacle.

The original mission of the American Society for the Prevention of Cruelty to Animals, founded in April 1866 by Henry Bergh, was to enforce anti-cruelty regulations for horses. Born in 1811, Bergh was the son of a prominent New York shipbuilding family. He attended Columbia College in New York but dropped out in order to travel around Europe; later in life, he was appointed by Abraham Lincoln to the American legation in the court of the czar of Russia. During his travels in Europe, he became sensitized to the poor treatment of animals. Bergh believed that "mercy to animals meant mercy to all mankind." In nineteenth-century America, horses were the most visible symbol of animal abuse, their presence in the city streets an inescapable fact of life. The ASPCA adopted as its mission the enforcement of anti-cruelty regulations designed to protect urban workhorses, noting, "Among the punishable offenses: overuse of the whip, driving a lame horse, furious driving (until a horse was foaming at the mouth), knowingly selling a diseased animal, or killing a horse without a license." In other words, only the most blatantly cruel practices were targeted—those that would be readily noticeable to the untrained eye. Even these modest reforms were considered difficult to enforce. There was nothing to stop a teamster from pushing his horse to just short of these limits.

Another early humane society crusader, George Angell of Massachusetts, was inspired to act when, in March 1868, two horses, each carrying its rider over forty miles of rough roads, were raced until they both dropped dead. Angell wrote a letter that appeared in the *Boston Daily Advertiser,* where it caught the attention of Emily Appleton, a prominent Bostonian who was interested in animal welfare. Within weeks, the pair had managed to produce the state's first anti-cruelty laws and founded the Massachusetts Society for the Prevention of Cruelty to Animals. The MSPCA passed out copies of *Black Beauty* embossed with the seal of its organization: an angel descending from heaven to stop a teamster who was whipping his horse.

Early reformers like Sewell, Appleton, Angell, and Bergh felt strongly that horses were living creatures and thus should be afforded basic rights, but that point of view was not widely adopted. Both Sewell, a Quaker, and Bergh, a Unitarian, had religious underpinnings to their anti-cruelty stance, as their faiths gave great emphasis to the humane treatment of all living things. Among the general public, however, the horse remained a work engine, and the public could spare little room for softhearted sentimentality.

Our language is rich with examples of the horse as engine; we describe a hard worker as a "workhorse" and a car's engine as having "horsepower." Though the role of the workhorse diminished significantly after the advent of the automobile, horses performed vital tasks well into the twentieth century. The city of Pittsburgh still owned three hundred draft horses in 1930, and the city fathers claimed that all of them could understand traffic lights. In the 1940s, horse-drawn carts were seen even in highly urbanized areas like Baltimore, where the clip-clop of hooves on pavement announced the arrival of the junk peddler, the ragman, and the fruit-and-vegetable cart. In city neighborhoods, the milkman's horse knew the route so well that he would pause at the next stop and wait patiently unattended as the milkman ran back and forth across the street to deliver his bottles. In these "route-driven" professions, the horse's intelligence allowed the deliveryman to complete his job faster than was possible in a motor-driven vehicle, and it was in these jobs that the horse-driven conveyances lasted the longest. As late as 1950, there were still hundreds of livery stables and riding establishments within New York City's boroughs.

By the mid-twentieth century, the horse business had shrunk considerably from its heyday, but its basic infrastructure was still in place. Horses were born and raised on farms or western ranches, auctioned off to dealers who served as middlemen, then sold to individual owners. Noble steed, heroic beast, partner for man—the horse fulfilled all of those functions. But the average horse was born and bred to be a stalwart servant—harnessed up to drag a burden behind him until his useful days were over, then to survive only as the products that had been made from his flesh and bones. That is the way it was in the horse business. The animals had a purpose, and that purpose was to serve man. Sentiment had no place in the transaction.

Whether Snowman knew it or not, his second chance at life, his tenure as the brand-new lesson horse at the Knox School, came about because of one unpredictable chance encounter. For all of the hundreds, thousands, and untold millions of horses who were tossed away like so much detritus as soon as they reached the end of their working lives, here was one who crossed paths with the right man at the right moment.

As with every horse, Snowman's melted-chocolate eyes hid the secret of his thoughts; but right away, when he arrived at the Knox School, he seemed to appreciate his good fortune. From his first day on the job, Snowman carried even the most timid beginner with the gentle care of a four-legged nanny.

Some horses are born to be teachers, and Snowman had a true vocation for his new profession.

5

A School for Young Ladies

The Knox School, St. James, Long Island, 1957

Bonnie Cornelius probably would have died of sheer boredom at the Knox School if it weren't for riding in the afternoon; it allowed her to escape from life in the big brick house that served as a combination dormitory, dining room, and classroom building. Everything about the place felt *heavy*. It looked more like a museum or an old mausoleum than a place for young, vibrant teenage girls.

The paneled double front doors opened into a vestibule hung with heavy curtains that collected dust; dark oil paintings stared from the walls, and an ornate chandelier dripped light over the spiral staircase.

The 1950s was a time of sock hops and drag racing, soda fountains and poodle skirts, but Knox, an all-girls boarding school, was a relic from another era. Knox girls' days were strictly regimented: from wake-up, room inspections, and a proper breakfast to dinner, evening study hall, and lights-out. The curriculum was traditional: music and history, Latin and French. The girls started the school year in summer uniforms, and no matter the weather on the last day of October, they were required to switch to their winter equivalent: navy blue blazers sporting the school's insignia and motto, *Semper ad lucem*—Always toward the light—and itchy wool skirts that hung modestly below the knee. They all wore white cotton socks that slouched around their ankles and scuffed lace-up saddle oxfords. Every night, the girls had to change into matching dresses for dinner. Bonnie hated the dinner dresses and thought they looked like waitress uniforms. The dining room was paneled in dark wood, with fireplaces taller than the girls' heads flanking each end. Old hunting prints and more muted oil portraits covered the walls. Through the French doors that overlooked the terrace, students could glimpse the beach at Stony Brook Harbor. Meals were plain and hearty. Seated at the head of each table, schoolmistresses carefully scrutinized the use of each knife and fork, as well as the topics chosen for conversation. Every meal, but especially dinner, was a lesson in deportment.

Miss Mary Alice Knox had founded Miss Knox's School for Girls in 1904. The daughter of a prominent Presbyterian minister in Elmira, New York, she had been impressed by her father's early championing of higher education for girls. He served on the board of trustees of the Elmira Female Seminary (now Elmira College), which was the first institution in the United States to grant college degrees to women. Miss Knox (as she became known), who studied at Elmira, became a prominent educator, first teaching history at Wellesley, then taking over as headmistress of the Emma Willard School, the first private college preparatory school for girls in the United States. In the early 1900s, Miss Knox was such a prominent educator that she was listed in *Who's Who in America*. Higher education for girls, considered radical in the 1870s and '80s, had quickly gained a broader appeal, and schools for young ladies, often named after the woman or women who founded them, were proliferating. At the age of fifty-three, Miss Knox left Emma Willard to found her own school along the Hudson River in Briarcliff Manor, New York; Miss Knox's School for Girls promised to provide "water from artesian wells, courses taught by specialists, and rooms with or without private bath." Mary Alice Knox envisioned a school that would be rich in music and art and close to the cultural life of New York City. When the school was founded, on the bluestocking principles of the Emma Willard School, it was considered modern—even daring. The well-rounded curriculum, including physical education, was designed to educate the modern woman, building a strong mind, body, and character.

But Miss Knox would remain in charge for only seven years. One Saturday afternoon in 1911, the headmistress and her students were returning from a performance of the Metropolitan Opera in Manhattan when they were caught in a devastating train wreck. Several of the students were killed, and Miss Knox, who survived the accident, was so distraught that she "succumbed a short while later." Louise Houghton Phinney—a widow, and an 1891 graduate of Smith College—was appointed to replace her.

For more than forty years, Mrs. Phinney ran the Knox School. Her imposing bearing tamed generations of girls. Her manner and style of dress, even in the 1950s, suggested the Victorian. The school had weathered significant changes during her tenure. First, in 1912, the school in Briarcliff Manor burned to the ground; though no one was hurt, the school had to move to a new location in Tarrytown. Then, outgrowing that facility in the 1920s, the school moved again to Cooperstown, New York, where it took up residence in an enormous Victorian-style hotel on the shores of Otsego Lake. From June through August, the hotel was a resort. When the summer pensioners left, the Knox School set up shop in the building, using the cavernous, empty rooms for dormitories and classrooms. Every May, the school vacated the premises to make room for the incoming hotel guests. This arrangement continued for over thirty years.

But by the 1950s, the Knox board of trustees had set about looking for a permanent location for the school. Among the board's criteria was that the school needed to be located on a sea or lakeshore, because many of the traditional school songs contained verses referring to looking out over the water. In 1954, the buildings and grounds of Land of Clover were purchased for the school. Mrs. Phinney formally ceded the headmistress-ship to her handpicked protégée, Miss Laura Wood, who had taught at Knox since the 1920s. Though officially retired, Mrs. Phinney remained actively involved, busying herself transforming the estate's buildings into dormitories and classrooms, and making sure that the school's traditions carried over to the new location. But what had seemed advanced in the early twentieth century had become dated and stodgy. By the 1950s, the life of the school was anything but progressive. Together, Mrs. Phinney and Miss Wood held tight to the reins of power, doing everything they could to see to it that the postwar changes that were sweeping the nation stopped at the school's front gates.

Every moment of a Knox School girl's day was considered a moment for self-improvement. Little room remained for relaxation or levity. If a housemother saw a girl sitting with her legs crossed at the knees, she would remind her that Knox girls cross their legs at the ankles. Even off

Knox students wearing saddle oxfords and school blazers collect their mail from the campus post office.

campus, the girls were told that they were ambassadors for the Knox School and correct deportment was expected. On the Long Island Rail Road, a Knox girl was easy to spot by her camel hair coat and white gloves. In school, girls vied for the Poise Cup, first awarded in 1917, which honored "a student embodying graciousness and dignity of character." In the parlors and sitting rooms of Knox, with their Persian rugs, paneled walls, and stiff brocaded furniture, Knox girls learned the life that was assumed to soon be theirs, as mistresses of the great estates at the pinnacle of East Coast society.

While many of the girls hailed from the New York area, others came from out West and even abroad. There were glamorous ranchers' daughters from Texas and Idaho, and rich girls from Puerto Rico and Venezuela. Famous names were not uncommon there: Mia Fonssagrives was the daughter of Lisa Fonssagrives, the Swedish beauty sometimes called "the first supermodel," and the stepdaughter of Irving Penn, the famed fashion photographer for *Vogue* and *Harper's Bazaar*; the journalist and television personality Dorothy Kilgallen sent her daughter to Knox. According to one former student who attended the school during the 1950s, the only criteria for admission was the ability to pay the tuition. The school, with its isolated location and all-girls student body, was considered a good place for poor little rich girls—mixed-up girls, girls from dysfunctional families and broken homes. Knox would not get you into the Seven Sisters, the elite women's colleges, such as Bryn Mawr, Radcliffe, and Wellesley, that were considered the female Ivy League at the time. But parents hoped it would keep their girls out of trouble—and as one student commented, "It was like being in jail. . . . It was so confining."

In the manor house, behavior was a subject of public comment, and from wake-up to bedtime the girls were never far from their housemothers' prying eyes. By the 1950s, academic achievement had taken a back seat to cultivating the social graces. While some Knox girls went on to attend four-year colleges, most completed their educations at the private women's junior colleges that were often called "finishing schools." But cultivating the social graces got very dull. Girls flouted the rules by slinking out to the woods to smoke and inviting boys to sneak onto the campus after hours. Students were frequently punished for infractions small and large; the punishments ranged from losing permission to leave

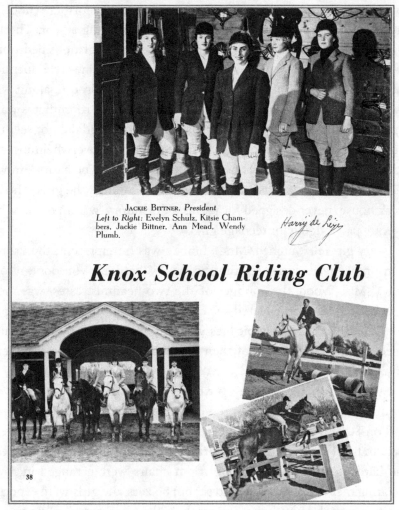

JACKIE BITTNER, *President*
Left to Right: Evelyn Schulz, Kitsie Chambers, Jackie Bittner, Ann Mead, Wendy Plumb.

Harry de Leyu

Knox School Riding Club

38

The Knox School Riding Club.

the campus to sequestration, or confining a girl to the infirmary for a few days. All in all, life at Knox was very regimented, extremely proper, and often boring. Few alumnae of the era describe it as a happy place.

Bonnie Cornelius grew up riding horses near her home in Buffalo, where she was a good student at a private day school for girls. But her home life, with her father and stepmother, was stressful, and when she was a freshman in high school she discovered boys and her grades dropped. Her parents made the decision to send her to Knox, and her arrival was a shock in many ways. Far from home, she was disappointed to find that the classes were less rigorous than at her former school, so much so that she almost felt as if she were repeating a year. The living conditions were a shock as well. Upstairs, the enormous bedrooms of the manor house had been converted into Madeline-style dormitories: five twin beds lined the walls of her shared bedroom, along with five dressers and five desks. Her first year, one of her roommates was a homesick European girl who barely spoke English and did not seem to want to bathe. Eventually, when her body odor got overwhelming, the other girls had to ask the school nurse to intervene. The bathroom was down the hall, as big as a bedroom and shared by all of the girls. The big brick house, never designed for use as a dormitory, was an opulent but ill-equipped lodging for teenage girls.

Every girl felt watched. Mrs. Phinney was omnipresent, the expression on her face always seeming to say "What have you done wrong now?" Miss Wood, the younger of the two headmistresses, was more reserved but also more feared—she was sharp, and nothing slipped past her. With this claustrophobic lifestyle, the girls had no privacy and little freedom, and every aspect of their personal life was fair game for scrutiny.

Even Sundays were given over to self-improvement. The girls were required to attend services at the house of worship of their choosing, and on Sunday nights, for their cultural education, they had to attend staid musical events, such as performances by string quartets. For these, the hard, straight-backed dining room chairs were arranged in rows. Wearing their dinner dresses and school blazers, the girls were expected to sit up straight, not slump against their chair backs, and, of course, to cross their legs only at the ankles while struggling not to allow the music to lull them to sleep.

On weekdays, sports started at two o'clock. The girls raced out of the dorm, then headed up the grassy lane toward the barn or fields. Every girl was required to participate. Besides horseback riding, girls could choose tennis, field hockey, or basketball. Those in the riding program pulled on their riding togs and hurried up the hill to the stables. As they approached, Harry heard laughing and giggling before he saw the girls. Rarely was one late. Most years, Harry had at least fifty girls come through the riding program. Among these, some were passionate about the sport, and others were beginners who were just giving it a try. The five-day girls, the ones who chose to ride every school day, were the most skilled, and the members of the Riding Club—Wendy Plumb, Bonnie Cornelius, Jackie Bittner, Ann Mead, and Kitsie Chambers— formed the dedicated nucleus of the program. These girls would look for any excuse to come down to the stables. A few would even show up on weekend afternoons when Harry was feeding, offering to lend a hand. In return, Harry gave them extra opportunities to ride. Up at the barn, the atmosphere was rigorous but fun and can-do. An everyone-pitch-in spirit prevailed.

The focus on sports and an emphasis on horseback riding as a suitable occupation for students was not particular to Knox. Many influential women educators of the late nineteenth and early twentieth centuries had attended schools of physical education, and they incorporated gymnasiums as integral parts of their schools. Charlotte Haxall Noland, who founded Foxcroft, a girls' school in Virginia well known for its riding program, studied at the Sargent School of Physical Education at Harvard. M. Carey Thomas, another early proponent of girls' education, built a state-of-the-art gymnasium in downtown Baltimore when she founded the Bryn Mawr School in 1884. In the nineteenth century, college preparatory education, such as that afforded to boys, was believed to divert energy toward women's brains at the expense of their reproductive organs, sapping their strength and rendering them unhealthy. Early female educators, believing that girls needed to be both healthy and well educated, favored including rigorous physical education in their curriculums, and horseback riding, with its perceived health-promoting benefits, was often included in the mix.

Horsemanship promoted posture, grace, and confidence, while providing exercise and fresh air. At an all-girls school, there were opportunities to play other sports, but perhaps none that provided the exhilaration, challenge, and freedom of riding, and certainly none that allowed girls to participate in a sport that was fast, dangerous, and thrilling. Horseback riding was equally popular with boys and men at that time, and girls experienced much more parity with boys in riding than in other sports. Girls wore breeches and boots instead of tunics or dresses, got muddy and dirty, and often took dramatic spills. Sprains, concussions, and broken bones were thought to go with the territory. Horseback riding afforded girls a unique opportunity—it was both feminine and socially graceful, and at the same time, it was exciting and rough-and-tumble.

At Knox, the riding program provided a place where girls could escape the school's confining environment. Some girls, like Wendy Plumb, whose father was an expert horseman and whose brother was an eight-time member of the United States Olympic equestrian team, had come to the school as skilled riders. Wendy spent her summers racking up ribbons on the horse show circuit and devoted her year at Knox to keeping up her technique.

In Harry de Leyer's stables, the rules were different from those in the rest of the school. No doubt the handsome young riding master was an additional draw to the afternoon program. Among a faculty of dour, serious, mostly spinster women, Mr. D, as he was known, stood out—he was younger, more fun, and male. Harry was not worried about the girls' dress or manners, their deportment or social etiquette. He wanted to make riders out of them.

It was rumored that after his job interview, a healthy debate had gone on among the teachers, many of whom were unmarried women "of a certain age." Was it really appropriate to leave him alone with the girls up at the stables? Of course, he was married and he was a family man, but he was also young, and once he was hired, he was like a lightning bolt cutting through that school, always smiling and quick with a laugh. The girls loved Mr. D, sensing immediately that he was on their side. But from around every corner, a woman with a tight bun, horn-rimmed glasses, and a disapproving air watched him, immediately summoning him to the manor house whenever anything seemed amiss.

Bonnie Cornelius was one of Mr. D's best riders—quick to lend a hand around the barn, always one of the first to arrive and one of the last to leave. Each day, when the girls arrived at the stables, Mr. D called out a stall number. Bonnie never knew which horse she'd have to ride that day, but she was always game for a challenge.

In the narrow track that ringed the inside of the circular stable court-yard, Mr. D set up fences for the girls to jump. Some days, he'd keep raising the fences higher and higher. One by one, the girls peeled away, until only the boldest were left. Other days, he saddled up and took them galloping out in the fields, looking for natural obstacles to jump.

Riding instructors typically stand in the middle of the ring, calling out instructions to their students from the ground, but Mr. D preferred to ride along with them. You did not say no to Mr. D unless you wanted to go home, untack your horse, groom him, and return to the ladies in the manor house.

Harry de Leyer,
riding instructor.

One day, Bonnie was riding one of the new horses in the stable, Chief Sunset. Like many of the horses Harry bought, he had a streak of brilliance almost equally counterbalanced by some terrible flaw—a flaw serious enough to have put him within Harry's price range. Chief was an off-the-track thoroughbred with bloodlines that traced to Man o' War, but the stallion was hot-tempered and difficult. Only Bonnie was good enough to ride him. The horse was especially unruly that day, and she could not get him to settle down in the ring. He pulled and bucked, refusing to listen to her commands.

Mr. D told her to take Chief outside the ring and let him go at a flat-out gallop across the fields, to work off some of his steam. Bonnie, who was having enough trouble managing the horse within the confines of the ring, told him that she didn't want to do it. She braced herself for his reaction, but to her relief, he just smiled.

"It's all right," he said. "I'll do it."

Swinging lightly onto the horse's back, he guided the stallion out of the fenced riding ring and into the big open field beyond. Rising up in his stirrups into the galloping position, Harry let the horse out to his full speed—the flat-out gallop that is sometimes described as a run. Not a pace normally used by amateur riders, it's the gait typically seen on a thoroughbred racecourse. Fleet of foot, this thoroughbred stretched out across the field, with Harry crouched close to his wind-whipped mane. To Bonnie, it was a breathtaking sight.

A few minutes later, he slowed the horse and circled him back to where his student stood, in awe of the unleashed speed she had just witnessed. Sure enough, when the horse got back in the ring, he was calm and well-mannered, for once. Harry hopped off and tossed the reins to her with a smile and a twinkle in his blue eyes.

"You gotta talk Dutch to him, Bonnie."

The teenager sheepishly climbed back on the horse, disappointed in herself for not rising to the challenge. As promised, the horse behaved like a gentleman for the rest of the afternoon.

The girls may have learned manners and deportment, Latin and French from their mistresses, but under Mr. D's friendly but exacting eye they learned courage.

Harry's life had taught him that sometimes courage is needed—not manners, not breeding and white gloves and nice coats, but the bravery to do what is required of you when the going gets tough. Harry had first learned courage as a small boy, looking between the ears of a horse at a fast gallop, not knowing that the same daring would someday lead him past Nazi checkpoints. He fervently hoped that these girls would never have to display courage when bullets were flying, and that war would never come to this place, but no one who had lived through the terrible war in Europe could afford to be naïve.

Harry was determined to teach his girls to be brave, to be tough. You never knew what life would throw your way. Out in the field, over the outside course, the girls flew, balanced in their stirrups at a fast gallop, wind whipping into their faces. Harry liked nothing better than leading the girls on a breakneck gallop across woodland and field, riding in a pack, taking fences as they came, adapting seat and balance to uneven terrain—these were the skills needed to foxhunt, and these were the skills he wanted for his girls. From the school, you could ride all the way to the beach or into St. James—though the girls got demerits for leaving the school grounds without permission. Harry had noticed that girls and horses were the same: you couldn't keep them cooped up for too long.

Harry hollered his lessons above the cold wind whistling in from the sound. In the ring, he raised the bars up on the jumps and shouted, "You got it! You got it!" He saw the shine that came into the girls' eyes when they conquered their fears.

Harry saw that their rigidly controlled lives made them timid. He remembered his own days in Catholic boys' school—perched on the edge of his seat, back stiff, feet on the floor. In 1940, when the Nazis invaded Holland, everyone followed the war's progress by listening to the radio. When Rotterdam fell, only seventy miles away, his father came to the school to gather up Harry and his brothers, and took the whole family—his mother and all twelve of his brothers and sisters—to a small two-room cottage out in the country. They huddled together, listening to the radio reports of the Nazis' progress toward St. Oedenrode. Five days later, the family emerged and returned to a town under Nazi control, and a world forever changed. Quiet but determined, Harry's family fought back in their own way. The German army had commandeered all of the valuable food and supplies in the area, taking the best for themselves and rationing out meager and inadequate supplies to the occupied Dutch. People had scarcely enough to eat, and what they had was of poor quality. The priest in charge of Harry's school did not have enough food to feed his students and asked Harry's father, a brewer, for grain from his hidden stores. In the dark of night, they sealed wheat and rye into beer barrels and loaded them onto a horse-drawn cart. Thirteen-year-old Harry was chosen to drive the horse cart the thirty miles back to the school, in the hopes that a young boy on a beer wagon would attract little notice. Harry drove that route at least half a dozen times, holding the reins steady as he approached the armed checkpoints. Surly Nazis stared at him, then let him pass since he was just a skinny kid driving an old wagon through town. Courage and a view of the world seen between a horse's ears—the two would forever be linked in Harry's mind.

Now, as a riding instructor, Harry pushed the girls to find and surpass their own limits. One November weekend, he took them to the Junior Olympics, a contest in which teams from all of the local riding schools competed. Bonnie was back on Chief Sunset, whose recent gelding had

done nothing to soften his temper. In the arena during the warm-up before the competition started, the horse refused a jump, in what's called
a "dirty stop": the horse skids to a halt after the rider has already risen
in the stirrups and shifted her weight forward. It is very difficult to stay
mounted when this happens, and this time Bonnie was thrown. Frustrated with Bonnie for "letting" the horse stop, Harry prepared to get
on himself, ready to teach him a lesson. "We feed these horses," Harry
liked to say. "We groom them, clean their stalls, and tend to them when
they are sick. And all we ask of them is to jump. So *make* them jump."
Harry took the reins from Bonnie, swung into the saddle, and galloped
toward the fence.

Oftentimes, riders are slightly afraid of jumping, and a horse has a
fine-tuned sense of his rider's underlying fears. When the rider is afraid,
the horse is afraid too, and will hang back, reluctant on the approach.
But when Harry sat astride and confidently approached a fence at a
gallop, horses *knew* that he meant business. Bonnie watched Harry approach the fence at a good clip; she saw Harry rise up in the stirrups,
keeping his legs and heels firmly pressed into the horse's sides, the signal
that means *go forward*. But at the last second, the horse ducked his head
and skidded to a stop. Just as Bonnie had, Harry came unglued, flew out
of the saddle, and landed in the dirt. Harry stood up, dusted the dirt off
his pants, and chuckled. Undeterred, he climbed aboard and tried again.
This time, prodded by Harry's swift application of the whip before takeoff, the horse jumped the fence. Harry dismounted, handed the reins to
Bonnie, and nodded toward the fence—it went without saying that she
was going to try again.

Whenever Harry fell, the students gently poked fun at him, but he
didn't mind. That was the great thing about Mr. D; he never acted above
the girls. That night, before going to sleep, Bonnie recorded the event
in her diary: "Rode Chief—Olympic Course—wouldn't go. I fell off.
Mr. D got on. He fell off." She would be sore the next morning, but
Mr. D had taught her that you always get back in the saddle. A Spanish
proverb says, "It is not enough for a man to know how to ride; he must
know how to fall." Harry de Leyer knew how to ride, and he knew how
to fall, and he taught his girls the same lesson. It was not the trip into the
dust that mattered, it was the way the girls got back on and rode again.

Harry still struggled with English, and one day, one of his crackerjack riders, Jackie Bittner, made him a deal: English lessons for riding lessons. If he would give her a little more time to ride, she would teach him to speak better English. Sure, Harry told Jackie, one of the youngest and bravest riders, teach me English. What's the harm in that? He was happy to give any girl extra time to ride.

Not long after, Harry was summoned to the headmistress's office. Miss Wood stood up, escorted him to a chair, and closed the door behind him. Harry's world revolved around the barn. He felt awkward up in the manor house, conscious of his muddy boots and the horsey odor that clung to his wool coat. He held his hat on his knees and looked at Miss Wood's long face with apprehension.

"Which girls have been teaching you words down at the barn?" she asked.

Harry hesitated for a moment before replying. He did not want to get his girls in trouble, but the question seemed innocent enough, and maybe Miss Wood wanted to praise the girls who were helping him. Helping others was held in high esteem at the Knox School.

"Well, Jackie has been giving me English lessons . . ."

Miss Wood frowned. "Very well, then," she said. "Thank you for your time."

The next day at the barn, Jackie didn't come for her lesson; nor the next day, nor the next. Worried about his pupil, Harry asked the other girls what had happened. Was she sick? Had she left school? There were giggles and silence, and then one of the girls admitted the truth: Jackie had been confined to the infirmary for three days. Jackie's "English lessons" to Harry had specialized in four-letter words.

Harry laughed to himself, secretly savoring the story. The girls made him laugh and helped him feel at home, despite the school's rarefied environment. He liked spending time with them and the horses in the barn, and now he liked seeing his workhorse Snowman looking content, his head hanging over the Dutch door to watch the goings-on in the stable courtyard. Snowy had made a good transition to the barn at Knox, toting the girls around their lessons with his unflappable sense of calm. Among the thoroughbreds that belonged to the rich girls, Snowman stuck out—but Harry felt sympathy for the horse. Both of them knew the rigors of working a plow. Sometimes—a lot of the time, actually— Harry felt like an impostor. Snowman was an impostor, too. Harry had a hard time shaking the idea that his horse knew that he needed to be on his best behavior.

Not just weekdays were devoted to horses. One of the best things about the riding program was escaping the school on weekends. Many Sundays, Harry took the girls to meetings of the Smithtown Hunt. Foxhunting, a passion imported from the English, was a favorite pastime of the landed elite along the eastern seaboard, with strongholds on Long Island and in Pennsylvania and Virginia's Piedmont. Foxhunting on Long Island dated back to the colonial period. The Meadowbrook Hunt, Long Island's oldest hunt club, in nearby Old Westbury, boasted that General George Washington had been a member. Teddy Roosevelt extolled the pleasures of Long Island foxhunting in an 1886 article in *Century Magazine*. The Smithtown Hunt, the closest hunt club to the Knox School, had traditionally moved its meeting from large estate to large estate. But by the late 1950s, a combination of less open land and waning interest had caused the hunt meetings to get smaller and smaller. Many feared that the Smithtown Hunt was a dying tradition that would not survive.

Originally, the sport of foxhunting on Long Island had received stiff opposition from the Quakers who had settled the farmland of Suffolk County. Quakers were opposed to foxhunting on principle, on the grounds that it was cruel to foxes. Even Henry Bergh of the ASPCA eventually got involved, drafting letters of protest to the Meadowbrook Hunt. But the Smithtown Hunt had met no such opposition as it pounded across the countryside around the Knox School. Though foxes were plentiful in the area, the landscape was covered with dense scrubby brush where foxes could hide; as a result, the hunt was most often conducted as what's known as a "drag hunt," where hounds track a scent rather than a live fox. The advantage of the drag hunt was that the horses could follow the hounds over a course that had been predetermined to be suitable for riding; also, a live fox was not the target.

At that time, the master of foxhounds, the person in charge of the hunt, was a veterinarian named Arthur Frederick. Like many aficionados of the sport, he believed in the good side of the tradition: a respect for open lands, an interest in hounds and horses, and an abiding sense of tradition. Frederick took his duties as master of the Smithtown Hunt seriously. To be invited to ride with the hunt, you had to pass muster as a horseman. Frederick was even known to hide behind bushes as riders came through to observe their skills in the field. Nobody hunted with the Smithtown Hunt who did not meet Frederick's exacting standards of horsemanship. Foxhunting—where large groups of horses follow hounds across open lands, jumping over fences and natural obstacles— takes particular skill. Unlike the controlled environment of a riding ring, riders and horses meet the unexpected: rough terrain, obstacles, wild-life, and unpredictable behavior from the other horses. A badly behaved horse or unskilled rider can put everyone else in danger. Frederick met Harry de Leyer when he was called to care for an ailing horse. Impressed by Harry's skill with horses, Frederick invited Harry to ride with the hunt, and said that he could bring the Knox girls along as long as he would make sure they were skilled enough.

But foxhunting takes more than riding skill: the girls needed to mas-ter a complicated code of etiquette. A rider's formal dress, the order in which they rode, and even the forms of address were all governed by complicated unwritten rules. The dress code required attention to the last detail: a melton wool jacket, a flat bowler with a string cord, and a white stock tie pinned with a gold stock pin whose point faced away from the rider's heart were among the strict requirements for hunt members. The Knox School girls were expected to ride well and, at the same time, respect the manners and traditions of the hunt. As tradition warranted, the students, who were guests rather than full-fledged mem-bers of the hunt, rode at the back of the pack, careful to be quiet and not to get in the way of the huntsmen or hounds.

One day, Harry and his girls, bringing up the rear, came across a clus-ter of riders bunched around a "chicken coop"—a slant-sided obstacle named for its resemblance to a henhouse. Every single horse had re-fused to jump the obstacle, in a chain reaction in which each horse had been frightened off by the previous horse's behavior. The large group was gathered off to the side, preparing to make another attempt. As the Knox girls followed Harry and his horse, Harry sailed around the corner and flew over the coop with ease, and each of the Knox girls followed, their horses willingly taking their cue from Harry's lead. That day, the girls were proud of themselves. They might have been mere teenage guests riding at the back of the pack, but Harry had taught them to be brave and bold, and their hard work and training had been on glorious display.

Knox had a rule that every girl needed to attend a church service on Sunday morning. Harry never missed a Sunday mass, and even though most of the Knox girls were Protestant, the early Catholic mass at the nearby Saint Philip & James Church was the only service that would get them to the hunt on time.

With the truck idling in the parking lot and the horses munching from hay nets inside, all of the girls of any denomination, clad in boots and breeches and wool hunt coats, their hair up in nets, traipsed into the small white church. Parishioners grew used to the sight of the girls and the young riding master kneeling in their riding habits at six A.M. Sometimes the group would sneak out before mass was over, doing their best to tiptoe in their riding boots, then climb back into their waiting limousine. Once Harry jumped into the horse van, they'd be off toward the hunt meeting.

The hunt started at a different place each week, and usually ended with a formal breakfast at one of the grand estates around Smithtown. Bonnie remembers a hunt breakfast at the Gould estate, otherwise known as "Castle Gould." Designed by Howard Gould, the son of railroad financier Jay Gould, the house, built of limestone and granite, was 225 feet long, 135 feet wide, and had three floors, forty rooms, and an

Knox girls in their camel hair coats standing near the Knox School limousine.

80-foot crenellated tower. The girls and their riding master, sweaty and dirty from a morning spent galloping pell-mell on horseback, stood around eating and socializing in the most opulent of surroundings.

But the sight of polished silver and the sound of tinkling teacups in the halls of large mansions were familiar to the well-to-do girls. Often, it was the simpler times that stood out in their minds—ordinary occasions that normal teenagers took for granted. Knox girls, boarders, did not drive their own cars but got chauffeured around town in a big black Packard limousine. At the end of one day's hunt, however, it was late—too late to find a driver to pick them up. Mr. D told them not to worry; he was heading back to the school anyway. He'd give them a ride in the van. The girls giggled as they climbed into the back and sat down in the straw, where the air was warm and heavy with the scent of horses, hay, and well-oiled tack as the truck rattled along the streets of St. James. They were all going to miss their dinner, so on the way home, Mr. D took the hungry girls out to dinner in a local diner, where they spent the meal dissecting the day's activity. No dreary housemothers, no lessons in etiquette, just hamburgers and lively discussion—an opportunity to feel like ordinary teenagers. In a life filled with a tedious procession of stiff white-glove social events, laughter and chatter at a hamburger joint with Mr. D were a special treat.

Back at the stables, the girls were bone-weary, but they helped unload the van, put the horses away, and stow all of the tack. At last, their day over, they said good night to Mr. D and trudged back to the manor house to confide their memories in their diaries.

In the morning, the girls would get up and put on their scratchy wool skirts and cotton socks and saddle oxfords. They would sit with ramrod-straight posture in the stuffy rooms of the manor house, where the light leaked in through windows half-covered by heavy damask drapery. They would decline verbs in Latin and submit to the house-mistresses' questions and commentary during their meals.

Then, at two o'clock in the afternoon, they would rush up the hill to the barn, and the routine would start again. Up on the backs of horses, under Mr. D's tutelage, the girls would unlock their inner lionesses.

The two-legged teacher would join forces with his four-legged teachers, having an influence that would last the girls for the rest of their lives.

6

Hollandia Farms

St. James, Long Island, Spring 1956

Snowman's winter and spring in the stables passed in a pleasant succession of lessons and trail rides. In the spring, the dogwoods ringing the fields bloomed flaming pink. As the weather warmed, the girls
had permission to ride down to the beach after their lessons, where they
discovered, to their delight, that Snowman loved swimming. Many of
the horses hesitated at the water's edge or took a few steps in to paw and
stamp, but Snowman waded past them until the water was chest-deep
and then, head stretched out and nostrils flaring, plunged forward. In a
moment, his hooves left the firm anchor of the sandy shoals and he was
waterborne. Any lucky rider—clinging to his wet mane or throwing her
arms around his strong neck—went along for the ride, the salty water
churning up in a froth around them. His broad back grew wet and slick,
and the strong scent of the horse's coat filled the air as the girl wrapped
her bare calves around his barrel, and felt his coat prickling up against
her skin. When the beach was crowded with girls and swimming horses,
the sounds of splashing and laughter filled the air.

At the end of May, the school year drew to a close. In the summer,
to save money, the school grounds—including the stables—were shut
down. Harry moved the horses from the horseshoe-shaped stable back
to his farm on Moriches Road.

And every summer, when the Knox School girls left, money got tight in the de Leyer household. Harry's tiny property had just a few stalls and a small paddock to double as a ring—not enough space for a proper riding stable. During the school year, he needed to keep a string of horses big enough to accommodate all of the Knox students in the riding program. If he had had more space at home, he could have continued with lessons over the summer, but the Knox stable was three times the size of his. As the 1956 school year drew to a close, Harry faced a familiar situation. A few of the horses would have to go. This problem was typical of riding academies, camps, and dude ranches all over the country. When the season ended, the excess horses were trundled off for sale, often going back to the same auctions they had been purchased from. Harry's auction purchase had grown used to his roomy box stall at Knox. Every morning, Snowman greeted Harry with his trademark three loud whinnies, and each time a girl passed his stall, he seemed to look at her with a wink and a nod. Yet Harry knew he needed to find a buyer for the big gray. He tried to interest one of the girls in Snowman, but he was not the kind of horse they went for.

The girls preferred the regal thoroughbreds, like Wayward Wind. Windy had a fine, shiny coat and a silky mane and tail. Her coloring was a deep chestnut, and her white markings—a white blaze down her face and four white stockings—made her stand out from the other horses. Windy had been only three when Harry bought her from Belmont Park in New York. Nobody wanted her. She had gotten caught in the starting gate and torn a huge gash, from the tip of her withers all the way down to the point of her shoulder. A track vet had sewed her up—thirty-four stitches, just to close the wound, and not even careful work because the injury was so severe that her racing days were finished. Most buyers passed her over entirely—with a wound like that, who knew if she would ever fully recover? The wound might get infected, or the shoulder muscle might have suffered permanent damage. But Harry had bought her for a song and slowly nursed her back to health. Now she was a sweet-natured beauty. The students loved to show her, often bringing home blue ribbons. Riding Windy, a girl made an impression when she entered the ring. Snowman, at 16.1 hands, was similar in size to Windy (an equestrian "hand" is four inches, or the width of an average man's hand, and is counted from the ground to the top of the withers), but his broad chest and heavy-boned legs, all qualities that were bred into work-horses, were not attributes that would appeal to a horse show judge in the way that would Windy's sleeker, more refined form.

Nevertheless, Harry kept looking hopefully among his students to find Snowman a buyer. The horse was reliable and dependable, and more than that, he was a four-footed friend. Even a timid girl could ride this horse without fear. These girls had daddies with plenty of money. If even one girl had shown an interest, he was sure he could get her parents to agree. Snowman had the reputation of being the easy horse, the quiet horse, the one you rode if you needed a little help. He was the horse you relaxed on after your hard lesson was over, riding bareback down to the beach, the horse you moved past once you got a little better. The horse you were proud not to have to ride anymore, the friendly kid brother who kicked around the stable but got no respect. Most of the girls were looking for jumpers. Harry had tried trotting Snowman over poles on the ground, but the horse would not pick up his feet. He was clumsy—he just did not have the makings of a jumper—so Harry didn't press it. Some horses were born to jump, and others stayed earthbound. This horse was a plodder, but Harry still respected his gentle heart.

With no prospect of a buyer for the horse, Harry brought Snowman back to the house on Moriches Road. Years ago, his father had taught him that every able-bodied horse on a working farm had to earn his keep. Feeding hay and grain to an animal who had no job and was just growing fat in the barn . . . *ach* . . . if Harry were that sentimental, he might as well give up now. That was not a way to keep a horse business afloat.

The fastest way to sell a horse was to send him to a dealer, like Milton Potter up at the Mid-Island Arena. But then, Harry would have no control over where the gray ended up. People said that Potter never kept a horse for more than twenty-four hours. If it didn't sell, he was on the phone to the slaughterhouse at Northport. Potter claimed that it was better to sell a horse for a penny than to feed it for an extra day.

So Harry held out trying to find a private buyer, but he got no nibbles. Just when he was starting to run out of options, a local doctor showed up on Moriches Road, looking for a quiet mount for his twelve-year-old son. He was not a horseman, but he lived on a neighboring farm. He wanted a dependable horse. Nothing flashy. A horse that would be gentle and safe.

Harry smiled and brought the man back to the stable. He had the perfect horse. Around back, one of the children led Snowman out of the stall, and he stood quietly with a rope tossed over his neck, not even clipped into the cross-ties. The doctor was impressed. This was just the kind of horse he was looking for.

After a brief discussion, the two men shook hands. Harry sold Snowman to Dr. Rugen for $160, with just one condition: if the doctor ever wanted to part with the horse, he had to give Harry a chance to buy him back.

The next day, Harry prepared to load Snowman into the van to take him to his new owner's farm. All the children came out to say good-bye. Harry knelt down next to the horse, padding his legs in cotton batting, then wrapping flannel bandages around them and sealing the bandages with white adhesive tape. The gelding had fine strong legs, not a bump or deformity on them in spite of his hard-used life. His coat shone from grooming and good food, and his wounds had healed. The only traces of his past were the places on his shoulders where his coat had been rubbed off by the stress of pulling the plow. Harry lowered the ramp to the trailer, and the horse clip-clopped up the incline, not even turning to look back at the children. Where Harry went, that horse would follow.

Dr. Rugen's farm was only a few miles away, past farms and potato fields crisscrossed by quiet country lanes, so it wasn't long before Harry returned, the trailer now empty. The doctor had seemed a sensible man, Harry thought, and his pasture was pleasant and in good repair. Harry felt satisfied that he had made a good deal. Johanna kept a neat ledger where she tracked all of the expenses of the family and the farm; that night, she entered $160 into a column, on the plus side. From a business standpoint, Harry had made a profit, but it bothered him to let the horse go. He did not owe the horse a greater debt than what he had given him: a decent home, hay to eat, clean water, good treatment. But it was hard for him to sell a horse who had felt like a member of the family.

Each time Harry chose a new home for a horse, he saw it as a grave responsibility, ever since the first time he'd been tapped for that duty. When the Germans surrendered the horses they had stolen during the war, Harry, a member of Dutch 4-H, was assigned the job of examining the horses. No one would ever know exactly what atrocities these horses had witnessed during the war—or in what ways their horsepower had been harnessed to the Nazi cause. When the horses came back to St. Oedenrode, in many ways they resembled the Dutch people: once fat and shiny, now gaunt, with new scars on their bodies and a wilder look in their eyes. But like the people, they had survived. With his father and brother, Harry examined each of these horses, picked up their feet, looked over their legs, checked their eyes and wind, their tails and backs. Every once in a while, they recognized a horse—one with distinctive markings—and could return it to the original owner. But most of them came without pedigrees and would be going to new homes: one horse for a one-hectare farm, two horses for two hectares. Young Harry felt the weight of each decision. For each horse, he chose a new owner; for each farmer, that horse might make the difference between success and failure, between bringing back the farm and losing it.

Harry would never know exactly where Snowman came from, but he knew how it felt to be displaced, neglected, and undervalued, and still face the future with ears pricked forward. A farm nearby and a boy looking for a quiet mount—it seemed to portend good fortune. Still, on the evening of Snowy's departure, sadness hung in the air as Harry did his rounds and checked the other horses. The air on the spit of land where Harry had made his home often has a briny tang from the nearby sound. On summer evenings, it is filled with birdsong and the chirping of crickets. The familiar scents of the barn—straw and sawdust, Propert's boot polish and neat's-foot oil—were overlaid with the scent of the air that swept over the marshes bordering Long Island Sound. Thinking of Snowman, it was hard for Harry not to feel a lonely pit settle deep in his stomach. He thought of his mother and father and all of his brothers and sisters left behind in Holland; he thought of his brown mare Petra, who had made him proud in jumping competitions; and for a moment, he leaned on his pitchfork and looked out across the darkening horizon.

But soon he straightened up and set himself back to work. Here he was, on his own little patch of ground, his own Hollandia Farms, taking care of his wife and family. Harry so missed the gray's three friendly whinnies trumpeting from the barn like an equine reveille, but he brushed aside the hollow feeling inside. He knew that to make a go of it in the horse business, he couldn't get himself attached to every old plow plug that came through the barn.

7

How to Make a Living at Horses

High Point, North Carolina, 1951

Harry was twenty-two years old, he and his wife, Johanna, part of a wave of postwar immigrants who came to the United States from Europe, when the Dutch flagship *Volendam* pulled into the port of Hoboken in August 1950. Out of about two million new immigrants who arrived in the United States between 1950 and 1960, some fifty-two thousand were from Holland, or about five thousand Dutch immigrants each year.

The early 1950s was a time of brash new developments that would forever change the face of the country—the biggest of them being the advent of television. In 1951, Edward R. Murrow debuted his television show *See It Now* by showing a split-screen image of the Brooklyn Bridge and the Golden Gate Bridge—the first time the Atlantic and Pacific oceans had ever been seen simultaneously. In 1950, Diner's Club introduced the first credit card and Xerox manufactured the first copy machine. The cost of a gallon of gasoline was eighteen cents.

But it was also a fearful time. The Korean War had started, introducing a new era of Cold War tensions. In April 1951, Ethel and Julius Rosenberg were sentenced to death as Communist spies. These years would be dominated by international tensions and technological changes that arrived at a breathtaking, sometimes terrifying pace. But like generations of immigrants before them, Harry and Johanna were undeterred by the uncertainties of the future. They knew hardship first-hand, and they arrived with the intention of building a good life for themselves in this new land.

Harry and Johanna's families had scraped together enough money for the first-class passage that was to be their honeymoon, but when the young couple arrived in America, they had only $160 between them. The six-day crossing had been rough, and Harry had spent most of it curled up belowdecks feeling seasick. Hoboken, just across the Hudson River from New York City, was a loud, clanging urban port. As they debarked, it was hard for the young newlyweds not to be overwhelmed by the unfamiliar sights and sounds. Before arriving in Hoboken, Harry and Johanna had passed through Ellis Island, where immigration inspectors had cleared their papers and performed a brief medical exam. At the port in Hoboken, the customs inspectors cracked the lid of the small wooden crate that held all of the young couple's belongings—they did not have much. Harry and Johanna stood by as an inspector prodded at its meager contents. Harry's worn leather saddle and his tall riding boots took up much of the space. The inspector made no comment and closed the lid. The official proceedings complete, Harry and Johanna stepped off the ship into their new homeland without a backward glance.

Before the war, it would have been unthinkable that Harry, the oldest son of a prosperous brewer, would someday be standing with his wife on the dock in Hoboken with little more than his hopes and dreams and one small wooden crate. But for the war, Harry's future would have been assured. No one who saw them that day, walking tentatively through the port, would have imagined that this young man had shown such an exceptional gift for horses that he had already ridden before the queen of Holland. The couple's clothes were plain, they spoke little English, and they carried little with them, but they had a bright look in their eyes. Although somewhere, deep in that crate, lay a single photo album from home, right from that first day in Hoboken, the couple kept their eyes fixed on the future. They boarded the train south, headed toward a new life that they were determined to embrace.

Their patron, Bill McCormick, grew tobacco on a farm outside of High Point, North Carolina. The sharecroppers' deal seemed more than generous to Harry and Johanna. Accustomed to tiny Dutch farms, the new immigrants saw the large tobacco fields stretch out to the horizon with promise. The sharecropping system was simple: the owner gave the aspiring farmer land to work, housing, and enough capital to plant, expecting him, in turn, to split his profits fifty-fifty. In the sleepy rural area, life seemed to roll along as it had for nearly a century. The share-cropping system dated back to the post–Civil War period, when white farmers had leased fields to newly freed slaves, capitalizing on their la-bor without sharing ownership of the land. Tobacco farms were not highly mechanized: they commonly used mules in the fields, horses for general farm work, and large amounts of manpower.

Harry (front, right) carries the flag of St. Oedenrode in the parade to celebrate the queen of Holland's return from exile in 1945.

But after the Second World War, the American farm economy had started going through tumultuous changes. In the postwar boom times, many black sharecroppers had left the land and migrated to industrial jobs in the North. Already 1950 was shaping up as a weak year for farm-ers, with overall profits down 10 percent nationwide. With the recent technological advances, production had increased, but the need for la-bor had lessened. As the demand for farm labor decreased nationwide, Mexican farmworkers in the western United States were increasingly accused of "stealing jobs," culminating in the controversial Operation

Wetback in 1954, when more than 400,000 migrant workers were involuntarily repatriated to Mexico.

The "farm problem" was at the top of most politicians' agendas. Small farms were consolidating; workers were leaving or being pushed off farms; and the cost of government subsidies to farmers was skyrocketing. The entire way of life that underpinned the farm was being challenged from all directions. But when Harry and Johanna arrived, they knew nothing of the complicated economic, social, and political forces that swirled around farming at midcentury. They only knew that they were hardworking, and they intended to make a go of it in their new land.

Workers' cabins were lined up in a row along the farm's edge. Harry and Johanna's new home had been fashioned from rough plank boards; standing inside, you could see gaps through some of the walls, straight to the outside. Harry worked in the fields from sunup to sunset, while Johanna tried to spruce the place up despite their small budget, sewing curtains and making cushions. They lived carefully on their meager capital, expecting that in November, when the tobacco crop came in and was sold at auction, they would reap a good reward.

The tobacco country in Guilford County, North Carolina, was nothing like St. Oedenrode, the close-knit traditional Dutch village where Harry and Johanna had grown up. But they appreciated the buoyant mood in America. The Dutch countryside had been ravaged by the war, and the postwar atmosphere in Europe was pessimistic. Loss and destruction had marred the landscape that people had known and loved—fortunes had been lost, villages torn apart. Across the ocean, the United States beamed like a beacon, a place where peace reigned, the homeland of the brave young men who had risked their lives to come to the Dutch people's aid. It wasn't easy to get a visa to the United States. Most young Dutch emigrants had gone to Canada, where the government had extended an open hand to people with a background in farming.

Growing up, Harry had believed that he would lead a life much like his father's. While he wasn't interested in the brewery business, he loved the farm. As the oldest son, he'd assumed he would take it over. But after the war, so much had changed. The farms needed to be rebuilt, and the economy was sagging. In his boyhood, Harry had worked harder than anyone to help his father keep the farm running. The farm and the

Harry's father astride his horse. The church in St. Oedenrode is in the background.

brewery went hand in hand: the crops fed the animals and provided the hops for the beer. The one couldn't survive without the other. But after the war, without horses to work the land, the fields had lain fallow, and the whole farm had fallen into disarray.

Then, a year or two after the war ended, just when things were starting to look a little better, a tornado swept through town, knocking over trees and littering the fields with debris. The next morning, Harry, then eighteen, and his younger brother Jan, thirteen, headed out to clean up their land. Harry took two horses over to a field that needed plowing; Jan took a third to where the big cultivator had been left the day before. A short while later, Harry looked up, confused to see Jan's horse galloping toward him unhitched, with his brother nowhere in sight. Harry left his team and ran to the next field.

Jan lay on the ground unconscious. A tree branch had downed an electric wire, and some part of the metal cultivator must have been touching it. When Jan had grabbed the machine, a powerful electric shock had jolted him. Harry ran back to the farmhouse, shouting as he ran. The family poured outside to come to their aid.

Pale and silent, Jan lay in a coma for days. Each day the village doctor came around to check on him; but he said little, and often just shook his head. The family waited in a tense vigil, watching the handsome, fair-haired boy, hoping for some sign that he was going to take a turn for the better.

They prayed and lit candles, watched and waited, and after a few days, their prayers were answered. Jan opened his eyes and began to speak. It was a slow process, but he would eventually get better, making almost a full recovery. Jan had been a quick boy and good with his studies, but after the accident, he struggled in school. He was still good with the farmwork and the animals, but he was no longer able to learn the way he had.

Harry's mother (left) with some of his twelve brothers and sisters.

It had always been expected, by the entire family, that Harry, as the eldest son, would take over the farm. But Jan, like Harry, had always been interested in farming, and Harry could see that Jan was going to need it more than he did.

When Harry thought of leaving his homeland behind, he took strength from the idea of the American paratroopers he had met. They were cocksure and courageous. The young Dutch boys had flocked around them, eager to help them fight the Nazis any way they could.

Now the only soldiers left in St. Oedenrode were dead ones. The field where Harry used to practice his horseback riding had been turned into

The St. Oedenrode riding club meeting on the field that the de Leyer family later donated to the church to expand its cemetery. Harry, age sixteen, is on foot on the far right. He had recently earned his riding instructor's certificate.

a graveyard—donated by Harry's father to the Catholic church when its cemetery overflowed with war casualties. After the war, the village girls took it upon themselves to lovingly tend the fallen soldiers' graves. A good student who had learned some English, Harry's sister wrote letters to the families of some of the fallen American soldiers to let them know that their graves were being cared for. One of them, Nicky Schiltz, had come from a part of America they had never heard of—Greensboro, North Carolina. Neither Harry nor Johanna had met Nicky Schiltz when he was alive, but they had met other soldiers—young men who were friendly and brave. Nicholas Corbin Schiltz, a first lieutenant in the army's 502nd Parachute Infantry Regiment, had been killed in action on September 18, 1944. Harry's sister hoped that her letter would bring comfort to his family. She wanted them to know that his sacrifice had not been forgotten.

Ja, Harry would not mind moving to a place where people like that hailed from. He learned that Canada was accepting Dutch immigrants with agricultural backgrounds, so he applied for a visa and started saving every penny for his move. But shortly after Harry's sister mentioned to the American family that Harry would be moving to Canada, a telegram arrived in St. Oedenrode. The Schiltz family would sponsor him to come to America.

There was only one thing left to do. Harry had been sweet on Johanna for years. Her brothers rode with Harry in the 4-H riding club. Johanna was a brown-haired beauty who loved the same things that Harry did—animals, and especially horses. Johanna's sister had already immigrated to America, and when Harry talked about going there, Johanna's eyes shone, as though she too could imagine the fields that stretched out as far as the horizon.

Now, in spite of the dirt, and the heat and humidity far greater than he had ever known, in spite of the rough cabin with the cracks in the walls, in spite of the hard hours of work between sunrise and sunset, Harry and Johanna attacked their new life with the vigor particular to those who have known hardship.

Harry did not mind fieldwork—he had been doing it all his life— but he missed taking care of the animals, and most of all, he missed the horses. He would never forget the flying sensation of jumping in a huge arena festooned with bunting and bursting with the sounds of a brass band. Those cherished memories helped him get through his days. Harry wiped his sweaty brow and got on with his work.

In the afternoons, Harry often walked a quarter mile down the road to help out at his neighbor's dairy. Calvin Ross ran a small ice business and a farm. He had a gas-powered engine to blow the hay up into the silos, but he used a horse-drawn wagon to pull the corn in from the fields. Harry offered to drive the wagon. He enjoyed being around the animals, and the dairy, with its predictable rhythms, reminded him of life back home. Life in St. Oedenrode had been marked by activities that changed with the seasons—swimming in the summer and ice-skating in the winter when the ponds froze over. Every spring, the children had gotten excited when the circus came to town, bringing the Cossacks—Russian riders who performed tricks and daring feats on horseback.

One day, Cal told Harry to set aside the weekend so that he could drive him to the North Carolina State Fair. Harry had never seen so many tractors in one place. He and Cal walked around with awe, looking at the contraptions. In the early 1950s, there were still many small family farms in America, and many of those farms still used horses to pull their plows. The fancy tractors cut down on the time necessary to work the fields, making farming more efficient, but they also required much more capital. A tractor was many times more expensive than a horse. The shiny tractors and farm equipment that Harry and Cal admired that day would soon permanently change the face of American farming, as small family farms were sold off and consolidated, leaving in their place large industrial farms with sufficient money to invest in farm equipment.

Back at Cal's farm, horses still did much of the work. Nobody had thought to use the workhorses for riding, but one day Harry caught one out in the field and saddled him up—the ride was rough, but solid. Experimenting with all three horses, and making makeshift fences from old posts and rails, Harry found that one of them could even jump a bit. He called the mare Petra, after the beloved horse he had left behind in Holland.

People scratched their heads at the sight of Harry and Petra out in the fields, late in the afternoons, when everyone else wanted nothing more than to relax in the shade with a cold beer. They couldn't help but stare at the young man, dirty and sunburned from being outside all day, riding in the field on the clunky old plow horse. Still, if a person who knew horses happened by, it was clear from the way the young man sat in the saddle, from his erect bearing, the ease and suppleness in his back, and the light hands on the reins, that this man knew how to ride. The language he spoke to the horses was mostly silent, but sometimes he muttered a few words in Dutch.

Circling around, galloping, and jumping, for a few minutes Harry could forget everything and recapture that feeling of flying. Afterward, he groomed the horse carefully, gave her an extra measure of grain, and then released her into the pasture. Tomorrow, he would hitch her up to the wagon to lug corn to the silo, and he knew the horse would plod along, as quietly as before. But just because you are hitched to a burden does not mean that you do not sometimes want to fly.

The entry fee for the local horse show was three dollars; it bought a rider the chance to vie for a ten-dollar prize. For Harry and Johanna, the cost was an extravagance. But riding mattered to Harry, deep down in his bones. He worked so hard all the time, they reasoned, that it couldn't hurt for him to ride in the show. The old plow horse didn't stand a chance, but Harry groomed her as though she were a top thoroughbred. Back home in Holland, the same horses who pulled the plows and carriages were saddled up and ridden to horse shows on the weekends. This seemed normal to Harry. He dug out his riding breeches and jacket from his suitcase, and Johanna carefully mended and ironed them. He blacked his tall boots and slicked down his hair. Harry was ready to go.

There are no photographs to record the moment when Harry de Leyer arrived at his first horse show on American soil. He was riding an old workhorse, and his clothing was correct but simple. But he had taught the horse well, and Harry brought home the blue ribbon and the ten-dollar prize in the open jumper class. Johanna, standing at the railing, was mostly excited about the money, which would help pay for much-needed baby things. They were expecting their first child.

But someone else stood near the railing that day, a savvy Irishman named Mickey Walsh. With his broad smile, white linen jacket, and bow tie, Mickey was an immediately recognizable figure. Irish through and through, the fifty-year-old had wavy gray hair set off by bright blue eyes. Between 1950 and 1955, Mickey Walsh was the first person to win a total of $1 million in the breakneck sport of steeplechasing, where horses compete at full speed over tall solid-timber fences. Now at the very top of his game, Mickey had recently founded the Stoneybrook Steeplechase in Southern Pines, North Carolina, a horse-centered community not far from McCormick's farm.

Like many professional horsemen, Mickey had come up the hard way. Born into a family that had been in the horse business for generations, Mickey left home as a young man to seek his fortune in the United States. But he arrived in New York at a time when prejudice against Irishmen abounded and signs declaring NO IRISH NEED APPLY were emblazoned on shop windows throughout the city. Mickey finally found a job leading out horses in Central Park, until he managed to parlay his horse skills into a better line of work: on Long Island, as a horse boy for some of the grand estates.

Walsh soon became one of the most competitive jumper riders in the country, winning every major championship for a series of rich owners. That day in North Carolina, the dapper man with the nimble athletic build of a lifelong rider and the confident grin of someone used to winning looked up from whatever he was doing and saw a young fellow whose grace in the saddle was immediately apparent to an old salt like him. Maybe it takes a rider to know a rider, because Mickey—unfazed by Harry's plow horse mount and provincial Dutch riding habit—recognized him in an instant for what he was: a man with a gift.

After Harry had secured his blue-ribbon rosette and the prize money, the Irishman approached. Harry's understanding of English was still a bit rough, but he recognized the Irish brogue.

"What do you do, young man?" Mickey asked.

"I'm a farmer," Harry replied. "I work on a tobacco farm near Greensboro."

"You're no farmer. You are a horseman. You should be working in horses."

Harry's heart beat a little faster. He could not imagine anything better. But even here, in a local show, Harry saw the kind of people who were involved in horses in the United States: women in white gloves and hats with veils, and tweed-coated country squires whose farms were funded by the kind of sharecropping labor Harry did. He wasn't bitter; he was lucky to be in the United States, and he knew it. There were opportunities here and a land that seemed full of hope and promise, not scarred by the sadness of the aftermath of war.

But horses . . .

Harry remembered the times when everyone else had gone home, when the sky was darkening behind the church in St. Oedenrode, and he remained, bone-sore in the saddle, working on one move—a flying lead change or a tight turn—always trying to improve. Harry knew that he could read a horse, with just the touch of his fingers and the feel under his seat bones. He knew it absolutely. But he was a family man now; his wife was going to have a baby. Horses were for fun, and the tobacco farm was where his livelihood lay.

The Irishman looked at him with bright eyes and a broad, open smile.

Harry tried to form the word no, but it just wouldn't come to him. He sat astride that old workhorse and for a moment, just one moment, allowed himself to imagine a better life, the life he really wanted.

"I don't know if I'm good enough . . ." Harry said.

The blue-eyed man kept smiling. "Oh, you're good enough," he said. "I can tell you want to win more than most people, and believe me, son, that's all it takes."

Riding back to Cal's farm at the end of the day, Harry felt tired but satisfied. He had ten dollars in his pocket, and the words of the older man lodged somewhere deep in his breast. It was not until days later that Harry would discover that the friendly fellow was the legendary Mickey Walsh, the man who had started leading out ponies in Central Park and was now an influential millionaire.

Nonetheless, Harry turned over the words in his mind as he lay down to sleep that night. He couldn't imagine wanting anything more than he wanted to ride. But rows and rows of shiny green tobacco plants were implanted behind his eyelids, and he and Johanna were all too aware that they needed that crop to do well or they would be out of money. Harry was starting to understand that things didn't look good. Bill McCormick was a drinker who did not manage the farm very well, and even worse, the summer season had been hot and dry. They needed rain, and a lot of it soon, or the crop would fail.

In tobacco country, November is auction time. Ever since the Great Depression, the government had put in subsidies to support the price of the crop, but even so, there were great variations in the prices. Johanna was now seven months pregnant and their start-up capital, the $160 they had saved in Holland and brought with them as a nest egg, had almost been exhausted as the long, hot summer dragged into a dusty, dry fall. Each day, the locals searched the sky for rain that did not come. The glossy rows of tobacco started to shrivel and yellow.

Eventually, Harry and Johanna had to face the truth. All of their hard work had come to nothing. The tobacco crop was worthless that year, and their 50 percent take of the crop ended up being 50 percent of nothing. It was time for them to look for work somewhere else—Harry needed a salary, however small, to keep them afloat.

Harry had stayed in touch with Mickey Walsh, who promised to keep his eye out for work for Harry, but so far, there'd been nothing. With the baby almost due, they realized they had no choice. Johanna's sister, who lived near Greensboro, offered to take them in while they waited for the baby to come. Harry continued to pick up odd jobs. It was the only work he could find. The bill for the hospital was $130, and Harry worked round the clock just to get that amount. Paying the hospital bill in full, in cash, cleaned them out. Their son, Joseph, who quickly earned the nickname Chef, was born into uncertainty. Harry and Johanna just didn't know what their next move should be, and now they had another mouth to feed.

With all of the changes going on in the American farm economy, it was not a propitious time to be an immigrant trying to make a living in farming. In prewar Holland, the farm and brewery had supported their entire family—but as Harry had quickly learned, the gulf between working as a hired hand and owning your own land was vast. All over the country, droves of young people were leaving the land behind for higher education or factory work. Farms that had been in families for generations were sold off, the land consolidated into fewer larger farms, the beginning of a long-term trend that by the 1980s would mark the virtual end of the family farm.

When they'd stepped aboard the ship bound for America, it had never occurred to Harry that he would not be a farmer. He'd spent his entire life working the land. But times were changing.

Harry and Johanna needed a place of their own. They could not keep imposing on Johanna's sister. Harry traipsed the streets, continually looking for work. The furniture factories in High Point were hiring—Harry scanned the ads, wondering if it was time to consider that kind of job.

But Mickey Walsh had kept the young man in mind, and just when things were looking bleakest, a call came through. Mickey had recommended Harry for a position in a Pennsylvania riding stable. A job in horses. For the third time since arriving in Hoboken, Johanna and Harry packed up their suitcases and moved on.

8

The Stable Boy

Bakerstown, Pennsylvania, 1951

Harry and Johanna arrived at the Stirrup Hill Horse Farm, in Bakerstown, Pennsylvania, just north of Pittsburgh, in 1951. They had a place to live on the grounds of the stables—just a small apartment, but at least there were no cracks in the walls, and Harry was busy from morning to night working with the horses. A jack-of-all-trades at the stable, he was responsible for anything and everything: cleaning stalls and feeding the horses, riding the horses, looking after the riders who came to the stables for trail rides and lessons. He groomed horses to get them ready to ride, and he hot-walked them afterward, leading them in their halters and lead ropes to cool them down.

And now he had a regular paycheck: $35 a week. Even in the early 1950s, when the average American salary was about $3,500 dollars a year, Harry's new wages were next to nothing, a pittance, especially for a growing family. The lean war years had taught Johanna to scrimp and save, and she applied herself to the task with vigor. She was determined to find a way to stretch those dollars as far as she could. Baby Joseph was only three weeks old when they arrived at their new home. Johanna clipped coupons from the newspaper, mended clothes and darned socks, and never let a penny go unaccounted for.

No matter how hard he worked, Harry still felt that his new life was one of ease—compared to the hardships of the war years, the things that he had endured, and the even harder things that he had seen others endure. To be paid to ride horses seemed like incredible good fortune. Harry worked from the crack of dawn, when he got up to muck the stalls, till after sunset, when he came in, bone-weary and smelling of horse sweat and saddle soap. But in spite of the work, and the meager pay, he had the feeling that, at last, he was doing what he was meant to.

Harry's boss was happy with him; he was good at his job, a hard worker, and serious. Harry kept the stalls clean and banked up with fresh straw, and he groomed all of the horses, keeping their manes tidy and their coats buffed to a gloss. Harry even got to ride some of them. His boss had noticed that he had a gift—Harry could calm the nervous horses, handling even the most difficult ones without a problem.

Huge animals with lightning-fast reflexes, horses are built to take flight quickly. A startled horse will lash out with his hooves and attempt to bolt. In a battle of brute force, a horse will always win, outweighing a man by a power of ten, but men have devised many clever ways to control horses. A chain can be slipped under a horse's chin, then around the bony prominence of its nose. A more extreme method is to work the chain tightly around the horse's upper lip. Watch someone handle a horse who is hard to lead, groom, and tie, and you will normally see him stand at its side, holding tight to the lead shank, or chain, and giving the chain a series of sharp yanks.

Harry's method was different. He stood in front of the horse with the lead rope slack and looked it straight in the eye. Most people lack the courage to stand directly in the path of a frightened horse, but Harry had the uncanny knack of seeming to speak to a skittish animal with the language of his movements. Harry would calmly hold up one hand. The horse would snort and snuffle, then finally drop its head, reaching its nose forward toward Harry's outstretched palm.

Ja, Harry did a good job. But Johanna was worried. Thirty-five dollars a week was hardly enough to put food on the table, even with her thrifty ways. Joseph was one now, and she and Harry were delighted that a second baby was on the way. Harry and Johanna talked it over. Another ten dollars a week would make a world of difference to the young family.

Hat in hand, Harry approached his boss. "I've been here for a year," he said. "I've worked hard, and I think you like what I do."

Mr. Sterling nodded his assent. The young man was a hard worker and 100 percent reliable. And he was a family man, not off carousing like many of the young stable boys.

"I need a raise," Harry said. "Just ten dollars per week."

The boss didn't even pause long enough to give the impression that he was thinking it over. He said no—he was already paying the going rate.

"But—"

Harry did not get a chance to finish his sentence. His boss held up his hand. "There are a million more guys like you out there—guys who want to spend their days fooling around on a horse. Not my problem you've got mouths to feed. I got my hay and grain, vet bills and horse-shoes . . . all that stuff just goes up, up, up. I can find somebody who will be happy to work for sixty dollars a month."

No use in arguing. Harry was disappointed, but the year spent in the horse business had convinced him that he could make a living at it. Harry called Mickey again and asked him for advice.

Mickey might be living the high life now, but he had not forgotten the people who had given him an early break when he was just a horse boy in Central Park.

"I think I've got something for you," Mickey said. "Big farm in Virginia—the wife's Dutch. The man is older and he likes to ride out early in the mornings. A daredevil. She worries he'll get hurt. She wants someone to ride with him."

Virginia. Harry had heard enough about America now to know that Virginia was horse country. Harry and Johanna loaded up their station wagon. With Joseph tucked into the back seat, they headed off to their new home, a place called Homewood Farms.

Nothing could have prepared Harry and Johanna for the beauty of David Hugh Dillard's grand estate. The countryside around Amherst, in Virginia's renowned Shenandoah Valley, was storybook beautiful: huge rolling farms, lined with dark post-and-rail fences. From the long, tree-lined lane leading down to the house, to the prize-winning peacocks that strutted across the grounds, Homewood Farms was a showplace. Set on hundreds of manicured acres, the farm was a world unto itself: rough log smokehouses produced twenty-five Virginia hams every year, cured and smoked to perfection; acres of kitchen gardens yielded abundant fresh produce for eating and preserving; in the dairy farm Jersey cows produced rich milk and butter; and at the private racetrack at his adjacent Oak Park Farms, Mr. Dillard ran his thoroughbreds. All in all, it was the essence of a Virginia gentleman's plantation.

David Hugh Dillard strutted across the land like one of his prize-winning peacocks, making up in bravado what he lacked in height. Only two or three inches over five feet with his boots on, he was known for his devotion to his family, and for his high, exacting standards.

It came as no surprise that Harry was expected to do a lot more on the farm than just accompany Mr. Dillard on his morning rides. His boss fancied thoroughbreds and had his own racetrack, and now he wanted to start training some of the horses in the glamorous sport of show jumping.

When Mr. Dillard was off the farm, he told Harry, he should drive his Cadillac, "just to keep the battery charged," and he invited Harry and Johanna to stay in the big house to house-sit.

After Harry bought and sold a few horses for Mr. Dillard at a profit, the businessman, ever the entrepreneur, had an idea. He suggested that Harry might be able to start up a horse business, buying and selling horses.

"But I have no money," Harry said. Mr. Dillard loaned him some seed money, and Harry started buying a few horses and attracting students from the local high school for lessons.

Homewood Farms was only a few miles from Sweet Briar College, renowned for its equestrian school. One of the most famous horsemen in America, Captain Vladimir S. Littauer, often put on clinics there. At Captain Littauer's request, Harry started bringing his horses over to Sweet Briar so that the students could ride them—and Littauer also encouraged Harry to obtain a riding instructor's certificate by attending one of his clinics. Littauer, an old White Russian who had served in the Imperial Cavalry of Czar Nicholas II, lived on a large estate in Syosset, Long Island, and was well regarded throughout the horse community. Like Mickey Walsh, Littauer saw past Harry's humble circumstances and recognized his gifts as a rider.

Everyone at Homewood liked Harry, especially the children. Ten-year-old Sharon, the farm manager's daughter, was delighted when the de Leyers gave her a cast-off pair of wooden shoes; she happily clomped around the farm in them. The horses whinnied when they saw Harry coming, and the children followed him like a litter of puppies.

Johanna loved her new home, and she loved Mrs. Dillard, too—the kindly wife of her husband's boss was of Dutch heritage and always showed them the utmost respect. Their second child, Harriet, was born shortly after they arrived there, and then, like clockwork, a year later, another blond-haired boy, Marty. Mr. Dillard paid Harry a fair wage, and let him earn additional money from teaching and buying and selling a few horses of his own, and Harry's horses were starting to win ribbons at local shows. Life was pleasant; it seemed like a place to settle in and call home.

For Harry, however, it was not enough. As much as he enjoyed living at Homewood, he wanted a place of his own. In St. Oedenrode, the farm and the brewery had belonged to the family. Working for Mr. Dillard, no matter how pleasant, felt like relying on the good graces of others. Now, with his instructor's certificate in hand, Harry dreamed of starting a business of his own, a proper riding establishment where he could train horses and teach people to ride. But he lacked capital to set himself up in business.

Captain Littauer came to Harry with a tempting offer. Eleonora Sears, one of the top horsewomen in the country, needed someone to ride for her at her grand estate, Prides Crossing, in Massachusetts. Miss Sears was a demanding taskmaster. Anyone who worked for her would have the opportunity to ride some of the top horses in America, and quite possibly the world. It was a wonderful job—for the right person. Would Harry be interested?

Harry knew Miss Sears by reputation. She was one of the most formidable people in the horse business. But he wanted to talk it over with Mickey first. Mickey knew Miss Sears well. She had recently bought a large horse farm in Southern Pines, North Carolina, Mickey's home territory, and Mickey's own daughter Joan often rode for her. Mickey said, "If she'll let you bring the horses to Mr. Dillard's, then okay, but if you have to stay at her place, then say no. You'll be right under her thumb. You will not be able to be your own man." When Miss Sears would not agree to Harry's terms, he could hardly believe that he was turning down a job to work with one of the top horsewomen in America. But by now, Harry knew what he wanted: he wanted to be his own boss.

Working for Mr. Dillard had given him a taste of the life he wanted, one where he ran his own business and called all the shots. He could not spend his life catering to the whims of rich people.

A short while later, Captain Littauer had a new proposition for Harry: a school for girls on Long Island was looking for a new riding master. Would Harry be interested?

Now Johanna had three small children to tuck into the back seat, Joseph, Harriet, and Marty; another house to dismantle; and another new life to start from scratch. And who knew what they would find there—up in New York, where neither of them had ever been?

But it looked like a good opportunity, so once more the de Leyers packed up their belongings and moved toward the future.

Six years after his arrival in America, Harry had his own business in St. James, his own horses, and his own tiny piece of land. There were times when he had to make hard decisions—which horses to keep and which ones to sell. Selling Snowman had been one of the hard decisions. But he could live with it because it was his own choice.

9

Where the Heart Is

St. James, Long Island, May 1956

Up before dawn, Harry drank scalding black coffee, then slipped into his wooden shoes and headed outside just as a few pink streaks lightened the sky. Snowman had gone to his new home the day before, so Harry was worried. The horses always noticed a change, and the barn seemed empty. Snowman had been a calming influence, like the older Knox students who looked out for the younger ones. Harry always paired the novice girls with the expert riders, and the quiet horses with the skittish ones. In the months since Snowman had been there, the horse had taken on the role of a paterfamilias. It would take the horses a few days to establish a new pecking order and, until they did, they would be out of sorts.

As they heard the heavy shoes clump down the lane, the horses started to whinny and stamp. Harry still half-expected to hear Snowy's familiar nicker among the chorus.

Ach, he had a sentimental streak—not the best trait for a horse trader. He'd never be ruthless—never drug up his lame horses with painkillers to make them pass for sound, never wrap poles with barbed wire and then bang the horses' legs to make them jump clean. He believed you should treat a horse the way you would want to be treated. Simple enough. That rule, learned from his father, had served him well.

And there was the other rule inculcated by his father: that on a working farm, every horse must earn his keep. Snowman had taught his pupils well; they had been eager to move on to quicker mounts. At the doctor's house, Snowman could spend his days as a pleasure horse— a role he was well suited to. A happy horse to a happy home. It was a rule Harry could live by. Like the horses, Harry would get used to the new order in the barn; it would just take him a few days.

Sure enough, the horses were restless. They stamped and rustled inside their stalls, weaving back and forth as he went down the line, tossing flakes of hay and pouring oats into rubber buckets. Slants of early morning light poured through the barn windows, lighting up the dust motes that hung in the air. Snowman's stall stood empty, an ordinary school-horse halter hung on a hook next to the open door. There had been no painted name tag on his stall to remove, no personalized tack box like the private boarders had. The empty stall looked like any of the others.

As Harry went down the line, calling each horse by its nickname, an air of calm settled over the barn. A couple of German shepherds trotted at his heels as he worked; a few stable cats sashayed in the aisle or licked their paws and watched the goings-on from perches up in the straw loft. Harry was the only two-legged critter in the barn, but he looked as much at home there as any of the others.

He loved his quiet early mornings, before the family was up. It was a good time to think. This morning, he was thinking about the big hole Snowman had left in the stable, which felt to Harry almost like losing a member of the family. But then he chuckled to himself—Johanna was expecting again; if the four-legged family had shrunk by one, the two-legged family was still growing. That helped him to keep things in perspective. He had doubled his investment in the horse, and though it might not be much, it was money in the bank.

And money was what Harry needed. Some of the biggest horse shows in the country were within a stone's throw of the Knox School. Harry had seen the incredibly athletic animals that competed in the big shows—mostly thoroughbreds whose generations of fine breeding showed in every move and in every one of their refined features. With the right horse, Harry believed, he could compete in these shows. He was willing to put in the time to train a novice with potential. But even an untrained thoroughbred fresh from the racetrack could cost thousands—plus the board and feed needed for several years of schooling. It was hard enough to earn his living by teaching riding at the school; training a champion jumper himself—it just didn't seem possible. Harry had an old photo album with pictures of himself parading through Amsterdam aboard Petra carrying his equestrian club's flag. In those days, he seemed a good bet to make the Dutch Olympic team. But nowadays that album was kept high up on a shelf and rarely looked at. That world was long gone, and Harry always looked toward the future.

As he forked fresh straw into the wheelbarrow and pushed it through the barn aisle, he knew that the desire to compete was still there, a slow-burning ambition that never left him. Harry planned to keep his eye out for the right candidate, one that needed some training, a diamond in the rough. And each time he made a profit on a workaday mount like Snowman, it would get him one step closer to finding that horse.

By the time the round of barn chores was finished, Harry had gotten himself used to Snowman's absence. He took a last look around, satisfied. Everything was in order, and all was quiet except for the sounds of horses chewing their morning feed. The sun was rising, and Harry heard the kitchen door bang: the children were up. Quiet time was over. On to his day. From the look of the sky, it would be fine weather for riding.

After a few days, the horses settled down, and Harry wasn't thinking about the big gray gelding quite so much. But one afternoon, Harry got a call from Snowman's new owner—who was *not* happy. Dr. Rugen complained that the horse had escaped his pasture and trampled his neighbor's fields. Was Harry sure that the horse wasn't a chronic runaway? Harry reassured the man. Horses are not prone to jumping out of their pastures. Usually, if they're given enough food and water, they're inclined to stay put. Was it possible that the doctor had forgotten to double-latch the gate? A clever horse can nuzzle open a gate with his lip if the latch isn't closed tight.

Certainly not, was the doctor's indignant answer. Of course he had latched the gate. The horse had *jumped* out of the pasture. Harry repeated his advice to make sure to keep the gate firmly latched shut.

He hung up with a chuckle, expecting that he would not hear from the owner again.

For those who don't know equines well, it is always a surprise that horses are normally content to stay inside paddocks constructed of post-and-rail fences. It's surprising because those same horses, when entered in jumping competitions, will willingly leap these same fences with a rider aboard. Unlike, for example, deer, which must be restrained by fences fourteen feet high, horses will happily stay inside pastures fenced at three and a half or four feet.

Horses are born with the ability to jump—the skill helps them leap small obstacles when they are headed across open terrain at a gallop. The sport of horse jumping developed relatively recently, growing out of the European tradition of hunting on horseback. In eighteenth-century France, riders would follow hounds on staghunts across miles of countryside, which sometimes obliged the riders to jump natural obstacles along the way: ditches, banks, low stone walls, and small creeks. The tradition moved to England, where it evolved into foxhunting. Here, too, riders followed the hounds across country on horseback, clearing small hedgerows, ditches, and water obstacles along their way. By the late eighteenth century, however, the British government had begun to pass enclosure laws, and areas that had traditionally been common land for sheep grazing were fenced off. Private ownership of land became the norm. English foxhunting enthusiasts, mostly wealthy landowners, thus had to jump those pasture fences as they crossed from one estate to another. Eventually, people realized that the thrilling sight of a horse leaping a fence could attract spectators, and artificial "fences" were constructed inside the confines of riding arenas. Even today, the names and shapes of jumps reflect their history as natural obstacles found in the field: brush, chicken coop, ditch, water jump, and post-and-rail fence are now the names of common obstacles in the horse show ring.

But horses, which generally weigh over one thousand pounds each, do not often jump fences on their own. Galloping across a pasture, they will leap playfully over a small ditch or log, but will stop when they reach their paddock fence. Even a show jumper, trained to sail over elaborate obstacles five or six feet high, will, when turned out to pasture, veer off and circle to the side rather than jump to clear the fence of his enclosure. One of the most remarkable things about horses is their willingness to jump for a rider they trust. Though it is a natural ability, evolved from the need to negotiate uneven terrain at a gallop, there is little evidence from nature that a horse will choose to leap over solid obstacles at great heights on its own.

Still, a good horseman pays close attention to the condition of his fences and the care with which he locks his gates; otherwise, he may find one of his charges frolicking about the neighborhood. Pasture fences are always constructed with the boards nailed to the inside of the post, because a resourceful horse confronted with loose fence boards may lean against a fence until the crosspiece falls off, then step over to get to greener pasture on the other side. But with good fences in place, most horses, except in unusual circumstances—like a terrible fright or a mare trying to get back to her foal—will not jump.

That was why Harry assumed that the doctor, an inexperienced horseman, had either forgotten to lock the gate or had a broken section of fence. The idea of an old plow horse taking it in his mind to jump out of the pasture was more or less inconceivable. And sure enough, Harry heard nothing from Snowman or his new owner for the next few days.

But one morning when Harry went out to feed, a horse stood loose in the barnyard—a big gray glowing in the dawn light. He lifted his head and nickered three times.

"What are you doing here, you bandit?" Harry asked. He reached out his hand and the gelding took a few steps toward him, stretching his neck to nuzzle Harry's bare palm. His warm breath tickled. Harry would swear he had a pleased-as-punch look on his face.

A quick scan of the post-and-rail fences surrounding the stables did not provide a clue as to how the horse had gotten here: not a one was out of place, and the gate was firmly latched shut, as was the gate in the pasture beyond. The sun was just coming up, and the grass fields sparkled with silver dew. Dr. Rugen's property was several miles down the road. As Harry scratched his horse's favorite spot near the withers, Snowman rewarded him by curling his lip with pleasure. Harry looked thoughtfully back out across the fields, running his eyes along the rows of brown post-and-rail fences stained dark from the morning dew. Snowman had always had an intelligent look in his eyes, from that first day at the auction. Harry realized he might have underestimated the gelding.

Clipping a lead rope to the horse's halter, Harry led Snowman into the tie stall, threw a flake of hay into the metal feeder, and went to call Dr. Rugen.

"I've got your horse," Harry said. "You must have a fence down somewhere. I'll keep him safe until you get here."

"I checked the pasture fence myself yesterday," Dr. Rugen said. "But I'll have another look and be over to fetch him."

The next morning, Harry was thinking about Snowman's great escape as he headed out to the barn. He half-expected to see the big horse again. In the stable courtyard it was still dark, with no sign of a loose horse. Looked like the doctor had figured out how to keep the gate latched, Harry figured. He was relieved, but a little surprised to feel a slight sinking feeling. A second later, the big horse came into view. He had been just out of sight, lipping up dropped strands of hay near the hay pile. He raised his head at the sight of Harry.

"You . . . again . . . ?"

Snowman looked pleased with himself. This time he wasn't even wearing a halter. It was a drizzly morning, and he had mud on his legs. His forelock swept across his forehead at a rakish angle—his eyes were bright and his ears pricked forward at the sight of Harry—and with his broad chest and the arched line of his neck's crest, he almost didn't look like a plow horse. As he moved toward Harry, he whinnied a soft greeting.

"Well, we do like having you here, but you can't stay," Harry said, approaching Snowman. He took the horse's head in his arm and stroked the soft part of his muzzle. Snowman made no move to run away. He was quiet as ever, even standing there loose, not bothering the other horses in the stalls or trying to get into mischief, as other horses might. When Harry walked toward the tackroom to grab a halter and lead rope, Snowman followed him like a puppy, nudging his pocket for a carrot as he walked.

The doctor, though an affable man, was getting progressively more cranky. And no wonder. Harry had advertised Snowman as quiet and an easy keeper. Nothing looked worse than when a horse trader sold an animal without disclosing his faults. So either Harry didn't know much about horses or he was a crook—passing off a horse with stable vices to an unwitting new owner.

Nothing in the horse's temperament had made Harry think he'd try to run away. Snowman had never tried to stray from the de Leyer barn. But one dissatisfied customer could spread a lot of bad news about a horseman's business. There had to be a way to make this work. Harry offered to check out the doctor's pasture to see what the problem was.

Rugen's place was typical of small farms in the area: flat fields that used to grow potatoes; brown timber fences; a salt block; and a rubber bucket clipped to a fence post. Nothing seemed amiss. A nuzzle-proof snap held the gate closed.

Still, Harry walked around the entire fence line, testing each section to see if it would budge. Nothing did.

"You sold me a jumper," the doctor said.

Harry tried to repress a smile, but it was difficult.

The doctor wanted to know what was so funny.

"If I'd have known the horse could jump, I would have charged you more for him," Harry answered.

The doctor did not look amused.

"Consider him a bargain," Harry said, smiling again. It was true that the situation was a *little* funny. Here was a horse that couldn't jump a pole lying on the ground, and now he had gotten himself confused with Lassie Come-Home.

Harry studied the big pasture. A smaller paddock enclosed the far end, with an open gate connecting to the larger pasture.

"Can you keep him confined to the smaller pasture at night?"

The doctor nodded, and asked why.

"Well, let's just say he *is* jumping, and I don't see any other way he'd get out, then he wouldn't be able to get a running start from in there. Not much more than a couple of strides. That'd make it a much harder jump, and very few horses would do that."

The doctor agreed to give it a try.

Harry sure wouldn't mind finding a horse that could clear four feet with only a couple of strides to get a running start. *Ja,* if he had a horse like that, he'd be in the ring schooling him for the big Sands Point show in September. A friend of his, the trainer Dave Kelley, was going to be riding there—going for the Blitz Memorial Challenge, riding an incredible jumper, Andante. Harry liked being in charge of his own business, but that meant his budget was big enough to buy broken-down ex–plow horses, not trophy challengers. And ex–plow horses did not normally jump four-foot fences, certainly not without a running start. Harry was puzzled, but he was sure they could get the horse to stay put now.

Harry gave the troublemaker a scratch on the neck before he left.

"Now, stay here, you old bandit," he said. "You're making a lot of trouble."

Harry knew what it felt like to kick around without a real place to call your own. It was hard not to have a soft spot for a horse who wanted to come home that badly. At odd moments, Harry still remembered the first look exchanged between him and the horse, down at New Holland—the big dark brown eyes peering between the slats, the way the horse had stood so still and held his head up with the slaughterhouse truck behind him. Truth be told, Harry had never stood a chance against this big gray gelding. Harry was pretty sure that horses were a whole lot smarter than people gave them credit for.

The next morning, Snowman was back at Harry's; and the next, he was out of his paddock and in a neighbor's potato field. A couple of days later, he turned up at the de Leyers' again. The doctor swore that he had kept the horse confined to the small pasture, that no fences were down, that the gate had been double-latched each night. He was reaching the end of his patience, and the last thing Harry wanted to do was alienate his neighbors.

Harry did have one last trick up his sleeve, an old cowboy method that would certainly keep the horse at home. Out on the range, without anywhere to tie up a horse, riders needed to teach their horses to stay when ground-tied. A ground-tied animal stands quietly if his lead rope is simply dropped on the ground. To teach this skill, you tied the horse's lead rope to a big rubber tire. A horse could drag the tire around, but he wouldn't get far. The weight of the tire would keep the lead rope from getting tangled, and the soft rubber wouldn't hurt the horse's legs. When Harry suggested the technique for Snowman, the doctor at first thought he was crazy. But Harry assured him that it would work and would only be a temporary measure, a few days at most, until Snowman learned to stay put.

For the next few days, when Harry went down to the barn in the morning, he felt a mingling of relief and disappointment to find that Snowy wasn't there. Deep down, he had been rooting for the horse. But Harry reminded himself of his father's rules. If you want to make a living at horses, mind the dollars and cents. Never be cruel to a horse, never sell a horse to a bad home. Be thrifty, but don't scrimp on feed and care. Treat animals as you would like to be treated, but don't for a minute lose sight of the fact that you have a business to run.

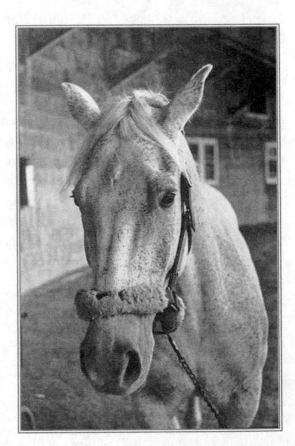

Snowman was a "man's best friend" kind of horse.

It doesn't take long for most horses to forget where they came from. A nice pasture and good food is usually enough to keep them in a paddock. After two days, Harry figured that Snowman was at last settled in his new home.

A new boarder came in that day, a customer who would pay eighty dollars a month, and Harry gave him Snowman's old stall. Snowman's halter came off the hook by his stall, moved to a nail in the tackroom with the other school-horse halters. The privately owned horses had leather halters with shiny brass name tags on them; the school horses' halters were interchangeable. As far as Harry was concerned, the Snowman saga was over.

But a few mornings later, Snowman was back. The big gray horse was standing in the middle of the stable courtyard.

First, Harry just stared. Then he started to laugh.

Snowman's head was high. When he saw Harry laughing, he shook his head, rattling the snap on his lead rope. Behind him dragged a big rubber tire, tangled with a piece of board ripped from the pasture fence. There was no mistaking the pride in the horse's eyes.

Standing in the barnyard, looking at the clunky flea-bitten gray dragging the heavy rubber tire, Harry realized that he had somehow missed the plain truth. He unclipped the tattered lead rope and led Snowman back to a stall. There was more to horses than columns of numbers, the profits and losses in his farm ledger. There is one thing no horseman can ever put a price on, and that is heart.

The Horse Can Jump

St. James, Long Island, 1956

Harry's kids celebrated their favorite's return, playing with him and clambering up on his back to ride. Snowy never minded—not even when two-year-old Marty tried to climb up his tail. He was always gentle around children, taking care where to put his giant hooves, lowering his head to nuzzle their hands, standing patiently while being groomed. Harry chuckled at the spectacle of Marty hugging Snowy's big leg, or the sight of one of the kids sitting on his back without a bridle or saddle. Harry himself had started sitting on horseback when he was two. That was the age when he started scampering up the manger to climb on board his own shaggy black pony. Even then, he could keep up with the older riders, jumping high obstacles by the time he was eight. Harry wanted his children to grow up just as he had, living and breathing horses. With Snowman, since the doctor had sold him back, his kids were learning to do the same.

Snowman was a perfect children's horse. Still, Harry could not forget the sight of the horse standing in front of him with a piece of fence board, barbed wire, and the tire attached to his rope. There were half a dozen five-foot paddock fences between home and the doctor's farm.

Maybe the horse was trying to tell him something.

Between riding with the Knox girls and running his own small stable, Harry de Leyer spent so much time on horseback during his first year on

Long Island that he wore right through the flaps of his old saddle. He often felt the rhythm of a trot or canter even when he was off a horse. He rode so much that he estimated distances not in feet or yards, but in horse strides, intuitively knowing how many it would take to reach a far-off pasture fence.

At night, he lay in bed thinking about horses. To Harry, every new horse that came into the barn was a puzzle to be solved. Snowman was a puzzle. If the horse could jump big sturdy paddock fences, why had he not shown any particular skill with a rider on his back?

There are different schools of thought about riding. Some people believe that you should educate the horse in the art of collection, akin to the training in classical dance, where the required movements are carefully honed until they become perfectly balanced and controlled. Others propound the forward method, believing that a horse knows how to move naturally and it is often the rider's interference that causes problems. Though Harry had received lessons from his father growing up, and had participated in his local riding club, most of what he had learned about horses had come through trial and error. He tried to think like a horse. Why tug on the horse's mouth all the time? He reasoned that if he had a bit in his own mouth, he'd want its use to be as gentle as possible.

So he always chose the softest bit a horse would respond to, such as a D-ring rubber snaffle. Its joint in the center keeps pressure off the horse's tongue, and the rubber is much softer than the hard metal of most bits. Most trainers' first instinct would have been to put a heavier bit in Snowman's mouth, a pelham, whose action is aided by a chain under the chin, or perhaps a kimberwicke, whose U-shaped mouthpiece puts a torque on the horse's tongue. But Harry believed that if you went easy on a horse's mouth, he would return the favor by being responsive. Some horses can be described as having a "soft mouth." These horses are acutely sensitive to any kind of pressure on the reins. Other horses are "hard-mouthed," having grown so used to having the reins jerked that only a severe bit will work. Harry thought there were many ways to talk to his horses; pulling on the reins and activating the bit was only one—and certainly not the most subtle.

Like other mammals, horses have five senses. Their acute vision, keen sense of smell and hearing, and exquisite sensitivity to touch are all designed to protect them from predators. Men have used the horse's sense of touch as an elaborate and detailed system of communication. A horse can "read" subtle changes, such as a slight movement of a rider's lower legs, a tightening of the reins, or an almost imperceptible shift in balance. A horse and rider who are working well together communicate in a subtle and fine-tuned nonverbal language—a sort of equestrian Braille. Messages are telegraphed from rider to horse in a way that, at its highest level, is almost invisible to a spectator.

All horses have some ability to jump, but most horses are not born to be jumpers. Three physical qualities factor into a horse's ability to clear high obstacles: speed, spring, and balance. Speed and spring are inborn, but balance must be taught.

Until 1878, the subject of a horse's exact series of motions at a gallop remained a subject of debate. Former California governor and racehorse owner Leland Stanford believed that there was a moment in the stride when a horse became airborne, but it was too fast to be seen by the naked eye. Stanford commissioned the British photographer Eadweard Muybridge, a pioneer in action photography, to do a series of photographs of a racehorse named Sallie Gardner. The series proved Stanford's contention. When a horse gallops his fastest pace, he propels off one rear leg into a gait that has four beats. The first three beats occur as his hooves strike the ground: one rear leg first, then the opposite front and rear simultaneously, then the other front leg. The fourth beat is a brief period of suspension when all four legs are off the ground. But when a horse jumps, he springs off his hind legs and lands on his front feet—as if he has split the gallop stride in two. The first half stride precedes the takeoff; the second half is after the landing. To take the next stride, he has to gather his haunches underneath him. Like ice-skaters who attempt tricky leaps and often fall, a horse has to perfect the ability to do something difficult over and over again, with the steady, reliable precision of clockwork. One jump is not much of a feat. A course of twelve or sixteen jumps of varying sizes and shapes is like an ice-skater's long program; with all of the practice in the world, the horse still may not succeed each and every time.

Harry knew that Snowman had spring; the horse had demonstrated that already by leaping paddock fences with next to no running start.

But the qualities of power and steadiness needed to pull a plow were nothing like the supple calisthenics required from a jumping horse.

Harry had a puzzle on his hands—and that is what he liked best. A horse with sufficient spring to jump out of a paddock should be able to carry a rider over a small fence, but Harry had already tried the most rudimentary step for a jumper, and the horse had tripped and stumbled. The gelding was willing, honest, and kind. What he seemed to lack was *ability*. Still, Harry was convinced that Snowman had *some* ability. He was determined to find out.

The first step in training a horse to jump is to teach him to negotiate a series of poles laid on the ground, called cavaletti. The poles are spaced six feet apart for a trot or nine feet apart for a canter, teaching the horse to pace himself and pick up his feet. In order to trot through the poles without rapping them, a horse needs to lift his feet higher than usual. This activity requires muscle, balance, and good training—the same way that sports require these abilities of human athletes. At first, an average horse stumbles, unsure about how to time his stride to avoid knocking into the poles.

With patience and repetition, however, most horses will learn how to trot over the series of poles without knocking into them. At this point, the horse understands the principle of regulating his stride to avoid hitting an obstacle. This is the first step.

Harry set up poles, evenly spaced on the ground, and headed Snowman toward them at a brisk trot. Snowman tripped, then stumbled, tripped again, then righted himself. Harry patted the horse, dismounted, reset the poles, and tried again. Not every horse mastered this right away—but Snowman showed no signs of being a natural.

Once a horse can trot through a series of poles on the ground, the next step is to add a raised pole at the end of the line. Most horses will make a small hop over this obstacle. The pole may be only six inches off the ground, but this is a triumph. The horse could just as easily trot over the bar, probably knocking it over, or refuse to jump it, ducking past it to the outside. That small hop signifies big progress. He trusts his rider enough to hurl himself airborne and carry his rider with him.

One of the hardest things for a young horse—or a horse like Snowman, who had never jumped with a rider on his back—is to learn how to balance with a rider aboard. Imagine a hurdler suddenly running a race with a toddler strapped to his back; a rider of over one hundred pounds changes the horse's natural center of balance. A skilled rider affects it less—but every rider has an effect.

As the horse gains in proficiency, the final pole is raised; then two jumps begin to follow the ground poles. Like gymnastics for people, this is known as gymnastic jumping, and as the horse practices through these lines, he learns how to control the length of his strides, gather himself at the right moment, and take off knowing that he will be able to clear the obstacle. With a skilled and sensitive rider aboard, a horse begins to trust in his own abilities.

A show jumper is an equine athlete. He performs feats that are based on a horse's natural abilities, but like those of a ballet dancer, those abilities have been honed to a level of control, skill, and grace that does not exist without hours of disciplined training. Not every horse is born to be a world-class athlete—but some are. Some horses embody that desire to excel seen in every great athlete. Those are the horses that eventually star in the sport horse pantheon.

What makes the sport of riding so unpredictable and endlessly alluring is that it requires a partnership. Just as the most brilliant rider is nothing without a great horse, so the greatest horse cannot excel without an equally talented rider. As Vladimir Littauer explained in his classic 1931 instructional manual *Jumping the Horse,* success over a jump depends largely on the rider himself. A "bad rider will disturb [the horse], a good one will not interfere with him; a very good one will help him over." In the 1950s, two main riding styles dominated in jumper competitions in the United States. One was the chiefly self-taught style of the professionals, mostly men, many of them Irish, who passed along horsemastership from father to son. The other was the American military style, influenced by the classical traditions of European riding.

The equestrian arts have a written history dating back to the Greeks. Styles of riding have evolved over the years; the very upright posture and long stirrups popular in the Middle Ages to accommodate knights in armor gave way to a more forward posture, where a rider keeps his weight balanced. In the past, people riding jumpers did not understand the physics of the jumping horse, and the rider allowed his weight to fall back over the fence—this is the position seen in old hunting prints. Federico Caprilli, the chief riding instructor of the Italian cavalry in the late nineteenth century, discovered that if a rider kept his weight forward over a fence, staying with the horse's center of gravity, the rider would be more secure and the horse could jump better. This forward position soon swept across Europe and the United States. With the change in the rider's seat, horses could consistently clear high fences, paving the way for the development of the sport of show jumping.

By the mid-twentieth century, even self-taught professional riders had adopted some version of the forward seat. But unlike the classically trained U.S. cavalry riders, whose refined style reflected the influence of the European riding schools, the style of self-taught professionals was often unorthodox. A classically trained rider will keep his lower leg mostly perpendicular over a fence, his back straight, and his eyes looking forward. His hands will release forward, giving the horse room to stretch out his neck. A self-taught rider may achieve the same effect but without the same style, hurling his weight forward over the big jumps, his back rounded, or he may duck down over the horse's neck, letting his lower legs slide out behind him.

Harry's riding style was a hybrid of these two. He did not have the military training that had influenced many of the top American riders, but his style was less eccentric than those of some of the other self-taught riders. His balance over the fences was impeccable, allowing him to stay with the horse's motion even over big obstacles.

Harry reset the poles and circled back again, approaching the cavaletti at a brisk trot. Again Snowman stumbled, scattering the poles. But Harry soldiered on, determined to find the key to unlock this horse's ability.

Again through the cavaletti, and again the poles scattered. Harry looked up at the darkening sky, circled around, and tried again. He dismounted, set up a low cross-bar, and headed toward it at a canter, rising up out of the saddle and crouching forward. He let the reins slide between his fingers, encouraging the big gray to stretch out his neck and lower his head. It was not a big obstacle—paddock fences were much higher—but with a rider on his back, the horse might be reluctant to try.

Approaching a jump, a rider must *believe*. The rider must go forward in unison with the horse. Riders learning to jump often lag a split second behind the horse, waiting in the saddle to make sure the horse will take off. These beginners often fall off as the horse lands. But a skilled rider always goes with the horse, giving the power to the horse—and thus if the horse skids to a stop at the last moment, the rider may be propelled out of the saddle and over the fence alone. As Prince Philip, the Duke of Edinburgh, is said to have quipped, "A horse which stops dead just before a jump and thus propels its rider into a graceful arc provides a splendid excuse for general merriment."

Snowman did not stop at the raised bar. But he did not jump, either. Rather than make a small hop, Snowy broke to a trot over the low cross-rail, not even bothering to pick up his feet. A hind leg rapped the bar with a crisp *thwock*. A moment later, the horse settled down to a walk. Harry laughed, urged the horse into a canter, circled around, and tried again—but this time, the result was even worse. Snowman trotted over the low fence, knocking the pole clean off the standard. So the first attempt at jumping the horse was unspectacular, but Harry could still picture the solid paddock rail fences that the horse had cleared on his own.

Day after day, in the small paddock behind their farm, Harry took the horse out and schooled him through the cavaletti series. Sometimes Chef, now a strong little boy of six, helped out, setting the poles and putting them back when Snowman knocked them over. The horse was not a fast learner but Harry was patient, and he was careful not to push Snowman too much. After a while, he could trot through the cavaletti poles on the ground, and even mastered a low jump at the end. To give the horse a break, Harry put the kids up on his back, or they rode him to the beach. The horse was good and he was honest—he was just a little clumsy with his feet.

The summer drew to a close. It was time for Snowman to return to his box stall at the Knox School. But if Harry thought that any of the girls would be happy to see him back, he was wrong. The girls still thought this horse was beneath them. He was still placid and kind enough for the beginners, but when Harry suggested riding him through the cavaletti or over a small fence, he was met with the arched eyebrows of astonishment. *Snowman?* Still, the girls did not have the guts to cross their beloved Mr. D.

As the fall semester wore on, Snowman's winter coat grew out. With his plodding gait and shabby coat, his ragged mane looked even less appealing. One of the beginning riders, Estella Quintana, was a tall girl, too big for many of the quieter mounts, and not brave enough to ride one of the big thoroughbreds. She rode Snowman in her lessons, and he would carry her over cavaletti and even small cross-bars, trotting over the fences without picking up his legs. The big gray was not an exciting ride, but he was steady, and even a beginner like Estella could handle him with ease.

Ever optimistic, Harry continued to school Snowman over low fences himself, hoping that the horse would progress enough to carry the girls over a course of jumps. They were an unlikely-looking pair in the schooling ring. Because of the rough winter weather, Harry bundled himself up in a thick wool jacket, but he always rode bareheaded. And Snowman's winter coat made him look like a shaggy teddy bear. The performance was predictable. He stumbled over the cavaletti on the ground, and he tended to just step over the fences Harry set up at the end of the series, rather than make a proper jump, using the minimum effort required to clear an obstacle. He was starting to clear low hurdles without difficulty, but a good jumper snaps his knees up over the fence, raising them almost up to his neck. Snowman did not bother to snap up his knees—he left his forelegs hanging down, and his hooves tended to knock the fences as he went over. It wasn't dangerous, but it was not stylish either, and it was a bad quality for a jumper, who would lose points for touching any part of the fence.

By the time February came, Harry had resolved to try something new. He wanted to get a better impression of the horse's style by watching him jump with a stronger rider aboard. He'd decided to put his gutsiest rider, Bonnie Cornelius, in the saddle. As he called out the stall numbers to the girls, signaling which horse they would ride for the day's lesson, he could see a look of bewilderment come over Bonnie's face. Normally, he paired her with the most challenging horses, Chief Sunset or Wayward Wind. But Harry wanted to watch Snowman jumping from the ground—studying a horse's form over fences was critical. Maybe watching him with someone else in the saddle would help Harry figure out a better approach.

By the end of the lesson, poles had gone flying every which way, and he saw the frustration on his talented student's face. Harry despaired a little. If his best rider could not make the horse jump, there seemed little hope that Snowman would ever carry the rest of his students over fences.

The horse could be used as a walk-trot-canter mount—a steady old plug who taught a succession of girls to gain confidence in the saddle—but he just did not seem to be able to move beyond that. The image of rows of pasture fences, big and imposing, lining up between Harry's stable and the doctor's house still sometimes came to his mind, but the pasture jumper, if he truly had a talent, was keeping it well hidden.

Still, Harry kept on riding the gelding. One day, when he entered the ring on Snowman for yet another schooling session, the jumps were already set up to four feet around the arena. He had been schooling Wayward Wind over the fences and was planning to dismount and lower the poles to an appropriate height for his novice jumper. He warmed up the horse at a trot, then a canter, rising up into a two-point position as he let the horse out into a gallop.

By then, one of the barn hands had come over to the side of the ring and was watching him. "You gonna jump that plow horse over those big jumps . . . ?"

Harry laughed. He hadn't been thinking about it, but he loved nothing more than a dare. Snowman had been coming along a little—without much trouble he could clear a three-foot fence, the height of a beginner course. Why not try a bigger jump? What was the worst that could happen? If the fence was too big, the horse would knock it down. Simple enough. Or he might stop at the last minute—but Harry reckoned he could stay in the saddle.

As he came around the turn, he shifted his weight slightly, and with the pressure of his hands on the reins and a slight squeeze of his far leg against the horse's barrel, he headed the big horse toward the jump.

Harry sensed a subtle shift. The horse pricked his ears forward and electricity pulsed up through the saddle. With a practiced eye, Harry saw the distance to the fence. He lowered his weight slightly, telling the horse to shorten his stride, and the horse followed suit, for one stride, two, and . . . Snowman's hindquarters gathered underneath him; his hocks sank down. Harry kept the reins loose and his balance forward.

Up and over the fence they flew, front legs well clear of the poles. Harry listened for the hollow thump of the horse's hind legs trailing over the rail, but there was none. Harry glanced behind him at the big fence they had just cleared, then threw the reins down and patted the horse with both hands. Snowman, relaxed as ever, slowed to a walk.

Harry trained Snowman to jump on a loose rein. Here he lets go of the reins, trusting his horse with total freedom.

After testing all of the keys, Harry had finally found the one that unlocked the lock. Snowman would jump—just give him a fence that was high enough to respect. Harry gathered up the reins again, feeling the groove of the laces against his fingers, then signaled to the horse with a cluck and a nudge. One of Snowman's ears flicked back—a sign that he was listening. He picked up the pace and Harry guided him toward the fence a second time. Again, in a perfect orchestration of movement, the horse sailed over with room to spare.

Flight.

No wonder in Greek mythology the gods' horse Pegasus has wings. A horse who loves to jump gathers toward the fence with a trembling electricity so patent that some horsemen say they can feel it in the roots of their hair. As the horse makes his final approach to a fence, it matters not how much the rider wants or hopes or prays. It matters not what whip he carries or how often he nudges with sharp spurs. The horse who jumps well jumps for the joy of flight; the rider he brings along with him receives a bountiful gift that is completely undeserved.

* * *

A horse's scope refers to its ability to jump high fences. Most horses clear three feet easily; some horses are comfortable at four or four and a half feet. By the time fences are raised above five feet, even the better jumpers are starting to reach their limit. Only a few horses are successful at six feet, and heights above seven feet—higher than a horse's withers or a man's head—are achieved only by a select group of elite athletes. Some jumping competitions, such as the Puissance (the name means "power" in French), measure only a horse's ability to clear the highest possible fence. The confirmed world high-jump record for a horse is eight feet, three inches. But the taste for horse high-jump competitions has waned over the years. While some horses can clear obstacles higher than seven feet, the likelihood of a crash is high, and the consequences of crashing from a height of seven feet can be shattering for both horse and rider. One wrong step can easily result in a horse with a broken leg or a rider with a broken neck.

Over a five-foot obstacle Snowman flew, snapping up his knees tightly. Next, Harry raised the fences to six feet. Snowman cleared that height with no problem, again snapping tight his knees, and reaching forward with his neck to create a higher arc. Harry brought the poles up again, until they were about six feet, six inches. Snowman continued to soar, as if he'd been born with invisible wings. Each time the horse cleared another high obstacle, it left Harry breathless, sensing the coiled power in this horse that had been so well hidden and then suddenly unleashed. He could not shake the image of the horse running home to him, across meadows and over pasture fences, dragging an old rubber tire and a fence board. Harry remembered Snowman looking at him as if to say, "Here I am."

How many times had someone told Harry about his special gift for horses, his gift for intuition, for speaking to horses in their own language? This time, the horse had stood right in front of him, calling out his message loud and clear—but Harry had not heard it. Harry considered himself a tolerant man; he could put up with a lot. But one thing he could not bear was to be underestimated, to be judged for something other than his true ability and the content of his character. And now, here before him, was a horse that would gather up and soar over fences so high that he could not see to the other side, sinking back on his hocks and lifting off on nothing stronger than his own belief that he would find solid ground on the other side. For Harry, it was a humbling moment. He was proud of his ability to judge horseflesh, but this time he had been dead wrong. His gentle plow horse had the heart of a lion.

How many years had Harry been looking for just one horse who might have the makings of a champion?

Sometimes a man can forget the most important lesson of all: big dreams are often best accomplished when you do what you can with the materials you have at hand. This eighty-dollar gelding, this lesson horse, this shaggy-coated, friendly, children-loving animal, had hidden his gifts under the plainest, most humble exterior. And Harry, keeping his eye on every hot-blooded renegade thoroughbred that came into the barn, shining like a copper penny, was guilty of not recognizing when the key to his aspirations, a natural born jumper, had landed right in front of him. Delivered right to his doorstep in a beat-up old cattle truck one cold February night. Dropped off like a newborn in a picnic basket abandoned on a church's front step. Handed to him for only eighty dollars and a moment's worth of compassion. As Harry himself later repeated, many times over, "I was foolish enough to sell the horse, but the horse, he knew better." He knew well enough to jump paddock fences to find his way home.

11

A Grim Business

St. James, Long Island, Summer and Fall 1957

The business of horse-trading is an ancient art, and prior to the early twentieth century, there may have been no more colorful calling in American life. Called "David Harums" after a turn-of-the-century fictional character whose dictum was "Do unto the other feller the way he'd like to do unto you, and do it fust," horse traders were proud of their ability to drive a hard bargain. As the popular newspaper columnist John Gould said, in a 1947 article entitled "Hoss Trading," "Horse swapping is an ancient rite of the race, it is a game of swapping wits especially dear to our pioneer stock. . . . A horse trade is a delicate and artful procedure, its cardinal principles deeply embedded in human nature."

A horse trader was skilled in the art of euphemism: a barn-sour horse, one who refused to leave the stable, was described as "quiet at the hitch," a lazy horse was "gentle," and a poorly trained horse was "spirited." Practices such as feeding old horses pepper to make them appear more lively, dying their coats, or stuffing their noses with rags to hide a wheeze were all tricks of the trade. Traditionally, horses were sold as "sound," meaning healthy and not lame; "strong-winded," which meant "able to work"; or "at halter," meaning in an as-is condition.

In the era of horsepower, the breeding, sale, and trade of horses was a big business. In 1897, the Chicago stockyards held the largest horse market in the world. At its peak, it auctioned as many as 60 horses per hour, for over 100,000 sold per year. The horse trade dwindled during the first two decades of the twentieth century, but the market for work-horses picked up during the Great Depression. Many Depression-era farmers had been bankrupted buying farm equipment on credit and of-ten lacked the cash to pay for gasoline. Bred on the farm and fed home-grown grain, the lowly workhorse was touted as a form of sustainable energy. Then came the war years, when gasoline was rationed, so plow horses retained their popularity. The Percheron Horse Association of America, one of the premier draft horse organizations in the United States, reported an uptick in registrations during the 1930s and 1940s, followed by a swift decline in the early 1950s.

By the late fifties, the "David Harums," seemingly once a permanent fixture of the American landscape, had begun fading from view. A 1962 *Palm Beach Post* article about professional horsemen called their work "a grim business." Their number having by this point dwindled to only about two thousand, they made money by searching for cheap horses, training them, and trying to sell them to amateur riders who were will-ing to invest money in show prospects. The horse trade had straight-ened out since the days when horse traders filed horses' teeth to disguise their age—but not much. A nag parlayed to a trader would get a crash course in how to be a riding horse; if the poor creature failed to learn fast, he might soon meet a miserable fate.

Men who were trying to make a living at horses became masters of the quick turnaround. Professional horse traders tried to eke out a liv-ing swapping horses before the beasts ate up all their modest profits in hay and grain. Horse trainers were always on the lookout for a talented horse, hoping to resell him quickly at a profit. Sonny Brooks, a New Jersey professional, described his method of trying to get a horse sold. "When I get him on the road, I try to win as much as I can real quick. If he wins good, he'll bring a better price. The faster I sell, the less I have to pay in upkeep."

Out on eastern Long Island, where suburban sprawl had not yet taken over, there were still men who made their living from horses. People called them "the last of the Mohicans." They were rough in their ways but skilled in horsemanship, and they knew a bit about every as-pect of the horse business: shoeing, vetting, horse-breaking, and saddle repair. There wasn't anything they couldn't do in a pinch. Equestrianism was a gentleman's sport, but the men who traded in horses were anything but gentlemen.

The other traders on the island would sell a horse off to the knackers at Northport without giving it a second thought. Board and feed was expensive, and for a horse trader, a horse sitting in the barn unsold was just another column in the red.

The luckier horses got sold to the growing cadre of young people taking up the sport of horsemanship.

Horseback riding, a sport that evoked both Anglophile gentility and rural roots, was popular among parents who wished to give social advantages to their children. The mid-1950s saw a growth in English-style pony clubs, where suburban youngsters could learn the intricacies of old hunting traditions and memorize the fundamentals of horsemanship from old-fashioned British manuals. When the U.S. Army cavalry auctioned off the last of its horses after World War II, it gave preference to veterans who wanted to start riding schools. Riding apparel was sold in the active sporting goods section on the sixth floor of Saks Fifth Avenue, where saleslady Elsa Granville-Smith proudly proclaimed that she sometimes outfitted "daughters, mothers and grandmothers" on the same day and extolled the virtues of riding for developing "poise, grace and skill." Up-and-coming Americans liked to associate themselves with the glamorous world of horses, thus seeming to gain entry to the gated enclaves of the upper class.

The Knox parents were eager for their girls to have these advantages. They came out to the school on the train from the city. The women were clad in furs, wreathed in the expensive scent of Chanel No. 5 or Joy. The fathers were all the same—these were men who had money and demanded the best for their girls. Part of Harry's job was finding horses that would make the Knox girls look good at the local shows. If a horse joined the lesson lineup and a girl fell in love with it, then later Harry might be able to make an easy sale. If he found a good prospect that was too difficult for a girl to ride, a parent might pay for the horse and hand it over to Harry to train, hoping that it would settle down enough to be a suitable junior mount. Harry had already discovered, while working for

Mr. Dillard, that the best way for a riding teacher to make money was to find a green prospect, sell it, and make a profit.

Easier said than done. Harry had no capital. Harry was also hampered by the fact that he refused to unload a horse, like so much excess inventory. He set his sights on reject horses, the ones that no one else wanted, buying only those for which he thought he could find a home.

While trips to the horse auction at New Holland did not often turn up pearls, there was another great pipeline available for young, green horses: the racetrack. Beautiful thoroughbreds, bred to race, were sold off to the highest bidder if they turned out to be slow. Many of these horses, with their fine bloodlines and elegant confirmation, were snapped up by trainers hoping to turn them into show horses. Thoroughbreds are specifically bred to be high-strung—they need to charge through a starting gate on a hair trigger at top speed. But many of these horses could be turned into jumpers with the right kind of training.

One of these off-the-track thoroughbreds might have the right stuff to become a champion jumper if a trainer had enough patience and skill. A thoroughbred would have a much better shot than Harry's pet project, Snowman. In the 1950s, Long Island had one of the top concentrations of champion trainers and riders in the world—it was a breeding ground for current and future Olympians. The competition here would rival that found anywhere in the world.

Harry wanted to compete. Without funds to buy himself a horse, Harry's best bet was to find a good prospect for one of his students—the father would put up the cash. Harry could season the horse for a year or two before passing it to the girl to ride, devoting a couple of years to a decent animal, and hopefully winning his share of ribbons. But that horse would not be Harry's *own* horse; it would belong to someone else. Still, that was the fastest way to get into competition—the pathway taken by other professional riders. Harry had a pretty good prospect in the barn right now: Sinjon. The horse was too challenging for the students to ride, but Harry had started him out himself in some smaller shows and had already brought home some blue ribbons.

Sinjon, a thoroughbred, came from the Charles Town racetrack. Right away, the gelding showed talent as a jumper, but he had too many vices. He was a "dirty stopper"—sometimes skidding to a stop right in front of a fence, a dangerous habit that could unseat even the most skilled rider. Not only that, but he also had a major stable vice: he was a weaver. This meant that he was so high-strung that he could not relax in his stall but hung his head over the Dutch door, rocking back and forth; the nervous habit kept him chronically exhausted and underweight. A Pennsylvania horse trader, Joe Green, did not want to bother with the problem horse and was looking to unload him cheap.

One of the fathers at Knox had been interested. He'd agreed to let Harry train the horse and take him to some shows in the hope that his daughter would eventually ride him. The bay was the dead opposite of Snowman. Where the gray plow horse was placid and easygoing, Sinjon reflected every inch of his thoroughbred breeding. Even though he had been too slow to race successfully, he still had the volatile reflexes and touchy disposition that is bred into thoroughbreds to make them fast.

When Harry could get Sinjon to keep it together, the gelding did pretty well, and he was a typically handsome thoroughbred—the kind of horse that looked as if he belonged in the show ring, not as if he used to work the fields.

Horse shows have different divisions, based on the different kinds of work equines traditionally did outside the show ring. For instance, a "working hunter" galloped and jumped over varied terrain while engaged in the sport of foxhunting. In the show ring, working hunters are judged on their skill, beauty, and style over fences. In Harry's day, the hunter division was the prestigious one—a place where well-heeled amateurs competed on the finest horses money could buy. Fences were of moderate height, and style, with all that designation entailed—expensive, custom-made riding gear, French saddles, and fine English leather bridles—counted in the judging. A horse like Snowman could never have competed in the hunter division.

If he ever made it to a show, Snowman would need to enter in the jumper division. This division, where the jumps were the highest and the courses the most complicated, was the only part of a horse show that was judged on skill alone. If a horse cleared a jump, he got points; if he knocked down a fence or refused to jump, he lost points. Open jumpers were not judged on looks, or style, or breeding—only on accomplishment.

Harry much preferred the open jumper contests. Few amateurs competed in open jumpers; the courses were just too high and too tough, and the stakes were high, too—a spill over a fence, in those days when protective headgear was not yet worn, could cause catastrophic injury. To Harry, the hunter division just did not carry the same thrill as the jumpers: too much emphasis on looks and style, not enough emphasis on pure adrenaline-rushing performance.

At several shows in the spring of 1957, while Snowman was still learning how to jump, Harry and Sinjon won the "green" hunter division, limited to horses in the first year of competition. Harry thought Sinjon might be able to compete over the bigger fences in the jumper classes, but his owner would have to agree to it, so Harry bided his time. Meanwhile, Harry kept working on Snowman, patiently teaching him to jump, one skill at a time. Snowman, the old paddock jumper, handled vertical fences—high fences with no element of spread or width to the jump—with ease, but he had more trouble whenever he had to jump not just high but also wide. Harry practiced gymnastic jumping with the horse, patiently adding height, then depth to the fences, teaching him to stretch out over a fence when needed.

A lot more training and testing would be needed to see if Snowman really had what it took to succeed in competition—but at least the horse could have a shot. It is almost inconceivable that a horse undergoing this kind of specialized training would not be removed from the toils of daily life and treated like a pampered athlete, but this is not what Harry did with Snowman.

Growing up on a farm had forever shaped Harry's view of horses. In the world he'd been born into, people and horses spent time on hard physical labor. For Harry, riding was much more than performing in a show ring. Endless hours of mucking and currying, doctoring and schooling went along with it. And horses had their work to do, too.

Snowman's job was to be a dependable lesson horse, and that was what he did, faithfully carrying the girls around on his back. The morning training sessions, the painstaking lessons where the former plow horse had to learn everything from scratch—those were simply added on to the horse's daily routine.

But Harry approached the training of the unglamorous lesson horse with the same care, attention, and dedication that he gave to the more obvious prospects like Sinjon. Deep within Harry burned one desire: he wanted to ride his *own* horse, a horse he had trained with his own hands, nurtured and fed and cared for—not as a hired hand but as part of a team. Snowman was not the most beautiful, not the most naturally talented—not even as good as Sinjon, a scrawny racetrack reject that Harry had to teach how to stand still in the barn. Snowman had only one advantage: he belonged to Harry. Against all odds, Harry was rooting for him.

Harry worked on both of his prospects, the owner's horse and his own—Sinjon and Snowman. The pair were a study in contrasts. Sinjon was hot to handle; Snowman was placid and friendly. Sinjon had the thin skin, refined features, fine coat, and air of hauteur common to well-bred thoroughbreds; especially in the winter, when he grew a shaggy coat, Snowman looked like a sheepdog with a sloppy grin on his face. Any horseman coming through the barn would have noticed Sinjon first. However, the two horses also had something in common. Both were at their best with Harry on their backs. Sinjon's talent was apparent to everyone. Harry's belief in Snowman's true talent was the secret he kept in his back pocket and shared with no one. As Jack Frohm, another professional rider on the circuit, told the *Palm Beach Post,* "A lot of guys are starving in the business. They live from hand to mouth and only stay with it because they love it." Harry did not seem close to finding a breakout champion, but at least he had a couple of horses to bring along—and if his eighty-dollar horse was the longest of long shots, it did not stop Harry from climbing back into the saddle every day and giving it his best shot.

Horses, Owners, and Riders

Huntington, Long Island, 1957

B y September 1957, Harry was prepared to take Snowman to his first show. September 5 was the first day of the North Shore Horse Show at the Old Field Club. Unlike the small horse shows at Knox, where Snowman had carried beginners around at a walk and trot, this was one of the majors. Many top horses from all over Long Island and even farther afield would be there, gearing up for the fall season. Aboard Snowman, Harry would be one of the few professionals, if not the only one, riding his own horse—his equine partner, who helped him in his lesson business, played with his children, and rode with him into the show ring.

If Harry had looked around the world of competitive jumping, he would not have found many role models for this kind of partnership. Horses belonged to people with money, who hired professionals to ride them. If a horse was good enough, it might become an Olympic prospect; it would then be loaned to the team, and taken over by one of the team's amateur riders. The Olympics were amateur-only, the province of men and women who could afford to ride and not get paid for it.

In the elite world of horse show competitions, the professional was still considered a second-class citizen. The "ideal" of amateur sport came from the English public school notion of "a sound mind in a sound body." Originally, even practicing sports was considered to be a form of cheating, since a person who worked on their technique would gain

an unfair advantage over those who simply went out to play. The British gentility, and the upper-class Americans influenced by that tradition,
truly believed that professional sports were vulgar and that only amateurs were truly engaged in "sport."

The reality was that, prior to the mid-twentieth century, lower- and
middle-class people had little time for play; a six-day workweek was the
norm for even white-collar workers, and the one day off, Sunday, was
a much-needed day of rest. The only amateurs who had the time to
ride seriously were usually rich enough not to be tied down by a job.
Yet professionals, who earned money from sports, were excluded from
amateur competitions.

This mentality was alive and well in the horse world in the 1950s.
Writers in horse-oriented periodicals discussed "the professional problem," saying that amateur riders could not compete against professionals because amateur riders "were busy managing their affairs during the
week," while a professional "had nothing to do but ride all day." That the
amateurs in the equestrian world were usually managing the affairs of
their inherited fortunes, and that the professionals needed to ride every
day in order to eat, did not seem to factor into the equation. Harry, who
made his living from horses, and who wore through the flaps of his saddle from riding so much, could ride a horse for an owner's pleasure, but
he could not join the ranks of the glamour boys who rode on the United
States Equestrian Team. This did not weaken his determination to be
more than a jockey for rich owners. He wanted to ride his own horse in
the top competitions, pitting himself against the world's best horsemen.

And in the fall of 1957, Harry was not alone in his sky-high aspirations. A dozen years had passed since the end of the war, and the social
landscape was changing. In Little Rock, Arkansas, the National Guard
came out to protect the black schoolchildren trying to enter Central
High School, and Elvis Presley appeared on *The Ed Sullivan Show,* though
shown only from the waist up, to hide his gyrating pelvis. Sports were
changing, too—big money was entering into games and recreations that
had once been strictly limited to upper-class amateurs, but were being
increasingly opened up to the general public.

September 5 dawned cool and gray, with a forecast for sunshine later
in the day. With his German shepherd Smoky at his heels, Harry headed
out to the barn. As usual, he loved the dark, quiet atmosphere of early

morning. With the wheelbarrow and pitchfork, he made quick work of the stalls.

Like every other morning, Snowy was the first to hang his head over the Dutch door, giving three loud whinnies when he heard Harry's footsteps. Even in the dim light, the gelding's coat glowed from all the extra grooming, and the braided forelock showed off his small ears. While he still wasn't much of a looker, he cleaned up nice.

One of Harry's summer students, Louie Jongacker, got to the barn early, carrying his polished boots and hunt coat covered in a wardrobe bag. Cast-off horses were not the only thing that seemed to show up at Hollandia. Teenage boys collected around Harry's farm just like stray dogs. Johanna always seemed able to set another place at the table, and Harry could always find something for a spare boy to do—driving the tractor, helping out with the horses.

The de Leyers didn't ask a lot of questions. There was enough work on the farm to keep kids out of trouble. Life wasn't easy in St. James for kids from the wrong side of the tracks, and boys who felt like fish out of water in the community loved to hang around with the de Leyers, understanding instinctively that these young new immigrants didn't care what your last name was or what estate you came from, but respected what you made of yourself. Harry and Johanna both radiated strength of character, and as long as you could live up to their expectations, you were welcome to spend some time.

Harry was taking Louie Jongacker along to the show. Louie was from Queens, but his grandmother had a small place about six miles down the road; in the summer, he helped with barn chores at Harry's farm. A tall, skinny lad, he was not a natural in the saddle. But the boy was a hard worker, and Harry wanted to give him a taste of riding in a competition. Over the summer, Snowman had been coming along well. He'd been trained to the point where he could negotiate the turns and pacing of a simple jumping course. Since Harry needed a mount for Louie, he decided to let him give Snowman a try.

Harry climbed in behind the wheel of the van, his mind spinning through the checklist of things that needed to be done and headed toward the Three Villages. The North Shore Horse Show was held at the Old Field Club, which had been founded in 1921 as a private swim club; its polo and horse show grounds abutted Long Island Sound.

Harry smiled as Snowman sauntered down the ramp. The gelding looked around the showgrounds calmly, as if he'd been doing this all his life.

The novice team would not win any ribbons, of course, but Harry trusted Snowman to give Louie a safe ride. The gelding did not always have the precision to avoid hitting fences, but he was an honest horse—he never refused a jump. The boy would experience the thrill of riding in front of a crowd. And Snowy would enjoy it, too. He did not have to earn a ribbon; just being here, fat and clean, braided up like a prize-winning horse, was a triumph in itself.

The North Shore show spanned three days. Stabling their horses in barns set adjacent to the arenas, competitors were outnumbered by trainers, grooms, and young helpers, all scurrying around. Slender girls lugged heavy rubber buckets, splashing water over the side with each lurching step. In the barn, elaborate custom-made drapery turned stalls into tackrooms where pampered riders leaned back on camp chairs while grooms blacked their tall, custom-made boots. Everyone's nerves were on edge.

Junior jumpers, Snowman's first class, was the last junior class of the day. Harry had butterflies in his stomach when young Louie swung into the saddle and settled on Snowman's broad back. The boy looked nervous and a little stiff—all eagerness, but not very brave. "Take it easy," Harry called out. "Just ride like you always do."

The schooling ring, where horses and riders warmed up prior to entry in the show ring, was crowded with riders bobbing and weaving, jockeying for space. Trainers yelled commands to the boys and girls on horseback, while nervous parents lined up two deep along the fence. Harry did not say much—he just watched.

He adjusted the bars on one of the practice fences, then nodded. Louie circled around toward the jump. When Snowman cleared the fence easily, Louie's body loosened up a little. When Snowman cleared the fence the second time, Harry held up his hand. Louie looked puzzled. They had only jumped twice, and some of the other riders had already been out here for half an hour. Harry leaned over and slid the pins out of the jump cups, then raised the poles to about four feet. He nodded. "Once more."

The boy's eyes widened, but he didn't protest, just circled around to take the fence one more time.

"Don't flap your wings like a chicken!" Harry called, signaling the boy to tuck his elbows in closer to his sides. He could see Louie's hands stiffen up on the approach, throwing the big horse just slightly off his stride, but then Snowman gathered up and cleared the fence with room to spare. Louie's face broke out into a huge grin. Harry smiled to himself.

"That's all," Harry said. Louie looked at him again. Three fences were not much of a warm-up. But Harry wanted the horse to stay sharp.

Snowman didn't go until late in the lineup. The course was not difficult—a simple round of eight fences, each set to three and a half feet—but so far, only one horse had gone clean. When the gray entered the ring, Harry thought the horse glanced back at him for a moment. Then they were off. Snowman headed toward the first fence at a placid canter.

Harry trusted Snowman to make no sudden moves. But he didn't know if he'd bother to pick up his feet. He couldn't bear for the horse or his young rider to be a laughingstock.

Steady and sure, the horse circled the course, ears pointed forward, as though this were just another day at Knox. With each fence, he gathered, tucked up his knees, and jumped.

At the end of the round, Snowman had no faults. When the class finished, he had the only clean round. The tall, skinny boy from Astoria trotted out of the ring with Snowman, carrying a blue ribbon. A huge grin almost split Louie's face. Harry stood at the in-gate, beaming as if Louie were one of his own children.

Finally, it was time for Harry to get on board Snowman. Harry had entered his horse in the two green jumper classes, and here, too, he did not expect a ribbon. His goal was simple: to make it around the course without being eliminated. Snowman needed to show that he was more than a paddock jumper. Jumping a competition course required more than just raw athleticism—it required a horse to marshal every one of his strengths, and to bring those strengths together in an artificial situation over a manmade course of obstacles. Nothing in the life of any horse, much less a horse who had spent most of his years on an Amish farm, would help him navigate a jumper course, nor would instinct or innate skill. Without the rider, the horse would be lost, confused, and overwhelmed. Either the horse would shut out all of the sights and sounds around him and tune in to his rider—or he would give in to the stimuli and be paralyzed.

Trainer Cappy Smith was known for his acumen about horses and his movie-star good looks.

When Harry entered the practice ring aboard Snowman, he noticed Cappy Smith standing near the fence. Six feet tall, with dark hair and a suave Tyrone Power look, Smith had a track record of national jumper championships spanning from 1938 to 1954. A stylist in the saddle, he had a sharp eye for horseflesh, and he was not easily impressed. He watched as Harry and Snowman circled the schooling ring, where Harry had set the practice jumps high, hoping to signal to Snowman that now it was time for business. In the junior jumper class, which Louie had won, the fences had been only three and a half feet high, and the course had been a simple sequence without too many turns. Now Snowman was going to face fences a full foot higher. Harry circled around, flew over one big fence twice, then slowed to a walk. No point in overtraining. After a few minutes, he sat astride Snowman near the railing to watch the other horses.

Cappy Smith came up behind him. "Looks like you've got a horse that can jump high," he said to Harry.

Harry smiled and chuckled. "Yeah, he can jump . . . but, you know, he's just a lesson horse. I use him for the kids."

Smith tipped his head and smiled knowingly. An old hand like Cappy could see past the plow horse's modest appearance.

Aside from Cappy Smith, nobody paid attention to Harry de Leyer when he entered the class riding a school horse. Harry even saw people in the crowd laughing into their hands and giving each other looks. Despite having been groomed and braided, Snowman stuck out from the fancy horses. Jumper classes were judged on skill, not style, but there was still a certain look associated with jumpers—they were sleek and twitchy, often chomping on their bits until they foamed at the mouth and flecks of the foam spattered their chests. Snowman showed none of this pent-up tension as he trotted into the ring. Harry knew that he and his mount looked out of place. The horses competing in this green jumper class represented some of the country's top prospects—most would be competing for the national championships in a year or two. Some might even reach the international ranks.

Harry watched a couple of the top riders put in clean rounds. When it was Harry's turn, he headed into the ring at a walk; then, gathering up his reins, he cued the horse to canter with a slight nudge of his lower left leg. Snowman lumbered along at a docile canter, his nose outstretched just the way it was when the pair was out for a country ride. Harry felt a flicker of apprehension. Was this horse even awake enough to ride this course? He squeezed his calves around the horse's barrel, and Snowman lengthened his stride without missing a beat. He was listening. Harry kept his eyes forward, his weight balanced, and his reins slightly slack. On this, the horse's first real horse show challenge, Harry needed his mount to know that he believed. Harry measured the distance to the first fence with his eyes, then looked up over the fence and beyond it. Through the reins, through his seat, through the gentle pressure of his calves on the horse's sides, Harry telegraphed a message: *You can do this.* Snowman pricked his ears forward, gathered his haunches underneath him, and flew. One fence accomplished, and Harry headed him toward the next obstacle with a steady hand. The first few fences, the horse jumped clean, but over the oxer, a spread fence, he brushed one of the top rails for two faults. This pushed him out of the running for a ribbon.

On the way out of the ring, Harry threw down the reins and gave his horse a big pat. Only two faults. A solid performance for the first time out.

Outside the ring, Harry saw Dave Kelley and Al Fiore sitting side by side, both grinning as if they owned the world. Fiore had a right to look cocky: he had been the leading point winner on the circuit for the past two years running. He was tall and broad-shouldered, over six feet tall, and, at 180 pounds, a good fifty pounds heavier than Harry. A self-taught horseman, the son of a livery stable owner in Queens, he was a crowd pleaser—his acrobatic style in the saddle made the crowds grip the edges of their seats. Al and Dave shared a laugh as they stared at Harry's flea-bitten gray. Neither of them would have been caught dead riding an old lesson horse into the ring in a top-rated show. This upstart on a plow horse was no competition for their big thoroughbreds. *Let 'em laugh,* Harry thought. Just a few short months ago, he had been walking behind the horse on a long line, teaching him how to steer. Now this horse could make a creditable performance in a jumper class. He may not have gone clean, but he had tried his best. There were several more classes. Maybe they were laughing too soon.

The next class in the green jumper division was the knock-down-and-out class. In this class, touches would not count, only knocking down poles. Because of this, the fences were much higher and time was a factor.

Harry saw Al Fiore and Dave Kelley jumping their horses in the warm-up ring, but Harry only cantered Snowman. He wanted to save the horse's legs. Al Fiore's mount, Riviera Topper, was from the Mann family stable, a breeding string that included Riviera Wonder, the winner of the national championships for two years running with Fiore in the saddle.

Riviera Topper was up first, and Fiore expertly guided the horse around the course. Fiore's flashy moves in the saddle made the course look difficult, but Harry saw that the horse had no trouble with the fences. Several more horses went, each knocking down at least one pole.

When it was time to get on Snowman, Harry swung up. This course was more difficult than the previous one. He wasn't sure how Snowy would respond to the challenge.

Waiting at the in-gate, the horse stood half asleep, his ears flopping at angles, looking every inch the lesson horse. When the gate swung open, Harry gathered his reins and urged Snowman into a trot. A quick glance around the stands revealed that few spectators were even watching. Harry had Snowman canter a tight circle, then headed for the first fence, and that's when he felt a sudden click of engagement. *Now Snowman was paying attention.* As Snowy gathered his hindquarters to take off for the first jump, Harry sensed the raw power coiled within him.

When they trotted out of the ring at the end of the round, they had gone clean. Harry looked over at Al and Dave; they were still laughing. One clean round was nothing—any horse could have a single good round. Winning in jumping required consistency.

The crew descended on the ring to raise the hurdles for the jump-off. Harry felt a small flutter of excitement. Now it was getting interesting. Snowman usually did better when the fences were higher. But he had never faced a course this big in competition—the fences' height was man-

The former paddock jumper excelled at high vertical fences, snapping his knees up tight to clear each obstacle.

ageable, but the spread might cause problems. Snowman sailed over the first fence with room to spare, but over the second oxer, a spread fence, he knocked down a pole, and as he crossed the last fence, another pole fell. Al Fiore's mount, Riviera Topper, won the class handily. Snowman's jump-off performance was good enough for third. The plow horse trotted back into the ring to pick up the yellow ribbon. When Harry came out, he handed the ribbon to his children, who squealed in delight.

In the classes that followed, Dave Kelley and Al Fiore traded back and forth for the top spot while Snowman took no more ribbons. Harry did not ride him too hard. Nobody paid attention to the gray horse who was so calm he sometimes dropped to a trot between fences.

During the green jumper stakes class, nobody paid attention when Snowman entered the ring. The stakes class had the highest jumps. Snowman put in a serviceable round, knocking down one pole. Over the challenging course, that was good enough to land him in sixth place out of about twenty horses.

Back at the stables, Harry untacked the horse, rubbed him down with liniment, then scratched his neck, chuckling when the horse curled his lip into a laugh. Snowman's yellow and green ribbons, plus the blue ribbon from the junior class, were hung proudly on the wire that stretched across the side of the van to show what Hollandia had won.

With Snowman settled, Harry returned to the arena and leaned against the fence to watch the open jumpers. It was the culminating event of the day, and the crowds were no longer milling around, eating food from the concession stands. Instead, everyone was pressed up against the fences and crowding the bleachers. It was the end of a long day. Children had sunburned noses; junior riders had sore muscles and were yawning from mornings that had started before dawn. Little kids had hands sticky from ice cream cones and lollipops. But everyone mustered their energy to focus on the main arena, where the fences had been raised up to four and a half feet—as a starting point. The poles would get even higher in the jump-offs.

Harry never sat in the bleachers. Taking a position at the fence, with one foot up on the bottom railing, he kept himself close enough so that he could get a good look at the horses, and where he could run into the ring if anyone needed help or a strong hand.

When Riviera Wonder, the reigning national champion, came into the ring with Fiore aboard, Harry snapped to attention. Like Snowman, the horse was gray, but the resemblance ended there. A thoroughbred gelding, he came from a distinguished line of show jumpers. His full sister, Miss Budweiser, was already an Olympic show jumper. Fiore and Riviera Wonder were two-time national jumper champions, in 1955 and 1956, and with the big show at Madison Square Garden just three months away, he was the hands-down favorite to win again.

A stylish and beautiful jumper, Riviera Wonder had been just four years old when he'd won at the Garden in '55, and he still had dark dapples across his hindquarters, which would eventually fade to white. Al Fiore's style over a jumper course was effective but unorthodox—at the fences he threw himself forward, leaning so far over the horse's neck that he appeared to almost click up his heels behind him. It made the crowds gape with surprise.

Harry watched quietly. He respected Fiore as a rider, but that crazy sudden motion he made with his upper body over fences would throw many horses off balance. Riviera Wonder, Harry saw, had pretty much everything: style, grace, athleticism, and heart. It was no surprise to Harry that he came from the most renowned thoroughbred jumping line in the country, the descendants of Bonne Nuit. His owner, Bernie Mann, a famous jazz trumpeter, owned a popular nightspot called the Riviera. Mann's string of jumpers, thoroughbreds with top-notch breeding, all had the word "Riviera" in their names.

Only one horse in this class could compete with Riviera Wonder, and that was Dave Kelley's mare, Andante. After the first round, everyone had been eliminated but these two. The jump crew worked fast, raising the fences for the second round. Now the smallest obstacle was over five feet tall.

Riviera Wonder came up first. Fiore was a rough rider, but his years of experience showed. He guided the horse around the course with panache; each time he seemed to click his heels behind him over the fence, the crowd gasped audibly, but each time, the horse landed with a thump, leaving the bars intact. Another clean round. Next up was Dave Kelley on Andante. An incredibly competitive rider, Dave had more championships under his belt even than Al Fiore, and Harry recognized the particular quality that drove Dave. He won a lot because he was so good, but he wasn't in it just to win. He was in it for the love of the game.

Where Al had made the course look challenging, Dave made it look easy. But on the last fence, Andante got a little sloppy with a hind leg; she rubbed the rail and sent flying the baffle, the light piece of balsa wood that sat atop the rail to detect any light touches. One half fault for a rear touch.

Riviera Wonder was the winner.

If he ever hoped to move up to the open jumper division, this was the level of performance Harry would have to compete against. In the open jumpers, there were no lesson horses, no former plow horses who'd just recently learned to jump—only high-priced horseflesh purchased by owners with money to burn, and tough-as-nails riders who had been competing at the national level for years.

Harry thought about the words of Cappy Smith: "You've got a horse who can jump high." In the green jumper stakes, Snowman had placed sixth, but this was a horse with almost no training, a horse who had been to only one or two schooling shows, going up against some of the best jumper prospects in the country. Even thinking about trying to train Snowman to compete against horses like Riviera Wonder and Andante seemed like a crazy gamble. Harry would have to devote many more hours to training, to somehow squeeze it in among all of his other duties—teaching, managing the barn, and riding his students' horses. Riding Snowman gave him no clear payoff except to stoke a distant and impractical dream. Riviera Wonder . . . Andante . . . the national champion horses had full-time professional riders and an army of grooms looking after them. Still, the only thing that could stop Harry would be a lack of gumption—and gumption was something that both Harry and his horse possessed in abundance.

The Knox school year was starting in just a few days, and it would be back to the routine—foxhunting and small schooling shows, lessons with the girls, trying to challenge the better riders and to encourage the weaker ones. That was certainly enough to keep him busy.

After the show, Harry loaded up the van and headed out for hamburgers with his children. Maybe nobody knew who he was. Maybe people wanted to laugh at him for riding an old plow horse. But he had ribbons on the dashboard of the truck to bring home tonight. Not the ribbons he had been winning for other people, like Sinjon's owner. These ribbons belonged to him, to his family, to Snowman, and to Hollandia Farms. From where he and Snowman had started out, those ribbons represented a huge accomplishment.

After the North Shore Horse Show, a desire lodged deep inside Harry and would not let go. He'd felt such pride upon hearing the announcement over the loudspeaker: "Snowman, owned by Mr. and Mrs. Harry de Leyer, ridden by Harry de Leyer." Sometimes it seemed to Harry that for a man in the horse business, his desire to be his own man worked against him. He still smarted from that time he had gone to his boss at the riding stable, cap in hand, to ask for a raise and had been turned down. But then he thought about Mickey Walsh, who had a particular jauntiness in his step because no man was his master. Harry could stand having the mistresses of Knox peer around corners at him because the one thing they never interfered with was the horses. Harry wanted his own champion—not a horse that would be sold away from him or that he would train for someone else's glory.

Back in Holland, especially during the war, his family had faced extreme scarcity. They had been forced to make do with what they had—and in comparison his life in the United States was one of abundance. He remembered the war years when there were no horses, and how they had cut corners to keep the farm going. If you want something badly enough, he understood, sometimes you have to work with the materials you have.

That night, in the barn, as Harry plied his pitchfork, bedding down the horses for the night, he reflected on Snowman and how the horse had jumped fences to come home. Harry was smart enough about horses not to be too sentimental about them, but he also thought that people could underestimate them.

He always visited Snowy last at night. They spoke the same language, the language of survivors. Just closing his eyes, Harry still remembered the day during the war when the thatched straw roof of the small Catholic hospital in St. Oedenrode caught on fire. He, along with many of the other young men of the village, were members of the volunteer fire department. They assembled close enough to see the flames, but there was gunfire coming from both directions. The much-needed fire hose lay behind enemy lines. The men decided to draw straws to see who would go. Harry looked around that circle of men, their eyes barely illuminated in the dark. He knew each one of them, had gone to school with them, worked alongside them, seen them courting their girls at carnivals, and sat next to them in the pews at church, their heads bowed. Harry was the youngest, and the only one who had no wife or children. Before giving it a thought, he volunteered. His father said, "You don't have to go, son," but he made no move to stop him. He was a quiet man, but Harry knew he was proud.

Crawling on his hands and knees down the alleyway toward the hospital, Harry could hear the *pock-pock* of gunfire, but he was so concentrated on his task that he didn't think about the danger. When dawn brightened the sky, the hospital was still standing, and the American and British troops had driven the Nazis out of St. Oedenrode. Among the patients at the hospital, there were two wounded American soldiers. The nuns invited Harry in to meet the soldiers he had helped save, and the GIs gave him a bar of American chocolate. After the war, Harry was surprised to receive a plaque for his bravery. He did not think what he'd done was brave—it was a job that needed doing, and he had done it. Some horses were like that too, Harry thought—born with a strong will to do what needs to be done.

That fall, life was as busy as ever—the family was still growing, with five children now. Every morning, Johanna put breakfast on the table, the family gathered to say grace, and after the meal, everyone set to work. The older boys were able to help out in the barn. Harriet handled some of the grooming. As soon as a child was old enough, he was given a job to do.

It was a good life, more than Harry might have expected, enough that he knew he should be grateful for what he had. Look what he and Johanna had built in just seven short years: a steady job, a growing family, a home of their own. They had worked hard and they had been lucky. Harry could look around and see that where he was, he could probably settle down for a long time, teaching the girls and then saying good-bye to them, watching his children grow, giving lessons in the summertime.

Harry and Snowman had not made much of an impression at the North Shore show. Getting a green sixth-place ribbon was not enough to make anyone pay any mind to the horse. But Harry kept thinking about that third-place ribbon in the knock-down-and-out class.

Harry knew what Cappy Smith had seen in Snowman, that special quality that nobody else had noticed. Snowy had a gift. No matter where it came from, it was a gift that no one could take away.

Sure, it was a good life, but Harry was only twenty-nine years old. He was far from ready to start marching toward the placid benefits of a routine existence.

Harry de Leyer imagined climbing aboard his plow horse and the two of them together soaring—not content with the ordinary, but buoyed along by the desire to take flight.

13

Sinjon

People who bet on thoroughbred racehorses often quote the adage "Blood will tell." Great champion racehorses—Man o' War, Seabiscuit, and Secretariat—all come from bloodlines that for generations have been bred for one goal: speed. But this adage is not as foolproof in jumping. The mystical component that separates a lackluster jumper from a great one is not so easy to pinpoint. Good natural balance is helpful, but it is not the most important characteristic. There is an elusive quality—personality or presence—that separates a good jumper from a great one. The well-known equestrian writer M. A. Stoneridge, the sister of the equestrian Olympic gold medal winner William Steinkraus, notes that even an ordinary horse is "a generous soul, good-natured, honest, anxious to please, endowed with a special brand of courage and a simple sense of justice." On their own, those admirable qualities are not enough to make a champion. In *The Complete Book of Show Jumping*, Judy Crago remarks, "If twenty of the world's leading show jumpers were turned out into a field with twenty hacks and hunters it would be impossible for anyone to pick the superior jumpers out." Most horses can jump, and a few can jump high, but only a very few have the courage, trust, and stamina to carry a rider over a course designed to test those very qualities.

By the end of September 1957, the outdoor show season was drawing to a close. That summer had been a good season for Harry—he had won a few ribbons, even though people still sometimes stared at him as though he had stumbled into their party without an invitation. Finding the right horse to show in the grueling, adrenaline-fueled open jumper classes was like looking for a needle in a haystack—that was why the riders on the United States Equestrian Team had strings of horses. For every ten horses with scope, only one would have the heart to match. This was the elusive quality that everyone was looking for—and that people with plenty of money at their disposal were more likely to find.

Among the horses in Harry's barn, Sinjon was definitely the best prospect to become a jumper champion. Ever since Harry had solved his weaving problem, he had lost his scrawny look and had filled out nicely. Harry had studied the horse and had figured out a way to help him relax in his stall by rigging up a system of hanging weights that the horse bumped into whenever he started his rocking routine, so that eventually the horse learned to stand still. When he was on, he was unbeatable. Wayward Wind, the beautiful chestnut mare, was a good jumper, but Harry did not think she had the makings of a champion; she lacked a certain spark. He also saw potential in Night Arrest, a filly that belonged to one of his students. Like Sinjon, she was a talented handful—brilliant in flashes, but hard to ride. And, of course, there was Snowman, the implausible paddock jumper. He had scope, and personality in spades—but he was clumsy. Of all the horses in the barn, he was the least likely prospect. Harry planned to keep training him; maybe he could improve by spring. In the meantime, Snowy had gone back to lessons, taking the girls swimming and on trail rides; and as ever, he seemed to enjoy his life.

Harry had a winning summer season with Sinjon, leading in points for the green hunter championship. But at Sands Point, the week after North Shore, a judge pulled Harry aside and told him that the horse held his head too high and did not have the right manner to be a champion in the hunter division, where judging was based on a horse's style. Harry was learning what it took to succeed in American horse shows. He understood jumpers, where the rules were clear-cut: a horse was penalized for hitting a fence or knocking one down; sometimes time was also an element. But hunter classes were like the talent portion of an equine beauty contest; the judges demanded a certain look as well as a good performance.

Harry felt sure that this touchy, erratic, hot-blooded horse had talent—and he wanted to give the bay gelding a chance to prove himself. Maybe Sinjon could compete in the jumper division; he was an excellent jumper with lots of spring, and in these classes no one would look at the way he carried his head. Only the ability to clear the fences would count.

But the short fall show season was nearly over now. The only horse shows left on the calendar were the top-flight competitions on the indoor circuit: Pennsylvania, Toronto, and the National Horse Show at Madison Square Garden.

Harry pitched the idea to Sinjon's owner, Mr. Dineen, the father of one of his students at Knox. The Pennsylvania and Toronto shows were too far away for Harry to make the trip. What if he tried out Sinjon at the National? It was a crazy idea. The National Horse Show was the top horse show in the country; called "the World Series of the horse show circuit," it was on a par with the best shows in the world. The horse had never competed in a jumper class, so Harry would have to enter in the qualifying rounds that were open to all comers. Scores of horses were entered in a single class at the National; the qualifiers would compete in heats in the morning rounds. Each day, only the top twelve horses would make it to the nighttime championships, where they would compete under spotlights in front of a glittering crowd that numbered in the tens of thousands.

Maybe Mr. Dineen liked the young horseman's outsized confidence—Harry could not get a whole week off from work, but he got permission to take Sinjon to the National to compete for a few days.

Nothing ventured, nothing gained. Entry was a long shot—not likely to lead to anything. Mr. Dineen and his daughter Eileen would be up in the stands watching. Harry vowed to do his best and make Sinjon's owner think the trip had been worthwhile.

The seventy-fourth annual National Horse Show at Madison Square Garden opened on November 5, 1957, with its usual fanfare. The show brought together the top equine competitors from the four corners of the country, and from all over the world. In an era when horse transportation was difficult and most competitions were regional events, the National Horse Show attracted horses and riders from the Midwest and the

West Coast, as well as six or seven international teams. The international teams, limited to amateurs, would vie against one another for the glory of their countries. In the open jumper division, only the top American professionals would compete. On the afternoon prior to the show's beginning, Mayor Robert Wagner entertained members of the international teams at city hall. Several of the top British competitors were women, which caused a bit of a stir, especially when the outspoken British champion Pat Smythe, in an interview that was broadcast on TV and widely covered in the papers, noted that the courses in the United States were not as challenging as those in Europe.

Meanwhile, back at the Garden, crews worked furiously, putting the last touches on the basement stables, layering ten to twelve inches of dirt over the steel platform floor, and hanging bunting and flags of all the represented nations from the balustrade. The National Horse Show social rituals, once interrupted by World War II and feared gone forever, were now back in full swing. The boxes in the "golden circle" around the show ring were known by their numbers—certain box numbers had been held by families for years, some as far back as the first show, in 1883. The names listed in the New York Social Register, the ultimate chronicle of snootiness, were originally taken from a list of box holders at the National Horse Show.

As society girl Tracy Lord said in *The Philadelphia Story,* "The prettiest sight in this fine pretty world is the privileged class enjoying its privileges." When people came out to watch horse shows, the spectacle of the rich in their finery was as much of a draw as the horses. A New York social columnist in 1900 complained that it had become "a great trial for members of the working class to save their money for weeks to see society in its good clothes" at the National Horse Show; not much had changed by the mid-1950s, when one young reporter, "a girl in black stockings, scribbling furiously in a notebook," wondered which cost more—the horses or the clothes. The expensive, tradition-bound, closed-off equestrian world was one of the last bastions of the upper-class elite.

During the eight-day course of the show at Madison Square Garden, the event featured in the *New York Times* no fewer than thirty-eight times. The annual spectacle was "the culmination of the social, sporting, and event calendars of the year," the paper noted. The opening ceremony was broadcast live on television. There were classes for roadsters and pleasure horses, saddle horses and walkers, but the thrills and spills of the open jumper classes stirred the most passion from the crowd. Whichever horse won the open jumper division was acknowledged to be the top jumper in the show—and the top horse in the nation.

This year, Riviera Wonder was the hands-down favorite for that title, expected to repeat his performances of '55 and '56. Eleonora Sears's gelding Diamant, a veteran of several Olympic outings, was considered a close second, after finishing reserve to Riviera Wonder two years in a row. Dave Kelley's mare Andante, the champion in '53 and '54, was also a strong contender.

For Harry de Leyer, the show offered a chance to try out Sinjon against the best. Any horse could enter the class—but few had the skills to try. The courses were challenging, and the fences were high—a horse jumping over a five- or six-foot fence catapults a rider more than ten feet into the air. Riders wore no protective gear, and spectacular crashes happened frequently in this high-risk, high-stakes game. Like jockeys in thoroughbred races, the ranks of open jumper riders were filled with paid professionals—often born into the life as the sons of livery stable owners or other professional horsemen. There were always a few intrepid amateurs and the occasional female rider was starting to sift through, but this was no sport for sissies, and no sport for green horses, either. One wrong move over fences this size could cause a catastrophic crash; sometimes a rider or a horse fell so hard that he or she would never walk away.

The qualifying classes were scheduled for the weekday mornings, when the crowds were sparse. The top twelve from all those rounds would ride in front of capacity crowds during the evening performances, which would be covered on live national TV. The coming of television to the National Horse Show in 1957 did not make a notable change to the spirit of the event. One of the greatest international equestrian competitions in the world had always been run as a decidedly amateur affair. Spectators came out in droves, but no attempt was made to cater to the crowd. The most popular classes, the open jumper classes, often ran late into the night, the jump-offs sometimes going until one or two o'clock in the morning. The program was famed for dragging on, with lags between each class as dignitaries jostled to get their pictures taken for the society pages. The television, like the spectators up in the cheap seats, could peek in and admire, but no nod was made to ever pretend that the show was for them.

Harry did not get caught up in the hoopla of the event. He had a job to do, and that was to ride Sinjon in the jumper classes. The life upstairs, where society swells posed for the *Vanity Fair* photographers, did not concern him. Harry did not expect to make it out of morning elimination, and in the first class, Sinjon, spooked by the strange sounds and smells at the Garden, put in a lackluster performance. He was not selected to perform in the evening round. Harry sat in the stands, high up in the cheap seats, and watched the chosen warriors battle it out. With his trained eye, he carefully sized up the competition. These horses were seasoned competitors—all sleek and beautiful, all bred to be equine athletes. Harry believed that Sinjon could vie against these horses, but the courses at the National were tough, nothing like the ones Sinjon had been competing on over the summer. The fences were high, the ring was small, and the crowds were noisy and distracting. Sure, Sinjon could jump fences like this back in the practice ring at Knox, but horses who were used to the big indoor shows had a huge advantage. For a moment, Harry imagined that he was under the spotlights riding Snowman. The thought made him smile. The big plow horse probably wouldn't mind the lights and the crowds, but Harry could practically hear the hoots of laughter that would greet their entry to the ring—the entire picture was so incongruous.

The next day, Sinjon was calmer, more settled. A new class was starting, and Harry had another shot. This time, Sinjon completed a clean round. On only his second time out, they had qualified for the nighttime class. That night, Harry would be facing off against some of the most seasoned performers on the circuit.

The experience of riding at night in one of the big indoor shows is like no other. The sights, sounds, and smells in the huge arena, under the lights, were completely foreign to a horse from a small rural barn. To get to the ring in Madison Square Garden, a horse had to be led from the stables up a steep wooden ramp. Adjacent to the stables, also on the lower level, was a cramped schooling area. It was narrow and crowded, filled with hotheaded horses weaving in and out. The schooling fences were set up in the center, with grooms in khakis standing by to adjust their heights, some holding broomsticks to rap the horses' legs as they headed toward the jumps, an illegal practice that some trainers believed made their horses sharp. Upstairs, the horses due up next waited in a narrow corridor. Beyond a high gate, the arena was hidden from view, its interior glimpsed only briefly each time the gate swung open to let a competitor in or out. Once inside the gate, the horse beheld a spectacle. The footing was soft, rumored to be the same dirt used for the Barnum & Bailey Circus, and many savvy old grooms spread Vicks VapoRub in their horses' nostrils to block the scent—common folk wisdom had it that the horses were afraid of the smell of circus elephants' droppings.

The arena in the Garden was smaller than most, with tight corners, giving the horses little room to maneuver. A walkway known as the promenade surrounded the ring; there, for generations, high-society New Yorkers had circled the arena, chatting with other box holders as they passed. The seats rose almost straight up, creating the effect that the spectators were seated on top of the ring. The lighting was strange—spotlights from different angles cast unexpected shadows—and the press box was stuffed with photographers, whose flashes popped frequently, punctuating the night. Even the most seasoned horse show competitor, man or beast, felt the pressure. Competing well required both nerves of steel and a relationship between horse and rider so profound that the horse could follow the rider's commands even through the panoply of distractions.

Upstairs now, in the waiting aisle for the night class, Sinjon vibrated like a live wire under Harry's seat. Harry let the horse walk, knowing how much he hated to stand still. The bay chomped nervously on his bit and flicked his ears back whenever he got close to the other horses.

Sinjon had performed well in the outdoor horse shows, but those had been big, rangy courses where horses could gallop freely and had plenty of room. At the outdoor shows, spectators were decorous and distractions frowned upon. The fences were lower in the green hunter classes that Sinjon had entered—with the object to show off a horse's beauty and style. Here, in this small, cramped ring with tight corners and short approaches to towering fences, Harry couldn't be sure what his horse would do. An attempt to get Sinjon's owner to see the horse's potential as a jumper, it had been a gamble to come here—Harry knew that. Most of all, he did not want Sinjon to fail spectacularly.

The moment when the announcer calls a horse's name and number,

at any show, no matter how small, is the moment when a rider realizes
that all of those days, hours, and years of training are coming into focus.

This is the moment. The time is now.

At the National Horse Show in 1957, that moment took place in a
noisy, smoke-filled, glaring arena. When the top competitors rode,
a hush fell over the crowd; but Harry and Sinjon were unknown, so
the low patter of conversation, the crackling of programs, and the soft
tittering of society laughter continued unabated.

Harry clasped his calves around Sinjon and lightened his pressure on
the reins just slightly, signaling the horse to bound ahead. The horse was
contained, but just barely. Sinjon craned his head around, looking at
the unfamiliar sights of the nighttime arena under the lights—and that
was not a good start. Harry nudged Sinjon into a controlled gallop and
kept him on a tight rein. He circled around, then headed toward the first
fence.

Sinjon took the first two fences cleanly, but Harry heard the crack
and felt the horse's foreleg drop a pole on the third. For the rest of the
course, the horse was clear.

Outside the arena, Harry watched the other competitors work. It was
a challenging course, and poles went flying. At the end of the class, Riviera Wonder was on top with a clear round.

But when they called the ribbons, Harry trotted with Sinjon into the
ring. Out of the twelve top competitors from the morning round, Harry
and Sinjon had earned fourth place—a staggering performance for this
all but unknown rider on his neophyte horse. Now, at last, Harry knew
that everybody could see what he had been saying all along. This horse,
though hard to ride, had the flash and brilliance to compete at the championship level. He just needed a year or two of seasoning. No need to
spend time trying to train a plow horse. Harry had a real thoroughbred
to train—a horse with the potential to be a champion.

The next day, Sinjon was off again and didn't qualify for the evening
round, but his brilliant performance from the show's second night, bat-
tling his way through the qualifying round to finish in fourth place, had
made an impression.

For the rest of the show, when he wasn't riding, Harry watched the
fanfare from the stands. He enjoyed the international competitions,
which brought back vivid memories of his own few years jumping in

Europe. Back then, people had speculated that one day Harry de Leyer would represent Holland in international competition. Maybe, he wondered, he would have ridden in the Olympics himself, if he had never left home. But Harry reminded himself to count his blessings. Here he was, at the National Horse Show. By any definition, it was better than he could have hoped for a few short years ago.

He admired Bill Steinkraus, the captain of the United States Equestrian team, a graceful rider who was as capable as he was elegant. He gritted his teeth through the German performances. He watched the pluck and determination of Colonel Humberto Mariles of the Mexican team, a perennial favorite who tore around the courses clad in military garb festooned with gold braid—he had an exuberant style that made him one of a kind.

On the last day, Mr. Dineen came to find Harry, telling him that he had good news. Harry was immediately excited. Being at the Garden, seeing the pinnacle of competition, he had begun imagining a glorious future with Sinjon. He was already envisioning their return next fall—how the horse would perform with another year of seasoning under his belt.

In the course of one short conversation, those hopes were dashed. George Morris, a young rider who had competed with the United States Equestrian Team in the 1956 Rome Olympics, had noticed the bay and believed that the horse could make it in international competition. Mr. Dineen had been asked to loan the horse to the United States Equestrian Team. With Morris aboard, Sinjon would be trained under the tutelage of Bertalan de Némethy, the brilliant Hungarian ex–cavalry officer who had recently been appointed as coach of the U.S. Equestrian Team. Sinjon would be given every opportunity to develop his talent, receiving the best coaching available in the United States.

Harry knew George Morris. He had watched him come up through the juniors—where his precise riding style had helped him win both the NHS Good Hands and the AHSA Medal finals. Each was considered the pinnacle of achievement for a junior rider. To win both was a rare and stellar achievement.

But Harry also remembered the time at a show a few years back when George had led his horse into the arena to accept a prize. Spooking at the fluttering rosette and dancing sideways, the horse somehow got his leg caught in a standard, the vertical support for a post-and-rail fence. If the animal panicked with his leg caught in this position, he could easily break it.

Harry and Joe "the Pollack" Keswyzk, his groom, had jumped into the arena to come to the young rider's aid. Harry steadied the panicking horse's head, while Joe braved flashing hooves to untangle the trapped leg.

Luckily, George's horse was not hurt. Harry took the ribbon and grasped the horse's bridle to lead him out of the ring. Young George was standing on the sidelines, looking sheepish, when Harry handed over the reins and the prize. From Harry's point of view, George was a kid. Talented—but a kid.

For a moment, Harry saw a flash of gray skies over Amsterdam. He remembered circling the hippodrome on his mare Petra, himself a brash, cocky, can-do-anything kid, ready to take on the world.

George Morris had talent, and he had opportunity. Harry de Leyer was not in a position to stand in his way. He reminded himself that this was precisely what he liked about Americans. The war had knocked the wind out of his compatriots. Not the Americans. They were still fresh and determined to take on the world.

In the gloom of the emptying basement, workmen were already starting to break down the temporary stables. They would collect the dirt and clean the floors, and soon the arena would be ready for a Rangers game or a prizefighting bout.

But one year from today, the army band would strike up and the drama and high-stakes pageantry would start all over again. Harry promised himself that he would return.

The closing ceremony of the seventy-fourth National Horse Show was broadcast on the fledgling medium of television, officiated by horse show president Joshua Barney and Major General Robert H. Booth of the U.S. Army. The First Army Band from Governors Island led the procession, followed by the five international teams, flanked on each side by a member of the NYPD's Mounted Unit, one holding an orange-and-black flag, the horse show's colors, and the other holding the team's national flag. Holland had no flag in the procession, nor a team at the competition, but that did not bother Harry de Leyer. He had already left the Garden, happy to be headed back to his family.

Harry's own show had ended earlier that day when he had handed Sinjon's lead rope to a groom for the United States Equestrian Team. He had watched Sinjon walk away from him, his bay haunches disappearing into the basement gloom. Harry knew that the horse was good. He probably knew better than anyone what he was capable of. Riders like young George Morris needed a lot of horses if they wanted to compete on the international stage. They didn't need to count on any one horse working out for them. But if someone had asked Harry right then, he would have bet money that Sinjon had the ability to keep on winning, to make a name for himself.

Harry walked back to his truck empty-handed. He had no horse to trailer back to Long Island, just an empty van, rattling along behind him in the cold November night. As he drove, he thought about the skinny bay bumping into the hanging weights in his stall, nervous as a cat. On the seat next to him lay the white fourth-place ribbon, embossed in gold with the name that had a magical sonority for every horseman: the National Horse Show.

Harry's life thus far seemed to be trying to teach him a lesson: don't wish for what you don't have. And yet, these past few days had given him just the briefest taste of life under the hot spotlights of big-time riding competition, enough to let him know that he wanted to taste it again. He did not have the money to buy a finely bred horse, and he was not in a position to keep a horse when the United States Equestrian Team came calling.

Generations of men just like him had contented themselves with working their magic on other people's horses—men who possessed the kind of knowledge that could not be taught to the pampered young amateurs with their clipped upper-class accents, good manners, and limitless funds. Horsemen like Harry gleaned their knowledge by sleeping beside horses on their straw beds, nursing them in sickness, and patiently watching their foaling stalls in the dark. Take a nervous, skinny, overcharged racetrack reject—too fidgety to stand still in a stable, not trusting enough to jump fences with a man aboard—and then study that horse, learn his language, and figure out how to speak to him in that language. Harry's hands were callused, and a couple of his fingers were twisted from having been broken. He did not think of his work as a gift; it was just the intuition of nearly thirty years spent around horses. But that was how it was—that talent, the one needed to make a horse, was not the kind that was given any importance.

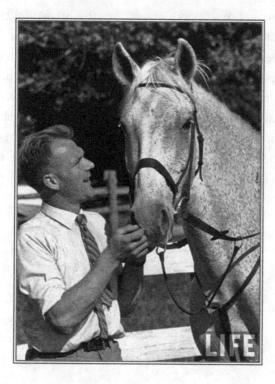

Harry and Snowman share a moment of affection.

Someday, Harry had no doubt, Sinjon would perform in front of European crowds, maybe even in the Olympic games. His rider would stand on a block wearing a scarlet hunt coat with a medal hanging around his neck and his national anthem playing. He would be proud, and rightly so. But when that horse was led back to the barn, the rider would hand his reins to a groom.

Making a horse and riding a horse were not the same thing. That was the way things were done, but Harry had never been one to accept the status quo. After all, he was here building a new life for himself and his family on the strength of his own crooked fingers and strong back.

Back when he was a young boy he'd had a village with a church and a school—it was an entire way of life that had seemed to him would endure forever. How wrong he was. Anything or anyone can change; Harry knew that now.

He belonged in that ring, with the men riding the open jumpers. He knew he could do it. A rider, however, is only one part of the equation. A rider must have a horse.

As he rattled east across Long Island, away from the bright lights of the city and toward Suffolk County, he thought about his next step.

Crazy as it might seem, his only hope was to make a champion out of his quiet lesson horse, Snowman—the placid mount that the timid girls rode during the day, that his children straddled to go swimming. Sure, getting a third-place ribbon in a green jumper class in a local show did not mean much of anything, but Harry felt it deep inside himself. He believed Snowy had untapped potential—unfulfilled promise that mirrored his own.

14

The Circuit

Sands Point, Summer 1958

In the 1950s, the average person had little access to the goings-on of the upper class. The wealthiest Americans—whom the social historian Paul Fussell dubbed "the rich-out-of-sight"—tended to live a life apart, playing in private clubs discreetly tucked away behind barely marked gates that protected long driveways. Called "coupon clippers" after the coupons they cashed to collect interest on their bonds, most of them did not work at all. Unlike the new middle class, whose members toiled from nine to five and commuted to offices, the rich golfed, played tennis, sailed, and, of course, rode horses.

The pathway to a spot in the nighttime finals of open jumping at the National Horse Show led through these hidden playgrounds. Meandering up the Mid-Atlantic, through the estates of New Jersey, across Long Island, and up the coast into Connecticut, through polo grounds and hunt clubs that occupied some of the choicest real estate in America, "the circuit" took riders inside the gates of the kinds of places that most Americans never saw. These all-white, all-Protestant bastions of "old money" were carefully cordoned off from ordinary folk. Membership requirements were not made public—if you had to ask what it took to gain entry, you were not member material.

A mix of amateurs and professionals competed on the circuit. The amateurs were mostly young men and women with limitless funds and abundant free time who devoted themselves to the pursuit of sport. Not every amateur was rich, but all had the right kinds of social connections. The professionals relied on the sponsorship of wealthy patrons. Attached to the barns of rich owners, the professionals showed the horses week to week, traveling with them, shipping them, caring for them, and handing over their ribbons and trophies to the owners. Side by side, amateurs and professionals competed, all eyes turned toward the National Horse Show in the fall.

Harry had never been one to settle for the expectations established by others. If he rose at four A.M. to groom, muck, and trailer; if the children helped out; and if his wife was behind him, then, he was sure, he and his horse, together, could do the work. Other horses might be fueled by their owners' fortunes, but Harry was a new breed of sportsman: fueled by an internal drive to excel, and a belief that the ability to do so was within his own hands.

Like many other breakthrough athletes of that era, Harry was competing for the right just to show up at the starting line. Like other ordinary working people, Harry had more than enough to manage with his daily life alone—family, work, children, and responsibilities. But Harry believed that it was possible to aspire to more than that—not just to exist and get by, to make ends meet. In an era when people were told to believe that the best you could hope for was a small house in a suburb where hundreds of other houses looked exactly like yours, or to don a suit for a corporation and become "an organization man," Snowman and Harry insisted that they had the right to rise above the ordinary.

The 1958 show season started at the Devon Horse Show, held yearly since 1896 on suburban Philadelphia's tony Main Line. A contemporary article from the *New York Times*, "PHILADELPHIA SOCIETY, CHANGING BUT CHANGELESS," described the Main Line as "a symbol as well as a location," characterized by a "subtly rigid code of manners." Devon's show grounds were elaborate: a large wooden sign over the entrance was emblazoned with the slogan WHERE CHAMPIONS MEET. The Wanamaker Oval, constructed in 1923, was advertised as "the largest horse show ring in the world." Spectators filled the ornate wooden grandstand and promenaded on a boardwalk that wrapped around the arena. Devon was the first proving ground of the equestrian year. Competitors from all along the eastern seaboard gathered to check out the competition, greet old friends, and hobnob in a social milieu that had changed little since Edwardian times.

There was, however, a sense that things were changing in Philadelphia in the late 1950s. The *Times* revealed that some of the grandest estates were being boarded up, ballrooms and banquet rooms shuttered. The upper class suffered from what they called an "inescapable problem with the help"—society people sharing butlers or "driving in their cooks for the evening from the city." Such were the travails of the spectators who came out wearing blue linen blazers and straw boaters to watch the horses perform at Devon.

But when the Devon Horse Show opened on May 15, 1958, Harry de Leyer was absent from the lineup. Back in St. James, dressed up in a jacket and tie, his hair slicked back and pomaded down, he was helping usher Knox students and their parents down the aisles for commencement, a duty he was not allowed to shirk in order to follow the horse show circuit.

And Snowman, too, was part of the school festivities. Out on the big lawn behind the manor house, the maypole was festooned with fresh flowers and gaily colored ribbon streamers. The girls, dressed in white organza dresses and wearing flowers in their hair, had practiced the intricate ribbon-weaving dance for weeks. As they skipped across the lawn in pairs, holding hands, Snowman, groomed to a spit shine, led the procession with pink ribbons braided into his mane.

Harry did not mind ushering the girls down the aisles; he was fond of his pupils and proud of them at graduation. But it bothered him to see Snowman dressed up in pink ribbons. Rather than lead the horse himself, as the headmistresses had suggested, he let one of the girls take charge of the horse for the day. Harry thought parading Snowman, a gelding, around in pink ribbons, was undignified, though the horse did not seem bothered. Snowy walked placidly in the sunshine, taking in the whole scene—the dancing girls, blue skies, excited parents with popping cameras, and fluttering ribbons—with an air of calm acceptance.

Harry watched the horse from a distance. He looked more like somebody's pet pony than an open jumper. Harry had strong feelings about dignity. He had worked hard to earn respect for himself and his horses. But the horseman in Harry noted how well this horse handled the noise and confusion of the day; any one of his thoroughbreds would have been prancing in place, spooking and fretting. Surely Snowy's quiet temperament would come in handy in the show ring, with loudspeakers blaring and stands teeming with spectators.

Harry could not wait to get those pink ribbons out of the horse's mane and give him a good training session tonight. Beribboned and bowed, Snowman was petted and praised by the Knox families, but the high-stakes world of show jumping, going on that day at Devon, seemed a million miles away.

The only taste of Devon Harry de Leyer would get would come when he read the results a week or so later in the *Chronicle of the Horse*. The seven-year-old bay mare First Chance, with Adolph Mogarevo from Ox Ridge stables aboard, won the championship; Dave Kelley's horse Andante came in second; and the veteran Diamant, Eleo Sears's horse, took third.

Late that afternoon, Harry pulled the pink ribbons from Snowy's mane, saddled him up, and put him through his paces. The horse was coming along. Harry felt him gaining in suppleness, handling the sharp turns better, improving his balance and coordination.

A big horse show was coming up in June, the first in a series of three Long Island shows known as the Seashore Circuit. Harry talked it over with Johanna. Showing horses was an expensive sport and the small purses would not cover the cost of attending unless a horse won one of the big stakes. But Harry was trying to build up his business, and so the visibility would help him. He had noticed that a lot of the local instructors did not ride in the shows themselves, and he thought it set a good example for his students that he was willing to give it a shot himself. Johanna agreed. A modest schedule of shows, as long as they were within an easy drive, could be squeezed into their budget. The first show on the schedule was A-rated. It was at Sands Point, west of St. James on Long Island's North Shore.

This show was to be Snowman's first test of the new season, the moment to find out whether all of the winter schooling had paid off. This year, he would not be eligible for green jumpers, the easier classes for horses in their first year of showing. He would move up to the open jumper division. Many horses seemed competent during schooling sessions but could not reproduce those results in the high-pressure, unfamiliar situation of a show ring. A show jumper needed to be able to negotiate a course of obstacles designed to test a horse's balance, consistency, and problem-solving abilities. Just as a gymnast needs to demonstrate different skills during a floor routine, a horse needs to jump fences that require different skill sets. Solid fences, where the landing is hidden, require bravery; verticals—fences that have height but no depth—force a horse to snap his legs up tight and make a short, high arc; spread fences require a horse to clear not just height but also depth. Courses are specifically configured to present challenges; certain combinations of fences require a horse to speed up, then slow down or spread out, then tuck up. Some fences are designed with visual tricks or with distracting shapes and colors. Harry had patiently trained his horse to jump over different kinds of fences, but there was no way to predict how he would handle an unfamiliar course in a new place. The only way to find out was to give it a try.

With Knox closed for the summer, there was nothing to stop Harry—no school events or anxious headmistresses. The summer season of 1958 was all his.

By the summer of 1958, America was ready for a hero. The country feared that the Cold War might no longer remain "cold"; Soviet leader Nikita Khrushchev had repeatedly threatened nuclear warfare against the United States. The relative prosperity enjoyed after World War II had come to an end as the world entered a global recession. It was the first major economic downturn since the Great Depression, and the public was fearful. The first quarter of 1958 had set a postwar record with a 10 percent drop in gross domestic product (a record that stands through mid-2011); five million people, or roughly 7 percent of the labor force, were forced into unemployment; and the automobile industry was struggling, with the rate of unemployment in Detroit reaching a high of 20 percent by April. In Kankakee, Illinois, members of the chamber of commerce constructed an effigy called Old Man Gloom, and staged a mock execution. International tension and the economic downturn both loomed as immediate threats to people's sense of security.

Perhaps looking for more cheerful distractions, Americans were riveted by sports, and that appetite only increased with the advent of television. The Kentucky Derby was televised live for the first time in 1952, and interest in the race was so keen that, two years later, the purse had doubled from $50,000 to $100,000. In May 1958, Tim Tam captured the Derby and went on to win the Preakness. He looked poised to win the Triple Crown for the first time since Citation's 1948 victory. But then— in the back stretch of the Belmont Stakes, as Tim Tam held a command- ing lead—disaster struck: a fractured sesamoid bone slowed the horse to a hobble, finishing his racing career and crushing the hopes of his fans—fans who were caught up in the drama of the moment because they were watching the race on television.

Spectator sports had entered a new era. Television exponentially ex- panded the audience beyond the group of people who were physically present in the stands, and the increased viewership brought in more money. At the same time, sports started to open up to new competitors. Pioneers in a variety of sports started to break down such traditional barriers to participation as race, social class, and gender. Even in ama- teur sports like tennis and golf that had been considered bastions of the country club set, minority, female, and professional athletes started to make inroads. In June 1958, the African-American Althea Gibson won the women's tennis titles at both the U.S. Open and Wimbledon. Babe Didrikson Zaharias, sometimes called the best female athlete of the century, helped found the Ladies Professional Golf Association in 1949, making golf the first women's professional sport. Ben Hogan, a black- smith's son from East Texas, so dominated men's professional golf that in 1953, when he was named the top professional athlete of the year, he was given a New York tickertape parade. These sports pioneers be- came popular heroes, and athletes like Didrikson, Gibson, and Hogan brought interest and spectators to sports that had traditionally been the private provinces of wealthy amateurs.

Television was shaking up the financial world of professional sports as well, with national considerations starting to reconstruct the landscape that had been dominated by local franchises and their devoted neighbor- hood followers. For New York City, 1956 was a year of triumph, as the World Series pitted two New York teams, the Yankees and the Brooklyn Dodgers, against each other in a contest dubbed the Subway Series. The Brooklyn Dodgers were the consummate everyman's team, and after

Jackie Robinson broke the color barrier in 1947, they became the first integrated team in major league baseball. Their beloved Ebbets Field, in the Flatbush section of Brooklyn, was just a subway ride and a ticket stub away for thousands of working-class fans. But by the end of 1957, both the Dodgers and the New York Giants had relocated to California, lured away by lucrative financial contracts, a betrayal that rocked New York's sense of identity to the core. Then in January, the Dodgers' beloved catcher Roy Campanella was in a car accident on Long Island. Campanella, the son of an Italian-American father and an African-American mother, had initially been barred from the major leagues, but then had gone on to play in every All-Star game between 1949 and 1956 and had received the Most Valuable Player award three times. Like other players of the era, he ran a small business in the off-season, a liquor store in Harlem. On January 28, 1958, after he'd closed his liquor store for the night and headed home, his car hit a patch of ice and skidded into a telephone pole. Campanella would never walk again. The loss of the Dodgers had left a void, and Campanella's accident dug that hole even deeper. New Yorkers were on the lookout for a new homegrown hero.

On June 9, 1958, the big bay thoroughbred Andante stood in her stall at the Sands Point Horse Show looking much like visiting royalty. Her stall was festooned with custom-made drapes in gray and black embroidered with a monogram. Duffy Stables' impressive stretch of the show grounds' stalls looked impeccable, with immaculately groomed thoroughbreds peering out over the Dutch doors. A hand-painted tack trunk sat next to each stall, and a rubber stall guard buckled across the top half of the door kept the horses from mussing their braids. Several grooms, immaculately turned out in khakis, some sporting driver's caps, tended to the horses—combing out tails until they were silken, polishing hooves with pine tar, or emptying plump grain into scrubbed-out rubber buckets. Each horse wore an oiled leather halter with a polished engraved brass name tag on it. Next to each stall a white lead rope hung, coiled in a perfect loop.

There was no mistaking which was the most important horse in the barn. In front of Andante's stall lay a lawn of artificial grass, so that the mare's polished hooves would not have to step onto the barn aisle's dirt. Curious spectators came by to see the two-time national jumper champion.

Everyone knew the owner of Duffy Stables: Ben C. Duffy, president of the second most powerful advertising firm in the country, Batten, Barton, Durstine & Osborn, and, according to *Time* magazine, "probably the best-liked man along Madison Avenue." A chain-smoker of Lucky Strikes, one of BBDO's big accounts, Duffy was conscious of images, and at Duffy Stables, everything was top of the line. Ben Duffy had worked his way up from the mailroom to become one of the most powerful ad men in America, and he understood the image horses projected: money, power, and an alliance with the ruling class.

No horse entered in this show would have a chance to beat Andante. If she won one more time, she would retire the challenge trophy. A horse had to win the trophy three years in succession in order to earn the right to bring it home. It would make a great photograph for the papers—the ad man and his prize horse, winning and retiring the trophy. Duffy had no doubt already imagined how that trophy would look gracing the mantelpiece of his Westchester, New York, estate.

Andante's rider, Dave Kelley, an affable man and a superb trainer, was thought by most horse people to be one of the best professional riders on the East Coast. An air force veteran who had served in World War II, he was liked and admired by everyone. With Andante, he had won the year-end high-point Horse of the Year Award in '53, '54, and '56. Most people thought he would have won in '55 too, except that he offered to ride his point rival Joe Green's horse Belmont at the 1955 National Horse Show after Joe broke his pelvis in a bad fall at Piping Rock. With Belmont out of the running, Andante would have been assured the crown, but thanks to Kelley's performances at the National, Belmont had ended up as the leading point winner that year, beating out Andante for the crown. At the big shows, Kelley sometimes rode ten or fifteen different horses, competing against himself. This year, Kelley and Andante looked to be an unbeatable combination.

On June 9, 1958, Harry rose at four in the morning. The de Leyers did everything together as a family, and getting ready for a show was no exception. While other trainers worked alongside professional grooms, Harry and Johanna treated the trip to the show as a family outing. Chef and Harriet were up early too, helping out with the horses, feeding, grooming, bandaging legs, loading tack and horses onto the van. Part of a generation that believed that boys and girls had different responsibilities, Harry did not think that girls should have to do heavy barn work, like mucking stalls, but Harriet was a spunky tomboy with a mind of her own and jumped right in to help in whatever way she could. She already maneuvered around the horses as well as a girl twice her age. When all of the barn work was done, Johanna took the children back to the house and got them cleaned up and dressed in their Sunday clothes—all but for baby William, who was going to stay with a neighbor.

Johanna and the children rode in the station wagon, and Harry drove the van with the horses. Sands Point was in Port Washington, about thirty-five miles west along the North Shore. When they arrived at the show, the grounds were already bustling with people. A thousand horses had been entered into the show. The stabling area was filled with grooms, riders, and trainers crisscrossing from the barns to the exercise paddocks and schooling rings.

The de Leyers did not have money for the kinds of fancy custom-made drapes, hand-painted tack trunks, and embroidered blankets that the other stables used to identify their horses. It was customary to hang a horse's ribbons next to his stall, on a wire suspended between two nails. At the beginning of the show, the de Leyers' wires were bare and their stalls undecorated. The halters that hung by the stall doors were well oiled and broken in, but they did not sport the fancy brass hand-engraved name tags that the other horses had.

Horse shows featured all of the color and splendor of thoroughbred horse racing, with none of the promise of financial reward. Even in the stake classes, the purses barely covered the cost of the entry fees. The fancy setups reflected the owners' fortunes; and these fortunes, in turn, most often predicted the results.

Harry had brought four horses with him: his chestnut mare Wayward Wind, a hunter named Cicero, his student's flighty and difficult horse Night Arrest to compete in the green division, and Snowman. Of the four, Snowman looked least likely to be there. While the other horses paced nervously in the new surroundings, Snowman contentedly munched on his hay while the de Leyer children clustered around him—excited that their favorite horse had come to compete in a real horse show. With the eager confidence of children, they were convinced that their Snowy would win.

In 1958, Sands Point was a new kind of horse show. The show, founded in the 1930s, had at first been held on the grounds of a private estate with a roster of exhibitors' names—Vanderbilt, Guggenheim, and Marshall Field—that excluded all but the most privileged. But Port Washington, in Nassau County, only twenty-five miles from Manhattan, was developing rapidly, and land once dedicated to equestrian pursuits had been increasingly crowded with postwar housing. The show had died out during the war, and had not been revived until 1954, when Bernie Mann, the trumpeter, nightclub impresario, and owner of Riviera Wonder, revived it as a fund-raiser to build a new ballpark for the town. On a twelve-acre plot loaned to the community by the sewer company, the local Lions Club built and maintained the new ball field, which doubled as a temporary show grounds. Youth groups, the Boy Scouts, the fire company, and local businesses all turned out to help make the horse show a success. The new Sands Point show did not have the stuffy feel of other Long Island horse shows—instead, the show grounds were packed with children and families out for a weekend spectacle.

The show's first events were the hunter classes, where horses are judged on style and performance and the judging is subjective. The competition is based on the old English sport of foxhunting, and the qualities of steadiness, beauty, and dependability are prized. The show started off well for Harry. He brought home a blue ribbon in the hunter class on Cicero, then another blue ribbon in the green hunters on Wayward Wind. Already the de Leyer stable looked more promising, with two blue ribbons fluttering next to the tackroom and two silver trophies proudly displayed on the station wagon's dashboard. The open jumper classes, in which Snowman would compete, would not get started until later in the day.

In open jumpers, only skill over fences—big fences—matters. Though the rules changed later, in those days horses were faulted for "touches," so that over a five- or five-and-a-half-foot fence, a brush of a front or hind hoof against one of the poles counted as a fault. After the first round, the jump crews raised the fences and only the horses that had jumped clean entered the jump-off. Very quickly the fences could tower higher than a man's head, steadily increasing the odds of a horrific crash. Sometimes a rider fell, sometimes a horse crashed; in the worst-case scenario, both tumbled. It was a high-skill, high-risk, high-thrill enterprise.

After the hunter classes were over, Harry got ready to ride Snowman in the jumper division. He took his blue blanket from the army-navy store and folded it four times, laid it carefully on the big gray's back, and then settled his saddle on top. The style at that time was to use a saddle pad made of real fleece, a soft and absorbent material that looked fancy and protected the horse's back. But a fleece saddle pad cost twenty-five dollars, an expense the de Leyers could not afford. The army-navy saddle blankets were not stylish, but they were cheap and functional. Harry had discovered that you could refold the blanket and place a clean side against the horse four times before you had to launder it.

Braided and groomed to a spit shine for his first class, Snowman looked more like a city slicker than an old plow horse. He'd been carefully clipped and trimmed, and his bridle had been taken apart piece by piece, carefully soaped and buffed to a sheen, then reassembled. Harry cinched up the girth, then slipped the soft rubber snaffle into the horse's mouth. He tucked the horse's ears under the crownpiece one by one, then tightened the throat latch.

The horse was ready to go. Johanna settled into the bleachers, but the children perched along the fence that led to the in-gate. They wanted to be close to the action, to see the horses prancing along, chomping at the bit, and to size up the competition.

Harry sits astride his flea-bitten gray with the calm of a prince.

Harry could not help but notice the way the spectators chuckled at the sight of him, laughing into their hands. He could guess what they were thinking: that he was a local yokel with an old farm horse, somebody who'd stumbled into an A-rated show by accident and didn't stand a chance. That day in the schooling ring, most people saw the parts—the chunky blue saddle blanket, the horse's coarse head, the young horseman's simple, homespun riding clothes, unlike the bespoke habits of the New York set. The amusement—perhaps even disdain—in the air was palpable.

Yet Harry sat astride his flea-bitten gray with the calm of a prince, surveying the ring with his penetrating blue eyes. The way a man sits on a horse cannot be faked. Historians surmise that the mythical centaur—half horse, half human—was actually based on an ancient race of men on horseback who were so much in harmony with their mounts that nonriders mistook them for a single beast. An old English proverb says, "Show me your horse and I will tell you who you are." Glancing at Harry and Snowman, a casual observer might have seen a horse and rider out of their rank, but an astute observer would have seen more. Even a cursory glance would have told a true horseman not to dismiss this unusual pair.

The judge was ready with his clipboard, the jumps having been raised and widened to new heights; it was time for the first jumper class to start. Part of the draw for spectators of open jumper classes is the chance of thrills and spills—in a similar way, NASCAR fans perch on the edge of their seats, not exactly hoping that something bad will happen but knowing that it might. Horses who jump tricky, complicated courses over five feet in height inspire breathless awe, even from those long familiar with the sport. The crowd at Sands Point that day was made up of many people who had never seen horses jump such high fences before. Families watched with an air of excited fascination.

All eyes were on Dave Kelley as the ring's in-gate swung open. Andante, a touchy mare, often cantered around a course with both ears pinned back, a sign of resistance or stress. But Dave's style with the bay was tactful and unobtrusive, and though the horse sometimes balked going through the in-gate, once headed toward a fence, she knew how to get down to business. Horse and rider were both veteran campaigners, rounding courses with an air of self-assuredness that came from frequent trips to the winner's circle. Harry watched from the sidelines, well aware that Andante had been winning national championships long before Snowman had stumbled over his first pole. The pair set off toward the first fence with an air of assumed victory. And the performance was flawless—almost. Andante rubbed one fence with a hind foot. Any horse with a clean round could beat her, but so far, nobody had.

After a few more rounds, the announcer called out Snowman's name. Harry heard a light smattering of applause from the stands. Most of the other horses had barreled along, held in check with tight reins, prancing in place and sometimes chomping at their bits until flecks of foam speckled their cheeks and spotted their chests. Many of the horses wore complicated leather straps—from standing martingales that tethered the horse's head to a strap around its neck, to draw reins that ran over the horse's poll just behind his ears, through the rings of the bit, and back to the rider's hand, acting as a pulley. Unlike Snowman, with his soft rubber snaffle, those horses were also outfitted with complicated metal bitting, whose ferocious names, like "scissor bits" and "double twisted wire," indicated their severity. Their riders had spurs strapped to their heels, and crops—short, stiff whips—in their hands, trying to keep their horses in a narrow tunnel between their two legs and two hands, giving their mounts no corner to duck out to the side of the fence to avoid jumping. On the approach, a rider often appeared to make a series of sharp jerks on the reins, followed by brisk application of the crop. Rider after rider seemed to be forcing the horse around the course. Judging from the other performances, jumping seemed to require a degree of brute force—an enterprise of coercion, not cooperation.

Snowman looked nothing like these other horses as he walked into the ring. Like a friendly kid entering the playground, he craned his neck around, surveying the crowd, and caught sight of the de Leyer children, lined up next to the fence. Later, the children swore he winked.

Harry cued Snowman to canter and headed toward the first fence. Unlike the previous riders, who had held their horses on a tight rein that kept their heads held high, Harry let Snowman gallop on a loose rein with his nose outstretched.

Harry, lean and wiry, balanced lightly in his stirrups, and as the big horse cleared each jump, he was quiet, seeming to anticipate the horse's movements rather than follow them. The big gray had a ground-covering stride, but he did not appear to be in a hurry. Most of the other horses scattered their energy, chomping and prancing, swinging from side to side, but Snowman loped along steadily, directing all his resources to the task at hand. Harry let the reins slip through his fingers as he felt the horse stretch out his nose the way they had practiced so many times. Harry believed that he needed to allow the horse to find his own way, just as he had done so well naturally, jumping paddock fences by himself. As Snowman approached each fence, with his head lowered, his neck extended, and his ears pricked forward, he never showed a moment's hesitation. Up and over. Over each fence, the reins went slack and drooped down over the horse's neck. Spectators' eyes were drawn to the big gray horse as, at the highest point of the arc in the air, Snowman's nose stretched out, as though he was trying to make sure to give that extra inch. The rider almost seemed to fade away into the motion.

Chicken coop, oxer, parallel bars. As they took off over the last oxer, Snowman cleared it with room to spare. A clean round.

Harry leaned forward, threw down the reins, and gave his horse a vigorous pat, beaming. But he kept his wits about him enough not to jump off the horse and hug him before leaving the arena, the way he had done in his first big show in Amsterdam. There was a pause, and then applause—but this time, it was genuine, not patronizing.

When the class was over, the announcer called out the ribbon winners over the PA system in reverse order, starting with the brown eighth-place ribbon.

Dave Kelley smiled and waved at the crowd as he went in to receive his red second-place rosette. To keep the chill off, a groom had covered Andante in a soft woolen blanket in Duffy Stables colors, with the horse's name embroidered on the side. But when the announcer called the winner into the ring, no fancy embroidered raiment graced Snowman's back. Harry jogged into the ring leading the horse on a loose rein, and as they entered, the crowd hooted in pleasure. Aboard the big horse were three towheaded children lined up in order of size: Chef in front, Harriet sandwiched in the middle, and Marty hanging on behind for dear life.

Harry accepted the blue ribbon, then smiled and waved at the crowd; the delighted children waved along with him. He caught sight of Johanna standing in the bleachers, smiling like she wasn't just going places but had already arrived.

This was the first jumper class in a horse show that would last three days. Already the crowd was rooting for the plow horse.

Marie Lafrenz, in charge of publicity for the Sands Point show, was up in the bleachers with her manual typewriter balanced on her knees. Orphaned as a child, Marie had grown up in Park Slope, Brooklyn, raised by her grandparents. She took up riding as a girl and was a fearless competitor—the first woman to win the Brooklyn Indoor Steeplechase, in 1939. During her years at New York University she began to write, and she now covered thirty annual horse shows as a stringer for the *New York Herald Tribune*. She also used her reportorial skills to drum up horse show publicity. This weekend, her job was to pound out press releases in the hopes that they would be picked up by the local papers.

Marie believed that horse showing had a future as a spectator sport. Harness racing, long a popular American pastime at country fairs, had recently started to win suburban fans. Attendance at Roosevelt Raceway, in nearby Garden City, sometimes topped fifty thousand people—and unlike thoroughbred racing, which was thought to attract an unsavory crowd of lowlifes and gamblers, harness racing was being pitched as a wholesome family recreation. Newly suburban Long Islanders showed up in droves to watch the races. Even an *I Love Lucy* episode showed Lucy and Desi at the Roosevelt Raceway, where she bet on a horse named Whirlygig. It seemed that the more horses disappeared from everyday life, the more iconic they became. By the 1950s, as families moved off farms and into suburbs, signs of nostalgia about horses—TV westerns, horse-themed books and movies—abounded.

Now a rarity, the workaday horse served as a reminder of a simpler time. In 1956, when an eight-year-old bay mare pulling a junk dealer's cart took off up Ninety-second Street in Manhattan and jumped several street barriers, she was dubbed the winner of the "Broadway Steeplechase," and received sugar, apples, carrots, and a half-page picture in the *New York Times*.

The horse as a fundamental archetype had lost none of its power.

Newspaper sportswriters looking for good copy were happy to be fed a horse story. The pioneering sports promoter Joey Goldstein had already figured this out. Helping to promote nearby Roosevelt Raceway, he started a campaign to gather artichokes for a French trotter who supposedly thrived on a diet of nothing but the exotic vegetable. The papers grabbed hold of the story and covered it extensively, bringing out droves of ticket-buying spectators toting bags of artichokes. Perched in the bleachers at Sands Point, Maria Lafrenz was looking for just this kind of attention-grabbing yarn.

It was a tough time for newspapers. The new medium of television was gaining ground rapidly, putting huge pressures on daily papers, which increasingly fought for readers. New York City alone had dozens of daily newspapers, published every morning and evening, as well as at least one smaller paper serving every locale; but the years from 1956 through 1958 were brutal for these papers. The number of closures and consolidations was dizzying, with mergers producing weird conglomerates with long hyphenated names, such as the *New York World-Telegram and Sun*. Even venerable grande dames like the *New York Herald Tribune* were struggling— a palace coup in the Reid family, owners of the *Trib,* had replaced Whitey Reid with his younger brother, Ogden. Trying to broaden the appeal of his paper by grabbing some of the *New York Post*'s more working-class audience, Ogden Reid would change the *Trib*'s image as a place where writing and reporting excelled. Competition for market share was fierce. Papers that failed to hold on to their audiences disappeared.

Ever on the lookout for appealing stories to fill their newspapers' pages, journalists often turned to press releases—short articles written up by publicists, like the story of the artichoke-eating trotter, that were geared to catch a newspaperman's interest. Marie, who knew the New York newspaper business, calculated that if she wrote something interesting about the Sands Point show, she might score coverage in the papers—coverage that would bring spectators, revenue for the worthy causes supported by the Lions Club, and increased visibility for the sport she loved.

Marie believed that horse show publicity would help the sport, pulling it from its corner of obscurity and making it a mainstream spectator sport—giving the extraordinary equine athletes their due. Unlike most horse show people, Marie knew the rules of the newspaper game. She took special care writing her press releases, sometimes crafting an article in the style of a well-known sports columnist, aware that if the reporter was short on time, he might use her article verbatim.

Marie had discovered that some words seemed to carry a special magic—and whenever possible, she tried to use those words. "Olympic rider," "ex-racehorse," and "thoroughbred" always seemed to get the press's attention. She also liked to come up with a catchphrase or a slogan. As one of the very few female sports reporters of her day, Marie knew from experience that she needed to try extra hard to carve out a niche for her work.

Daily newspapers hummed with the monumental activity of putting out an interesting, well-written issue every day. As William Zinsser described the scene at the *Herald Tribune*, "Phones rang incessantly. Every desk had an ancient typewriter in its sunken well, leaving only a wire basket for copy, an ashtray, a cup of coffee, and a spike for impaling any piece of paper that a reporter might later regret throwing away. The spike was where old press releases went to die." The best way for Marie to bring out spectators was to make sure that her press releases did not end up on that spike—and at Sands Point, the big white plow horse with the handsome young Dutchman aboard caught her eye.

On Saturday, Marie sought Harry out between classes. Where had he gotten the funny horse with the unstoppable jumping style?

Harry was happy to share, in his heavily accented English, the story of the trip to New Holland just two years earlier, of finding the horse on the slaughterhouse truck.

Harry specialized in buying cheap horses, green horses, rejects from here and there, and he did not find anything extraordinary about it; but Marie, who spent her time out among the spectators, saw something special.

For Snowman, four more classes remained before the big jumper stakes. Except for Harry and the kids, there was probably not a single person on the grounds who thought the big plow horse would be able to go the whole way.

Nonetheless, by Saturday afternoon, the gray horse and his brash young rider had attracted a following. Snowman had shown remarkable consistency. Horses earned points for their wins in each class. The entry with the best record over the course of the three-day show would be declared the champion on Sunday, the show's final day. Right now, going into the last class on Saturday afternoon, Snowman and Andante were neck and neck in overall points. Andante was ahead, but Snowman was performing well enough to be considered a threat. If he won this class, he and Andante would be tied for overall points going into the final jumper stakes on Sunday.

By the time Saturday's last jumper class started, a large crowd had gathered. Chef, Harriet, and Marty were watching with excitement while Johanna tried to keep them quiet. Dave Kelley went first. As he expertly guided the bay over the jumps; Andante looked every inch the seasoned competitor. The mare had been over courses like this a million times before, and it showed. When they pulled up at the end, the pair had only one fault. To win, Snowman would need a clear round. The gray had been jumping well all weekend, but this was his fourth class of the day—and the fences were formidable. Andante, with her years of experience, had a major advantage. On such a demanding course, after already putting out so much effort, an untested horse like Snowman might fall apart.

When Harry entered the ring, as nonchalant as a man out for a country ride, the crowd stilled. As Snowman circled the arena, there was no sound except for the thump of his cantering hooves on the sand and the trumpeting sound of his breath timed to each stride. There was a beat in silence as he passed over each fence, followed by the thump of landing. Approaching the last fence, the horse had no faults. Holding the spectators spellbound, the big gray galloped down toward the uneven wall of brush, then took off and soared, clearing the obstacle with daylight beneath him.

When his feet hit the ground on the far side of the fence, the crowd erupted in applause. But Harry did not hear. He was concentrating on the false step he'd felt as the horse landed. Snowman had overreached on the landing, clipping the back of a front heel with a hind shoe, scraping the hair and skin away. Harry looked down and saw bright crimson leaking from the horse's foreleg. At almost the same moment, Johanna jumped up from the stands and ran to the fence.

Harry hopped off and led the horse quickly back to the stable, with

Over a large spread fence, Harry reaches forward to give his horse full use of his head.

Johanna and the children following nervously behind. Back in the stall, Harry bent down to examine the wound. It was a deep gash across the pastern, too wide to suture. The skin over the pastern covers only sinew and bone; there is no fat there to provide a cushion. Any wound can turn serious—and Harry knew from experience that a cut this deep on the foreleg would swell. The pastern, the slender part of a horse's foreleg that joins his fetlock, or ankle, to his hoof, takes much of the brunt when a horse lands—any swelling there and the joint would stiffen up, making a jumping performance impossible.

Johanna saw Harry's disappointment, but said nothing. Harry and Snowman were tied for the lead going into the final stakes, but now it was likely he would have to scratch.

Harry was adept at handling all kinds of equine emergencies. He gently probed the wound as the big gray lowered his head calmly and snuffled, as if to show that he knew Harry was trying to help him.

"What are you going to do?" Johanna finally said. "You won't be able to ride tomorrow."

But Harry was not licked yet. He knew that if he iced the wound, there was a chance, however small, that he could keep the swelling down. It was a long shot, however.

Chef stayed with his father while Johanna took the younger children back home. Harry and Chef climbed into the van and drove off to look for a gas station with an ice dispensary. Harry bought bags of ice, as well as an old inner tube.

Back at the stable, Harry fashioned a sock from the tire and filled it with ice. He slipped it around the injured leg, then sat down next to the stall to wait, his son perching beside him. Around dinnertime, Johanna came back to take Chef back home. The boy was reluctant to leave his father's side, but Harry insisted. After that, it was just Harry alone with his horse in the dark, straw-filled stall. Occasionally, he muttered a word or two to the horse in Dutch, but mostly the pair were quiet, no sound but the faint rustling as the horse shifted his weight or moved around in the straw.

Each time the ice started to melt, Harry refilled the makeshift sock. Snowman calmly watched him and stood still when Harry tended to him. While the other riders were out at show parties or back in their motels asleep, Harry squatted in the stall and kept watch. When he ran out of ice, he drove to the filling station for more.

Through the night, Harry watched over Snowman, catching only snatches of sleep. His muscles ached. When, in the early morning, the grooms arrived, he awoke, stiff from the night spent hunched in the corner against the rough wooden barn walls. He looked out at the sky—it was barely dawn. Time to see how the wound had fared overnight. Harry cut the tire away. He cupped his hand and ran it along the back of the horse's leg, feeling the groove between the tendon and the cannon bone, the rounded prominence of the fetlock, and then along the pastern to the spot where the wound still gaped, fleshy and pink. Snowman watched, but did not protest or pull away. Gently pinching along the sides of the pastern, Harry assessed his horse's foreleg as much by touch as by view. Beneath his fingers he felt only the smooth sides of Snowman's lower foreleg—the pastern and the heel where the flesh met the rim of the hoof were firm and true, without a trace of swelling.

* * *

After Snowman was fed and groomed, Harry led him out of the stable, to an exercise paddock. Harry held his breath as he unclipped the lead rope and shooed the horse away from him. Snowman trotted away, happy to be out of the stall, shaking his head a few times. Harry watched closely for the telltale bobbing head of a lame horse—but Snowman showed no hint of soreness. Harry allowed himself to exhale.

Still, there was no telling if Snowy would be able to take the stress of the high jumps in the stakes class. When a horse jumps, all of his thousand-odd pounds comes down on his two front legs. The higher the fence, the more pressure is applied to those slender forelegs. A horse who is injured or sore will be likely to falter on the landing, and favoring one leg might cause the horse to be unbalanced—which can increase the risk of permanent injury or even cause a gruesome fall.

Snowman looked okay turned loose in the paddock, but the true test would come when he had to carry a rider, so Harry saddled him up. Harry had slept barely at all, and he felt stiff in the saddle, like an old man. This was hardly the first night he'd spent keeping vigil over a horse in a barn—he remembered the time he'd bought a horse with a bad case of colic and had stayed up all night squeezing black coffee and Jack Daniel's into the horse's mouth with a dropper. In the morning, the horse was all right. Harry would do anything for his horses. All he asked of them was to jump.

Harry spent the entire morning walking Snowman on a lead rope, then rubbing him down, then walking him more, trying to keep the gelding loose and limber so that the injured leg wouldn't stiffen up.

When it was time for the afternoon class, he carefully bandaged both front legs, then slipped rubber bell boots over Snowman's hooves to protect his heels. During the warm-up, he tested the horse for signs of tenderness, turning him first one way and then the other. Finally, reassured that the horse was steady on his feet, he guided Snowman toward the schooling fence. The gelding gathered himself and soared—then landed and resumed his measured gallop. That's when Harry knew for sure that his horse was ready to compete.

Soon it was time for the final jumper stakes. By now, the crowd was paying attention, anticipating a showdown between the reigning champion and the upstart. Even without being aware of his close brush with disaster, spectators had gotten behind the big gray horse. In the press box, Marie Lafrenz was one of many reporters present—nobody wanted to miss a good story.

At the in-gate, Andante was keyed up, her ears pinned back, nervously twitching her tail back and forth. But in spite of the mare's fidgeting, Dave Kelley looked completely unperturbed. Holding the reins bridged in one hand, his crop in the other, he sat loosely in the saddle, the relaxed grin of a winner spread across his face. Next to the mare, Snowman seemed to be half asleep. Harry sat astride with the reins held loose.

In the first go-through, both Andante and Snowman sailed to clear rounds, the only two horses to score no penalties. Now it was time for the jump-off. The jump crew moved quickly around the arena, raising the hurdles another six to eight inches and spreading the jump supports, called standards, farther apart to create more width. An American Horse Shows Association judge stood in the middle of the ring, supervising the modifications. After a few minutes, the jump-off course was ready, and in spite of the horses' fatigue from three days of grueling competition, this was the most daunting course of the entire horse show.

Andante was up first and made her usual fuss going through the gate—Kelley flicked his whip against her barrel and gouged her with his spurs. She catapulted into the ring with a burst, bounding toward the first fence at a gallop. Kelley held the mare's nervous energy firmly in check, keeping the reins short and his calves wrapped tightly around her sides. At first, they seemed in unbeatable form, but when they got to the triple bar, a huge spread fence with bars stair-stepping up in a steep incline, the pair failed to clear the uppermost railing—it teetered for a moment, and then it fell.

Four faults.

When Harry rode into the ring on a loose rein, the contrast between the two horses' styles was impossible to miss. Captivated by the big gray with the nonchalant manner, the crowd whooped its approval. Harry caught sight of Johanna sitting in the stands with Marty beside her. Chef and Harriet, preferring to be closer to the action, were perched on the railing near the in-gate. Even though Harry was the only one in the saddle, it was as though each member of the de Leyer clan was along for the ride. First prize would secure the championship for Snowman, and

Approaching the fence, Snowman is alert and Harry is balanced forward.

his share of the purse would cover the show's expenses. Harry would be the open jumper champion at an A-rated show, an incredible achievement for his first big test of the season, and Johanna would know that the time and expense the entire family had dedicated to this show were going to pay off for Hollandia Farms. For the children, it was a chance to know that the best horse in their stable was the horse they thought of as their very own.

But this was a tough course. The fences were all above five feet, with big spreads, and the horses were tired. Even veteran Andante had been unable to go clean. And Snowman's sore leg was more likely to bother him now that he was entering the second round. To jump this raised course without any faults was going to be tough. If Snowman knocked down a pole, the two would be tied, bringing another round of jump-offs with yet higher fences, increasing the risk that one of the worn-out jumpers would take a misstep and crash.

Harry headed toward the first fence at a controlled gallop. Snowman approached, nose outstretched, ears pricked forward, with the same sweet expression he bore when running free in the paddock. Somehow, it was clear that both horse and rider were having fun. Over each fence, everyone in the crowd held their breath, exhaling only when the horse's hooves thumped on the landing. Harry's style was unorthodox but fluid. His heels flew into the air, but his weight stayed balanced over the horse.

Over each fence, the reins looped loose so that the big horse could have full use of his head. They headed toward the triple bar and cleared it easily.

Down the line to the last fence, the big parallel bars, Harry galloped, reins still loose, doing none of the checking on the reins that most of the riders favored. The horse had no heavy bit, no complicated pulleys or straps. His neck stretched out and his ears pricked forward as he headed toward the last obstacle. The big gray horse took off and soared . . . and flew over the last fence, with no faults.

The lumbering plow horse and his handsome young rider had just won the championship stakes class. They had beaten Andante, the reigning champion. There was a special sympathy between this man and this horse—a kind of intuition that the crowd sensed. The horse wanted to please the man, and the man wanted to let him do it. This was more than an act of athletic prowess; it was an act of joy.

The judges hunched over their scorecards, their pencils scratching. A few moments later, the announcement came over the PA system: Snowman was the open jumper champion, winner of the stakes class and champion of the show, with the great Andante as reserve. Andante would not be bringing home the perpetual trophy. The trophy would be engraved with the names of a new team: Harry de Leyer and Snowman.

That evening, Harry pinned a tricolor ribbon next to Snowman's stall. Harriet, Marty, and Chef all gathered around the big gray, and the horse stretched his nose down to receive their pats and praise.

Marie Lafrenz had already captured the moment on her Smith-Corona and sent off a press release. The next morning, Marie's article ran in the *Herald Tribune,* under the title "THE CINDERELLA HORSE." The *Sun* referred to Snowman as a "refugee from the cannery." The story of the plow horse's triumph was repeated over and over again. Before he left the show that day, Dave Kelley came by to congratulate his friend, and as always, Dave's congratulations were genuine. He loved a good contest and never seemed to begrudge others their victories.

"You should come up to Fairfield," he said with a big smile. "I think you and your plow horse can win it."

Harry smiled, but he felt a flutter of excitement. Fairfield, in Connecticut, was another powerhouse of talent on the East Coast circuit.

He'd have to talk it over with Johanna. It was one thing to go to some of the local shows—there were several good ones within a short distance of their home—but following the circuit required a much higher level of commitment.

The 1950s was not a time when people got caught up in foolishness and chased big dreams. It was a time of conformity, a time when, as the writer Bill Stott said, people thought all they could do was "stoically keep muddling on, as we had in the war, pushing toward small, nearby, mainly private goals." Big, expensive, whimsical aspirations were the province of the rich—people who had time, money, and fewer responsibilities.

But some people automatically lift their eyes above the horizons and see more. Harry was such a person. In the lift and thrust that powered Snowman over fences, Harry sensed the same belief in his horse: a conviction that you can soar if you want to; you just have to want it badly enough.

By the time Harry pulled into the driveway of his tiny farm with the grandiose name of Hollandia, by the time he led Snowman back to his stall in the converted chicken coop and got him bedded down for the night, Harry knew that he was going to head up to Fairfield.

What he did not know that night in St. James was how starved for dreams the rest of the country was feeling, workers caught in their nine-to-five ruts that took them in cars or on commuter trains to their office jobs, then back to their matching houses with tiny front lawns to mow. Wedged between terrifying fears of nuclear age tensions and the more familiar specter of an economic downturn, the public was gloomy. Harry could hardly have realized how he and his old plow horse were going to lodge in a hope-starved people's imagination and stay there.

15

New Challenges

Joe "the Pollack" Keswyzk and Jim Troutwell had an ongoing wager with Harry. Not that Harry wanted to bet against his own horse, but the grooms had already picked Snowman to take the championship at Fairfield, too. Joe and Jim weren't exactly grooms. The two local men helped out around Harry's barn and sometimes went with him to shows as well. Joe drove a big rig during the week and pitched in with the horses on weekends, and Jim worked nights, then came over early in the morning to lend a hand. Jim was dark-haired, a sign of his Native American roots; Joe was blue-eyed and fair. Both men were over six feet tall and burly—Harry, with his medium stature and slim build, looked small next to the pair. They sweated alongside one another and sometimes shared a beer—and in the meantime, Joe and Jim had turned into Snowman's biggest fans.

After his Sands Point victory, Snowman had stirred up interest in the press, and in the days leading up to the Fairfield show, the horse's upcoming appearance was noted in the local papers. In 1958, it was clear that television was changing the nature of spectator sports, but it was not yet clear which sports would be swept up in this new tide of sponsorship.

The vast television audience watching on the virtual sidelines led to innovations such as Bert Bell's introduction of sudden death overtime in pro football, which played out in dramatic fashion in 1958 when the Colts beat the Giants for the NFL championship—the first game to be decided by the sudden death rule. The prime-time broadcast of that game, seen by a television audience of forty-five million viewers, helped make football the first sport to dominate the television era. Newspapers could not compete with the visual medium of television on its own terms, so they struck at a different angle—not live action, but great stories.

Back at Hollandia, Harry readied Snowman for Fairfield, along with Night Arrest, his student's flighty thoroughbred, and the pretty chestnut Wayward Wind. Harry had never left Long Island for a show before. Here he would be facing a whole new set of competitors, like Adolph Mogavero from Ox Ridge Hunt Club—one of the biggest and most competitive operations on the East Coast. Ox Ridge's young thoroughbred mare, First Chance, had cleaned up at Devon last spring while Snowman was leading the May Day procession. Andante, the tough old warrior, would also be there, looking to avenge her loss at Sands Point to the upstart plow horse.

On June 18 the weather threatened rain, but Harry loaded up Snowman, Windy, and Night Arrest, the two grooms climbed into the van, and off they went to Connecticut. The de Leyers wouldn't consider leaving the family behind, and so Johanna readied the children, including baby William, for the drive to Westport, Connecticut. The Fairfield Horse Show was held on the grounds of the Fairfield County Hunt Club as a benefit for the Children's Services Hospital. With Night Arrest and Snowman, Harry would be competing against himself in the open jumpers. The horses had different skills. Night Arrest was a flashy and talented dark dapple gray whose thoroughbred breeding and high-strung temperament gave her terrific speed, an advantage whenever time was a factor. Anyone would think her the most likely candidate of the three to win jumper classes, but she was a handful.

Harry knew that most people considered Snowman's victory at Sands Point a fluke. It had been a novelty when the eighty-dollar wonder horse won the stakes, but horse showing, like horse racing, has always featured its fair share of upsets. Sometimes a bad horse had an unusually good day on the same day that some good horses had a bad one. Snowman was the classic long-odds horse. In spite of his Sands Point win, the odds would still be against him to win this time.

But in the de Leyer household, Snowman was the odds-on favorite.

The whole family believed he could do it again. For his part, the gelding seemed nonchalant. It was always nice to have him along because he calmed the other horses.

The first open jumper class was held early on Friday morning, June 20, the show's opening day. This would be Snowman's initial test against the young mare First Chance, who a lot of people were predicting would be a strong contender for the national championship. Harry had entered Wayward Wind and Night Arrest in the green jumpers, and Night Arrest was also entered in the open jumpers, since he thought the promising young mare needed more experience. Riding more than one horse in a class was tricky. Harry had to rely on Jim and Joe's help. As he hopped off one horse, Harry handed the reins over to his grooms and jumped on another one.

By the time the first class started, the rain had begun to come down, but the footing was still fairly solid. After the first round, Andante had knocked down a pole. Out of the entire field, only Snowman and First Chance had had clean rounds. There weren't many people on the grounds that morning; the rain had kept away most of the spectators, so there were just the riders, trainers, owners, and their families. The jump crew, their white uniforms already splashed and muddy, raised the bars.

Johanna and the children huddled together under an umbrella, watching intently. The grooms had cleaned up Snowman between the rounds, rubbing down his legs with a soft cloth. His flea-bitten gray coat glowed softly in the rain.

When Harry came into the ring for the jump-off, nobody was paying attention except Johanna and the children. But Snowman, seemingly unperturbed by the rain, sailed around the course for another clean round. When First Chance came into the ring, she flew around the course, too. Back came the jump crew, scurrying around to raise the bars higher. Now the height was a daunting five feet, six inches.

On this round, First Chance knocked down a pole, but Snowman went clean. Johanna and the children jumped up from their seats in delight. The plow horse had won another blue ribbon. Maybe the victory at Sands Point hadn't been a fluke after all.

The next class up was the green jumpers. This class was limited to horses in their first year of competition. Since Snowman had been to a show the previous fall, he was not eligible. Harry was riding Night Arrest and Wayward Wind. The rain continued steadily, and helmetless Harry just kept riding. When the water dripped down his forehead, he wiped it away with the arm of his tweed jacket. At the end of the green jumpers, Harry had collected another two ribbons for Hollandia— a blue for Night Arrest and a second-place red for Wayward Wind.

When Saturday dawned, a steady summer downpour still was hammering the show grounds. The rain had deterred all but the most dedicated spectators. Men wore tweed hats and mackintoshes; women carried black umbrellas and wore muckers to wade through the mud.

While the footing in the big arena on the polo field had been decent the day before, today it was soupy, the worst possible conditions for jumping. The sandy ring surface collected large puddles. The most dangerous situation for a jumping horse is unsure footing—sliding on takeoff would ensure a crash; perhaps even worse, sliding on landing could bring a horse to the ground, possibly crushing a rider's leg underneath his thousand-pound body. Often, the worst injuries to riders occurred when a horse fell, then hit the rider's unprotected head with his iron-shod hooves as he was scrambling to his feet.

But Harry was not worried about the footing. He had years of experience riding with the Knox girls out in the hilly wooded fields around Smithtown with the hunt. Knowing that his mount was sure-footed and used to galloping in rain and even snow, over muddy bogs and sandy flats, made him trust his horse. Harry was confident that Snowman, more than any other competitor, would be comfortable galloping through the soupy sand.

The first class of the morning was the knock-down-and-out class, where any competitor who knocked down a pole would be eliminated. Snowman went clean on the first round, and Harry found himself back in a jump-off against First Chance. But then Snowman couldn't seem to hit his stride and ended up taking a pole down.

Harry was happy with the red ribbon, and he patted the horse on the neck as he exited the ring.

The grooms kept busy, scraping mud off the horses between each round. In the next class, Andante, who had not been jumping well, turned in a clean performance to win. The de Leyers were not disappointed in Snowman's performance. They clapped and applauded louder than anyone in the sparse crowd each time Snowman got another ribbon. There were seven classes leading up to the championship, and so far, Snowman had won a ribbon in all of them.

On the last day of the show, the rain clouds finally broke up, and by Sunday afternoon, the sun was streaming down on the polo field where the big jumps were set up for the championship classes.

Harry drops the reins over the fence, to the amazement of the crowd.

Harry stood by the side of the ring, surveying the course. Today, the families who had stayed home on Friday and Saturday had come out to see the show, and the atmosphere was festive. Snowman seemed to like performing in front of a crowd.

Going into the stakes class, two horses were vying for the title: Snowman and First Chance. Whichever horse won the class would bring home the show championship. First Chance—younger, lighter-boned, and pretty—was having a great season. Her rider, Adolph Mogavero, was a seasoned pro. Fairfield was almost home turf for them. Their base was the Ox Ridge Hunt Club, in nearby Darien, and Mogarevo had shown here at Fairfield numerous times. Snowman was heavier-boned than First Chance, and he had the unfortunate handicap of being not only older but less experienced. This would be his second-ever stakes class. After three days of slogging through the rain, Harry was not sure how much the horse had left in reserve.

Right from the start of the jumper stakes, it was clear that the crowd had a favorite: the blond man on the bulky gray horse. Some had read about them in the paper, and others were simply charmed by the handsome young man with the bright blue eyes and big smile.

The horses lined up at the in-gate: First Chance and Andante, Bon Soir and the other thoroughbreds. Joe and Jim had Night Arrest and Wayward Wind ready to go; the horses paced as the grooms walked them in circles, trying to keep them calm while they waited. The fences in the stakes class were formidable, all between five and a half and six feet tall. Each time a horse sailed over a fence, everyone in the crowd gasped and held their breath. Often enough, a horse balked at a fence and refused, sometimes almost sending his rider straight over his head. Horses approached the fences with their heads high, chafing against their bits. Riders jerked on the reins with each stride, trying to position the horse for the takeoff; then, a few strides before the fence, they gouged with their spurs and sometimes applied the whip. The overall impression was one of fear and danger—the riders seemed to be fighting their horses every step of the way. Horses knocked down fences or jarred them with a hoof, sending the light balsa marker flying.

Harry was first up on Wayward Wind and brought home a clear round, then tossed the reins to the groom and jumped on Night Arrest. The crowd clapped, delighted to see Harry ride again. Night Arrest danced and pranced when she entered the ring, a barely contained bundle of energy. Again, another clear round for Harry de Leyer. A few more horses went, and then it was Snowman's turn. The crowd had already seen Harry charge around the course twice, on the two thoroughbreds, and even though his previous rounds had been relatively smooth compared to those of the rest of the horses, they were still surprised when the big gray horse trotted into the ring on a loose rein. Snowman turned his head and appeared to survey the crowds—and maybe he saw Johanna and the children up in the bleachers, cheering him on.

Harry smiled in the direction of the stands, then eased the horse into an easy canter. There were still puddles on the ground, and the footing was sticky, though not as slick as it had been the day before. As Snowman cantered confidently around the course, his rider crouched forward, completely in sync with his horse. There was an obvious difference between this team and all of the other competitors: over each fence, the rider threw the reins forward, so that the horse could reach out freely with this nose. Over the last fence, a huge set of parallel bars, a woman on the sidelines jerked her hand up to cover her mouth in a gasp, as Snowman jumped up and sailed over with room to spare.

Snowman won the championship again. This weekend, ribbons and silver plates were piled on the front seat of the car. The purse was only a couple hundred dollars, but it was enough to cover their expenses with a bit to spare. The long drive up to Connecticut, the money for gas, and the grooms' pay—it had all been worth it. Harry was champion with Snowman and reserve champion with Night Arrest in the open jumpers.

But the show wasn't quite over. Jim Troutwell and Joe the Pollack had a proposition. There was still another class left. Dubbed the "grooms' bonus thriller," it was a fun experiment that gave the grooms a chance to ride, bareback, over a modified but challenging course. There were sure to be thrills and spills, since the grooms had to ride without saddles, and some were not very skilled. Best of all, there was a small cash prize. None of the open jumpers would be competing in the class: Andante, First Chance—those horses were all back in their stables getting rubbed down with liniment and carefully bandaged for the ride home.

Joe and Jim approached Harry with a plan: they had a friend who was pretty good on horseback. If Harry would let him ride Snowman, they could split the small purse three ways.

Harry gave Snowman a pat and handed over the reins. "Sure, no problem," he said. He knew that Joe and Jim had worked hard all weekend in the rain, and he wanted to pay them back. When Snowman, who had just come into the ring to receive a silver plate and a tricolor ribbon, sauntered back in with a groom astride his broad back, the crowd erupted in approval.

And sure enough, Snowman piloted the groom around the course with a clean round. Joe and Jim made sure he had an extra measure of carrots that day.

This was a horse that made everyone love him. Snowman had proven himself twice in succession, taking home the championship at two top shows back to back.

Entering the winner's circle, Harry often brought one of the kids along for the ride.

Something in the way he climbed up the ramp into the big green de Leyer van, as well as the calm look in his eye all weekend, his patience with everyone, whether children, adults, or grooms, and his seeming delight at the crowds told Harry that maybe Snowy somehow knew how close he had come to the end, and how much he should love life. Harry—who had watched young paratroopers perish, shot down by German snipers in the short distance between jumping from an Allied airplane with a parachute and floating to the ground—believed that, too.

After Fairfield, horse show fever hit the de Leyer household. School was out for the summer, Knox was closed, and the de Leyer family caravan became a familiar sight at every show. Everything the de Leyers did, they did together, and people smiled when pretty Johanna walked through the show grounds, shepherding her adorable towheaded children in front of her. No matter how hot and dusty it was outside, Chef, Marty, and William were neatly groomed, as well turned out as the horses. Even tomboy Harriet always wore a clean dress.

From one horse show to the next, it was the same routine: late nights braiding and washing in preparation for the show; early mornings, Harry up before four; and the long trailer trip to the next show—Lakeville in Connecticut and Stony Brook on Long Island, then out to Paramus, New Jersey.

The jarring trailer rides, the punishing show schedule, and the strain of the classes took a toll on most horses—but Snowman held up well. Every weekend, on the way home, the dashboard of the old station wagon was covered with silken ribbons. A few days later the preparations started again. The weeks passed in a whirlwind.

Johanna managed the family with skill and love, keeping the household going from dawn to dusk, keeping everyone happy, fed, and clothed and looking presentable. Harry had to care for the entire string of Knox horses with just a little help from Joe and Jim around the barn.

But through June and into July, Johanna and Chef, Harriet and Marty, were all rooting for the family horse: Snowman. It seemed as though the big gray, with all he had achieved, had shown that they, too, could achieve something. Every blue ribbon he brought home represented a triumph for all of them—a sign that this new life they were building was full of hope and promise.

But something troubled Harry. He'd begun feeling run-down. His tongue was sore. He tried to ignore it, just drinking milk and eating soft foods, but his weight kept dropping, and Johanna started pestering him to go to the doctor. Harry was too busy to think about himself, but by the middle of August, it was clear even to him that something was the matter.

16

The Things That Really Matter

St. James, Long Island, 1958

Growing up on a farm, Harry had learned to ignore small illnesses and injuries or to treat them with home remedies. One time, soon after Harry had bought his farm, he fell off a horse, twisting his ankle so badly that he could not walk. The ankle turned dark purple and swelled up until it would not fit in his riding boot. He could not put any pressure on it at all. But instead of going for an X-ray, he bound it up with adhesive tape and kept riding. A few days later the vet was out at the barn checking one of the horses. Harry held out his duct-taped, swollen leg and asked the vet what he thought of it. The vet laughed and said he had no doubt it was broken, and told Harry to go to the hospital for an X-ray and a cast. Harry refused; he just wrapped it up tighter and kept riding. Eventually, it healed.

Growing up during the war years had taught Harry something about endurance. He knew that the privations he'd faced during the war were nothing compared to the sufferings others had endured. It pained him to think about the St. Oedenrode tailor who had once altered school uniforms for young Harry. The Jewish tailor had been forced to wear a yellow star, and had survived the war only by hiding underground in a sealed concrete tank meant to store cow manure for fertilizer. A friend of Harry's had helped blow up a train bridge to impede Nazi movement, and he had paid the ultimate price: transport to a concentration camp, from which he had never returned. Harry's own father had been tar-

geted by the Nazis and had spent the last couple of years of the occupation in hiding, visiting his oldest son only rarely and in the dark of night.
Harry had grown up understanding that life was far from easy and that
sometimes people just had to endure.

So now he kept working the same long hours on little food and tried
to ignore the sore on his tongue. He kept himself going with extra milk,
but he had lost more than ten pounds. He was also getting so weak that
sometimes he felt dizzy in the saddle.

By late July, at Lakeville, in Connecticut, he could not swing up to
the saddle from the ground; he needed a leg up to mount. He trusted
Snowman to carry him around the course, but the horse had to make
up for the fact that his rider was almost too weak to stay on. When
Snowman took down poles in both classes, Harry tried to reassure the
gray, who was giving it his all, but he had to admit the truth to himself:
in this weakened condition, he was more of a hindrance than a help to
his horse.

Only then did he finally make an appointment to see his local doctor,
who was immediately concerned. He spotted a small tumor on Harry's
tongue, and sent a sample to pathology to have it tested. Still, Harry
put the soreness out of his mind. He was a young, strong, and healthy
man—not a likely candidate to develop a serious health problem. But
the doctor had laid down the law: no riding at all, until the pathology
report came back.

But the Smithtown Horse Show is coming up this weekend.

No riding, the doctor said. No exceptions.

Smithtown was one of the oldest and most prestigious horse shows
on Long Island, and it was right here, practically in his own town. Snowman had just won three back-to-back championships on the road, but
this was to be his first appearance at home. Also, Harry had promised to
supervise William in the lead line class, where the youngest riders walk
in the ring with a mother or father holding the horse on a line.

Harry confided in his friend Dave Kelley about his health problems,
and Dave offered to show Snowman for Harry. This would mean that
Dave would be competing against himself on Andante. But Dave was
always honest and fair, a true sportsman in the best sense. Harry knew
that Dave would ride true and give Snowman his best shot.

On the day of the Smithtown show, Harry dressed in regular clothes, prepared to join the throng in the stands to watch his horse perform. Because he was so gaunt his pants hung loose on him now, and he sometimes caught Johanna studying him with a worried look in her eyes.

That morning, Harry put his young son up on Snowman, looping the stirrup leathers three times through the irons to make them short enough for the toddler to reach. Feeling a little woozy, Harry walked the horse around the ring, among all the proud mothers and their budding horsemen and horsewomen. Snowman acted every bit the gentleman, and at the end of the class, they had won first prize.

Later that day, Harry sat in the stands and watched his beloved horse face off against Andante with Dave Kelley in the saddle. Snowman gave a flawless performance and took home the blue ribbon.

Harry chafed in the stands, frustrated that he could not ride.

A week passed. It was almost time for the next weekend's show when Harry got a phone call from the doctor's office. The lab results were in.

Harry drove through St. James, his mind full of other concerns. It was hard for him to take time out to go to the doctor on the day before a big show. He would have to be up early to get prepared to drive to New Jersey. Snowman was now leading in the points for the Horse of the Year award, and Dave had agreed to show him again.

The hamlet of St. James was just a village then: a church, a general store, and a fire station clustered around a V-shaped green. A blinking yellow light sat at the quiet intersection of Moriches Road and Lake Avenue. Small farms and tradesmen were mostly clustered around St. James, and the big estates led out to Long Island Sound. From the Knox School, you could look out over Porpoise Channel, a small coastal inlet that bordered the school's grounds on one side. Life here was peaceful; it seemed so far removed from the hardships of the war years. It was a safe, tranquil place.

Harry swung left toward Smithtown. The cheerful yellow plaster exterior of Saint Philip & James Church was just a couple of miles down the road. Here, Lake Avenue was lined with small shops and businesses, a diner, a hardware store, a liquor store. A few people were out and about, people wearing summer clothes, enjoying the nice weather. He was impatient and wanted to get this visit over with and get back to work. In spite of his weight loss, his frailty, and his fatigue, his mind was fully occupied with all the tasks he had left half done at home.

He pulled his truck into a parking slot and went into the office.

When the doctor greeted him, his manner was grave. He ushered Harry into his office and gestured for him to sit down. The doctor's look and tone gave Harry pause.

When the news came, it was sudden and shattering.

The slide had shown a malignancy: oral cancer. The only treatment possible was to remove his entire tongue. He would lose his ability to talk, and he would still be fighting for his life. This diagnosis came with no guarantees for a happy ending.

Harry sat in the doctor's office, trying to absorb the news. The weakness, the weight loss—he had attributed it to his inability to eat because of his sore tongue, not to any severe underlying cause.

Harry was a man of faith, and clearly his faith was being tested. On the ride back up Moriches Road toward home, he thought about his wife, Johanna, and the children, Chef, Harriet, Marty, Billy, and Harry junior. And he thought of the big horse Snowman, who did everything with all of his heart. Compared to his family, compared even to his love for his hardworking horse, all of the ribbons and trophies and write-ups in the newspapers, the sudden look of respect on people's faces, the cheering of the crowd—none of that mattered now.

As a young boy, Harry had thought life was heading him down a pleasant and predictable path, until the goose-stepping Nazis had intervened, catapulting life in St. Oedenrode into a completely unexpected chaos. And now, once again, Harry's life had taken a tumultuous turn. By the time he arrived home, he was already determined to bear it with grace.

He did not even need to confide in Johanna—she could see trouble from the look on his face. Johanna had gone through hard times with him before. This was an unexpected blow but they would get through it together.

The following day, Harry drove to Branchville, New Jersey, to watch Snowman compete. There had been a festive air following the de Leyer caravan all summer, but now the mood had turned somber.

Harry was a practical man, and he knew that there was no point in complaining about the hand he was dealt.

At the beginning of the war in Holland, the Dutch had mustered up an army, gathering all of the young men, horses, and provisions they could, but their army had been defeated without ever engaging in battle. The inevitability of the German conquest was overwhelming. One minute, young Harry, age twelve, lived in a free country. Then, in just the blink of an eye, the queen had fled to England, the Nazis had taken over, and whole segments of the Dutch population were under siege.

The de Leyer family had not given up without a fight; they had done whatever they could, however small, to resist the occupation. His father had used his status and influence in the village to organize resistance, and had ended up having to hide from the Nazis or risk deportation to a concentration camp. Harry knew what it felt like to face odds bigger than you are. He knew how to fight, but he had no experience with an enemy like this one, an enemy from within. And he was not just a fighter; he was also a practical man, a man with a wife and a family to support. He was determined to face the reality and come up with a plan. Johanna could not manage the horses alone. He needed to sell them off now, while he could still function.

The doctor had told him point-blank: Harry would lose his power of speech—signaling the end to his career at Knox, even if he did beat the odds and survive. Harry would need to put his financial affairs in order. The shining pathway that had opened up in front of him—the circuit, the blue ribbons, the shows—all of it faded into the background. All that mattered was to figure out how to provide for his family.

Branchville was another big event. This show drew the New Jersey and Pennsylvania crowd, but the competition was just as stiff.

In the open jumper stakes, Dave Kelley, once again competing against himself, was slated to ride both Snowman and Andante. Harry helped saddle up the horse, and Dave watched as Harry gave the gray a pat and whispered something in his furry ear.

Earlier in the afternoon, Harry had pulled Dave aside and told him about the diagnosis and that he was going to have to sell his horses. Dave had agreed to buy all of them. Dave knew that Harry's horses were healthy and well cared for. He could use them for his own riding establishment.

In the bleachers, Harry watched with grim satisfaction as Dave steered the gray horse around the course. Dave rode bareheaded in a light-colored tweed jacket, canary pegged breeches, and black boots. Over each fence he released his hands, his balance so good that he maintained a straight line from each hand to the horse's mouth, even over the large fences. Unlike Harry, he did not ride on a loose rein, but he had watched Harry's style with the horse and was careful to give the horse room to stretch out his neck and head. The horse went clean, then clean again. Once again, Snowman won the open jumper stakes. Harry walked him into the ring to accept his owner's prize, but there was scant joy in it, and Harry sensed that the big horse felt his mood. Snowman had been showing all summer and had brought home the championship or reserve championship at every show. Right now, he stood first in the standings for the Professional Horseman's Association year-end award.

Harry took the blue ribbon from Dave and thanked his friend. "What do you want to do with this horse?" Dave asked. Harry knew that plenty of people would like to buy the gelding now. With his string of wins, the big gray was by far the most valuable horse in the de Leyer stable.

But Harry shook his head. "Not this one," Harry said. "This one stays with me. I won't sell him."

Harry had made a solemn promise when he'd bought Snowman back from the doctor, and Snowman had already repaid him a hundredfold. Snowman was part of the family. Harry had sold the horse once; he would never sell him again. Dave didn't press him. Both men understood that sometimes there were bonds between horse and man far greater than money.

Late that afternoon, Harry was stunned when he heard his name being announced over the PA system. He was needed back home at Hollandia immediately. Harry suppressed the impulse to panic. Calling long-distance and trying to find him at the show could only mean one thing: disaster must have struck at home. Harry's mind flitted through the possibilities—Johanna would not call unless there was a real calamity at home, perhaps a barn fire or one of the children seriously hurt.

Harry rushed home feeling sick with apprehension. His own problems were bad enough; he could not bear to think that something had happened to someone else in the family.

But after the long drive back from New Jersey, his mind spinning away with the possibilities, he arrived at the house to see that nothing appeared amiss. Inside, he found Johanna.

"You need to call the doctor right away," she told him. "There was a message that it's urgent."

Harry had a sinking feeling. What could the doctor possibly tell him that was that important? He already knew the worst. How much worse could it be?

Harry picked up the phone and called the office, and the receptionist put him right through. The doctor had astonishing news. Something just hadn't sat right with him; Harry was young and healthy and did not smoke or use tobacco, which would put him at risk. The doctor had been so concerned, in fact, that he had driven into New York to check on it.

And it turned out that his hunch had been right.

Harry's slide had gotten mixed up with that of another fellow—an older man who was a heavy smoker and had been in for a biopsy on the same day. Harry's slide had been fine—the abscess on his tongue was nothing serious. It was totally benign, nothing more than a nagging virus that would heal on its own. No need to sell his horses or give up his career.

The whole world opened up again in front of Harry de Leyer.

With a little time and Johanna's cooking, Harry quickly regained his strength. It was August now and the summer season would soon draw to a close. Once Knox was in session, Harry would not be able to continue traveling to shows.

There was one last important show before the school year started: Piping Rock, farther west on the island in Locust Valley, near Oyster Bay, the famed enclave where the Roosevelts had their summer home.

The competition here would be stiffer than any Harry and Snowman had ever faced before. The U.S. Equestrian Team would be back from the summer season in Europe. Sharpened from international competition, they would be competing at Piping Rock in preparation for the fall indoor season leading up to the National in November.

As summer drew to a close, the trees around St. James formed broad leafy canopies, the air was humid, and a low buzzing of mosquitoes hummed in the background, but soon enough there would be a fall nip in the air. Harry was feeling stronger; he was still putting on weight, his illness almost just a memory.

The beginning of the Knox school year was pressing in fast, but right now, his mind was on Piping Rock.

17

Piping Rock

Locust Valley, Long Island, 1958

The satirist Dorothy Parker once said, "If you want to know what God thinks of money, look at the people he gave it to." She might have added, "And if you want to see the people he gave it to, head to the Piping Rock Club." In September 1958, the Piping Rock Horse Show was in its fifty-third year.

It was not a long drive from Harry's converted chicken farm in St. James to the grounds of the Piping Rock Club, but what a world away it was. Set along Long Island's Gold Coast, the area made famous by jazz-era novelist F. Scott Fitzgerald in *The Great Gatsby,* the Piping Rock Club prided itself on its exclusivity. The elite of New York society congregated in Locust Valley at its cluster of genteel clubs. The Seawanhaka Corinthian Yacht Club, the Creek Club, and Piping Rock were gathering places for the country's "elegantsia." It was in the woods of the Piping Rock Club, in 1937, that society songster Cole Porter fell from a horse and broke both his legs. He claimed to have composed the song "At Long Last Love" while awaiting his rescue. In fact, breaking a leg at Piping Rock had a long society tradition. Lida Fleitmann, one of society's most eligible debutantes in the 1920s, was famed for her daring exploits on horseback, not the least of which involved fracturing her femur during a Piping Rock jumping competition, an event considered noteworthy enough to appear in her wedding announcement in the *New York Times.*

The entrance to Piping Rock was unprepossessing—just two stone pillars that barely set off a path into the piney woods. But let there be no misconception: the humility of the entrance was designed with only one goal in mind, to turn away outsiders. According to the code of ethics on which the club was founded, in order to see the grandeur, one needed to be invited inside.

Eleonora Sears, wearing her trademark fedora, at the Piping Rock Horse Show, flanked by United States Equestrian Team members Frank Chapot (left) and Bill Steinkraus.

Behind those gates, out of sight, was one of the most elegant clubs on the eastern seaboard. Designed in 1913, the club had a rambling but elegant Georgian-style clubhouse fitted out with rooms for guests, who enjoyed sitting on the broad veranda that overlooked a courtyard with a fountain. The golf links were known to be among the finest in the nation. There were grass and clay tennis courts and an equestrian facility, including polo fields where the Prince of Wales had played on several occasions. The horse show's jumping contests were held in a beautiful grass arena the *New York Times* had called "the finest exhibition field in the world for the purpose." The arena was bordered on one side by a steeplechase field and on the other by a grandstand made up of tiered white boxes. In the stands, Vanderbilts mingled with foreign ambassadors and high-ranking government officials, chatting in the distinctive tight-lipped upper-class accent made famous by Franklin Roosevelt, known as "Locust Valley lockjaw." Perhaps this was what Fitzgerald meant when he said of Daisy Buchanan that "her voice was full of money." The people of Piping Rock's voices dripped with privilege. They were not a welcoming bunch.

Eleo Sears posed for a photo with her usual forthright gaze. She stood in the center, looking directly into the camera. Her face was shaded by her trademark white felt hat; her skin sported a perpetual suntan. She wore sensible heels, a skirt, a cardigan, and a white blouse. In the summer of 1958, Eleonora Randolph Sears had recently celebrated her seventieth birthday, but from a distance Eleo, as she was known to members of her set, looked easily twenty years younger. No longer the beauty once voted the best-dressed woman in America, she still had the erect bearing of an athlete. On each side of her stood a handsome young man wearing pegged breeches and riding boots, his velvet cap tucked under his arm. Bill Steinkraus and Frank Chapot, both members of the United States Equestrian Team, had shown Miss Sears's horses successfully in Europe. She regularly marked her return from these equestrian trips abroad with an appearance at Piping Rock, and 1958 was no exception. The photographer snapped the picture of a woman who looked quite used to being the center of attention.

Eleo Sears was one of the best-known female athletes of the early twentieth century. In addition to being a fearsome tennis champion, she was also famed at squash, had pioneered women's entry into polo, drove her own car in an era when few women did, and had piloted a plane. Once, in the middle of a tennis match, she managed to divert a loose cart horse careening toward a crowd of spectators, then calmly resumed her match. Miss Sears was so well known in her day that the *New York Times* ran an article about her sartorial habits while out ice-skating; it was considered newsworthy when Eleo switched from a skating muff to mittens. She had popularized the sport of long-distance walking—regularly striding from Boston to Newport, Rhode Island, a distance of seventy-one miles. As she paced, she was trailed by her chauffeur driving her green Salamanca-bodied 1914 Rolls-Royce Tourer, a thermos and sandwiches on the back seat. She was also followed by a coterie of photographers, who plastered her picture across the newspapers of Boston, Rhode Island, and New York. Equally famous for her equestrian skills, she had won numerous blue ribbons at the National Horse Show. She was one of the first women who switched from sidesaddle to riding astride. Prior to Miss Sears's time, women competed only in ladies' classes, riding and even jumping sidesaddle, an absurd feat that, while considered "more ladylike," was also much more difficult than jumping with both feet planted firmly in the stirrups. In 1958, Miss Sears, the still-handsome woman who'd once been painted by John Singer Sargent, was one of the most formidable doyennes of the horse world.

And Harry de Leyer had done the unthinkable: he had turned down a job working for her, preferring instead to be his own man. And there was nowhere like Piping Rock to show just how difficult it was to be his own man. It is hard to imagine a more closed world, one in which fortunes were more entrenched or traditions more hidebound. The inherited wealth behind Eleo Sears dated back to shipping fortunes and land grants made in the colonial era. The United States was a land of increasing diversity and opportunity, but among the East Coast establishment, there was no sign that change was coming.

But sometimes change doesn't just come; people need to make it happen. Harry de Leyer was famous for being stubborn. Too stubborn to let a perfectly sound horse go to a glue factory. Too stubborn to take a job working for one of the top horsewomen in America. Too stubborn to accept the fact that he couldn't ride against anyone he chose to—and to compete on the basis not of birthright but of skill. People might have considered him crazy for turning down a job at Prides Crossing, Eleo Sears's Massachusetts estate; any rational person would have thought he was nuts to believe that he and his plow horse could compete against horses who had just flown in from Europe in specially equipped equestrian airplanes. Maybe he *was* nuts. Only time would tell.

Piping Rock was devoted to the concept of amateur sport. In 1913 a *New York Times* reporter stressed that at Piping Rock, "Any professionals seen were on the outside of the ring." Amateurs competed for silver trophies only, the reporter noted, adding that the lack of prize money caused "an outpouring of entries from people who competed for the love of the sport." By the late 1950s, the show had evolved to the point that professionals were allowed to enter, and monetary prizes were awarded. The purses at Piping Rock were generous, attracting the top horses to the yearly event. But the mind-set—that profession-als were not on a par with amateurs—continued unabated. "Amateur" was a code word for the privileged class. Like the climbers who claimed victory in the conquest of Mount Everest, hardly mentioning the local Sherpas who climbed along with them and carried their gear, it was the owners and amateur riders who were important at Piping Rock. Pros may have been allowed inside the ring now, but "professional" was still just another name for the hired help.

By 1958, Miss Sears no longer showed, but contented herself as an owner-spectator. Her two horses, Diamant and Ksar d'Esprit (pro-nounced kiss-AR dess-PREE), fresh from their European triumphs, would be piloted by the two gentlemen stars of the USET who'd posed beside her in the photograph, Bill Steinkraus and Frank Chapot.

In 1958, the press had been abuzz with the exploits of the United States Equestrian Team in Europe over the summer. On July 18, 1958, Hugh Wiley, riding Nautical, had been the first American ever to triumph in the King George V Gold Cup in London—arguably the most prestigious jumping competition in the world. Then, later in the same competition, the young all-male American team won again, taking home the team gold. It was a triumph of huge proportions. Two of the horses ridden in the competition, Ksar d'Esprit, with Bill Steinkraus aboard, and Dia-mant, ridden by Frank Chapot, were among the top four. Steinkraus, a tall, slender man from Connecticut, was widely admired for his effort-less elegance on horseback. A Yale graduate, he was a veteran of the U.S. cavalry and had been stationed in Burma during World War II. Frank Chapot, another Ivy Leaguer, was considered a fearless rider. For both of these horse-and-rider teams, showing at Piping Rock marked their of-ficial return to the United States, and the first stage of gearing up for the U.S. indoor season, which would culminate in the National Horse Show.

For Harry, the summer's end was bittersweet. Right now, Snowman stood in the lead for the Professional Horseman's Association Champi-onship, but that would soon change. The rest of the horses and riders would stay on the road all fall, while Harry returned to his daily routine of tending to the barn and teaching lessons in the afternoon. His week-ends would be taken up with small local shows and foxhunting with his pupils. Maybe he could get to a few of the bigger shows, but for all intents and purposes, his show year was over.

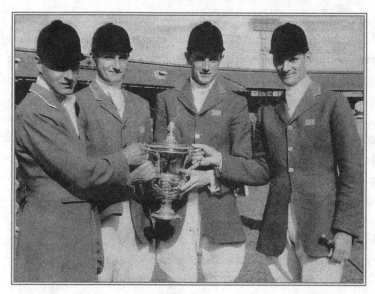

The glamour boys of the United States Equestrian Team fresh from a winning season in Europe. (Left to right) Frank Chapot, George Morris, Hugh Wiley, and Bill Steinkraus.

Between now and then, however, there was Piping Rock. Snowman was sharp after the summer's competition and Harry knew not to over-train him. A horse had only so many good jumps in him, and Harry did not want to take advantage of Snowy's good nature or ruin his legs. Harry wanted Piping Rock, the season's swan song, to be the horse's best show.

On the morning of September 10, 1958, Harry, Johanna, the children, and Snowman headed off to the Piping Rock Club certain of one thing: they would give it their best shot.

The William S. Blitz Memorial Gold Challenge, a large gold perpetual trophy, would be awarded to the horse that amassed the most points in competition over the course of three days. Each year, engravers cut the champion's name and the year onto the loving cup, which was displayed in a case inside the Piping Rock's white Georgian clubhouse. This trophy seemed to belong to Eleo Sears. Her horses had won it in 1955 and 1956. The Blitz carried a one-thousand-dollar prize, a much bigger purse than most other cups. But the money prize would not have been of interest to Eleo, a great-granddaughter of Thomas Jefferson's. Miss Sears was one of the primary supporters of the fledgling United States

Equestrian Team. The riders, in order to maintain their amateur status, could not get paid, but an October 1958 article in the *Chronicle of the Horse* estimated that it would take $500,000 to support the team for two years, until the beginning of 1960. To Eleo Sears one thousand dollars was irrelevant. In any case, she did not even believe in prize money. She thought that people should compete for the love of the sport alone.

Nobody who knew him would contest that Harry loved the sport, but for Harry, that one-thousand-dollar prize would be an enormous boon. The purse would be split among the top four horses, with the top horse taking home the largest chunk of it. With Johanna's frugal accounting, the money would be put to good use. It was clear that the de Leyers would need to find a new home. The horses were splitting the chicken coop farm at the seams, and one and a half acres was not enough room for all of them. Harry had his eye on a property that was larger—about five acres—and just adjacent to the Smithtown polo field. By scrimping and saving every penny, they might be able to move to the bigger place.

At Piping Rock, Harry was introduced to a whole other level from what he had seen at shows over the summer: not just the cream of the crop from Europe but the best of Connecticut and Pennsylvania were there. This was where the competition would start to shape up. Everyone eagerly watched to see who would dominate the fall circuit. The summer shows suddenly seemed far away, their victories almost bush league. Sure, it had been exciting to win back-to-back championships at North Shore and Sands Point, Lakeville and Fairfield, but now people in the crowd were talking about the equestrian team and its riders' performances in Europe, and in comparison the summer circuit seemed like small potatoes.

One thing was for sure. Over the summer, the de Leyer family, competing week after week, had learned to work like a well-oiled machine. They had their routine down pat. Arriving at the grounds of Piping Rock, they wasted no time staring at the grandeur of the setting—they had gotten used to arriving at these clubs and to moving among these fancy people. Johanna always had all of the children dressed to the nines, but when they arrived at the show grounds, everyone changed into wooden shoes and coveralls. Everyone, even the children, had a job to do. Harry slipped on coveralls and got the stable set up; the children helped to carry buckets and brushes. Harry stacked bales and filled the stalls with

Bill Steinkraus riding Eleonora Sears's champion jumper Ksar d'Esprit.

Frank Chapot riding Eleonora Sears's expensive German import,
Diamant.

fresh straw. With the help of Joe the Pollack and Jim Troutwell, he set up the tackroom. Soon Hollandia's stabling area was spick-and-span—even if they did not have the fancy tackroom drapes that others had, Snowman's impressive array of ribbons, tacked up next to his stall, certainly livened up their stable area.

The big green horse van Snowman traveled in was comfortable enough, but it could not begin to compare with the specially equipped airplane on which Eleo's horses had traveled home from Europe just a few days before. Transatlantic horse travel was hardly the norm in 1958. Fewer than twenty horses made the trek to Europe for the summer tour. Specialized air transporters, such as the Seaboard & Western All Cargo Freight line, carried horses overseas in air-conditioned turboprop Lockheeds, fitted out with carefully padded stalls. The crossing took eighteen hours, as the airplanes needed to stop for refueling. These were among the most pampered horses in the world.

Eleo Sears's horse Ksar d'Esprit, like Snowman, was a gray, but that was the only similarity between the two geldings: he was lithe and fine-boned, with a snappy action over fences and a lovely, refined thoroughbred face. Bred in the United States, then sent to Canada, this horse was already a veteran of several European tours and a former champion at the National Horse Show. Steinkraus was an elegant and tactful rider, as well as a Wall Street businessman and a concert violinist. Loved by people in and out of the horse world for his style on and off a horse, he would be featured later that year in a *Sports Illustrated* article entitled "Thinker on Horseback." Close to Harry in age, Steinkraus had already competed in two Olympic Games: 1952 and 1956. Of all of the competitors, he came closest to the platonic ideal of the scholar-athlete. Bill Steinkraus and Ksar d'Esprit on a good day were unbeatable. Harry had to hope that they would not be having a good day.

If possible, Miss Sears's other horse, Diamant, was even more impressive. Diamant was a German-bred jumper purchased from Fritz Thiedemann, one of Germany's leading riders. The horse had already been a seasoned champion in Europe when Miss Sears bought him for "an undisclosed sum," rumored to be close to $30,000. He had made a strong showing in Europe over the summer for the young American team. The press had been impressed by "the expensive German import," and he arrived at Piping Rock as a strong favorite. In any case, people figured that the main competition would be between the two young Olympians, mounted on two of the best horses in America. Everyone else who entered did so at their own peril.

Snowman had been an entertaining diversion during the summer months, but now the fall equestrian season was in full swing, and people who took the sport seriously were there. Sure, the gray horse had won some championships, but against whom? He had had his moment in the sun, and the fans' interest returned to the glamorous boys of the USET.

Harry de Leyer, not easily cowed by pretensions, did not concern himself with these things. When it came to riding, no amount of hauteur could take the place of seat-of-the-pants skill. Harry didn't spend a lot of time thinking about the competition. Reputation was all relative. Harry remembered the honor of being chosen to bear the flag, and how it had felt to parade in front of the crowd on his mare Petra during that glorious time in Amsterdam when the war was over. The crowds in the stands that day had been ecstatic, and all eyes had been upon him. That day, he'd seemed important and feted and respected.

And then there'd been other days, dark days on the tobacco farm, trying to please an alcoholic boss, watching the tobacco plants go from glossy green to shriveled and brown with the drought. On those days, he'd been sweaty and grimy and dressed in coveralls. On those days, he'd driven the milk cart down a dirt lane, about as invisible as a man could be. But Harry knew he'd been the same man in both circumstances. It was not his surroundings or his appearance or the opinions of others that mattered. The only thing that mattered was his belief in himself. So he did not give much importance to the closed-off, snobbish world of Piping Rock.

Harry had brought three horses to this show: Night Arrest and Wayward Wind to compete in the green jumpers, and Snowman to compete for the Blitz. The gray settled right into his stall, his calming presence helping keep the other two on an even keel. As long as Harry was around, Snowman never minded showing up in a new place. With his head hanging over the half door, he took in the scene with a calm air. He seemed to know he was part of the family, and if the family wanted to make a gypsy caravan to a new place every weekend, that was fine, as long as he got to come along.

Snowman was braided up and spotlessly clean, groomed until his shiny late-summer coat showed dapples if the light reflected across it the right way. His whiskers had been trimmed and his hooves painted, and like the children, he looked dressed up in his Sunday finery.

As Harry bedded his horse down for the night, he knew that he would give his very best, and Harry could not ask for more than that. The children were excited. School would be starting soon, and their long summer spent following Snowman from show to show would come to an end. Harry loved their simple childish belief in their pet. Only he and Johanna understood that their lesson horse had just stepped into a whole new level of competition. This show would not pay for itself unless Snowman won the Blitz prize—and that meant he would have to be cumulative champion across three days of grueling competition. As always, Snowman looked at his owner with the big brown eyes that had earned him the nickname Teddy Bear. Sometimes Harry felt that the old horse all but opened his mouth and talked to him. The gelding's steady dark gaze told Harry that, as always, he would do his best.

Friday dawned gray and cool, perfect riding weather. The bright green turf field was as neatly groomed as a golf course fairway. At Piping Rock, it was traditional for society folk to line up around the arena in their fancy cars, these prime parking spots playing the role of the reserved boxes at the indoor shows. Schooling jumps were set up out in the woods. Some riders took advantage of the hidden fences to pole their horses. A groom stood on each side of a fence holding a pole, and as the horse went over the fence, the grooms lifted the pole and rapped the horse on the tender, bony part of the cannons. This practice was supposed to surprise the horse into jumping even higher to avoid the painful smack; it was also illegal. One prominent rider had been asked to "sit down" for an entire season after being accused of it. Still, at a place like Piping Rock, the temptation was great. The stakes were high, and the trek out to the woods to pole, while avoiding the prying eyes of the horse show officials, was a yearly ritual for some.

All of the fences at Piping Rock were white: white standards, white poles. The jump crew dressed in white from top to toe. Against the green turf field, on a sunny day, the effect could be blinding. The morning started with hunter classes. Harry kept busy around the stables, mucking and cleaning tack. There was always work to be done.

Finally, it was time to tack up. Even though Snowman was spotless, Harry went through the entire ritual: he picked the horse's feet, pinching the tendon gently, and cleaning out the underside of the hoof. He started with the left front foot, then circling around to the left rear, right rear, and right front. There was a right way to do everything around horses, and that was how Harry did things, those habits so long ingrained that he performed them without thinking. He ran the curry comb over the horse, though there was no dirt or dander to collect, then clapped the hard rubber comb against the barn wall. Next came the soft body brush, which drew up the skin's oils to bring out the coat's natural shine.

Even now, Harry could not work over this horse without remembering what he had looked like just a couple of years earlier. Judging him by his appearance, one would not think he was the same horse. But Harry knew that the new look did not change him. Every person and every horse was a combination of what you could see on the outside and what he carried with him on the inside.

Harry still did not have a fluffy sheepskin saddle pad and Piping Rock was far too fancy for the army-navy blanket, so he settled his saddle right on the horse's satiny back. Harry was like a proud father. Johanna always made sure that the children looked perfect; Harry wanted Snowman to look his best, too.

Harry slipped a finger into the horse's mouth and slid the soft rubber snaffle into place, then folded down each ear in succession, settling the bridle's crownpiece into a comfortable position. The carefully oiled leather felt buttery and familiar under his callused fingers. He fastened the throat latch and gave his horse a pat on the neck.

"We're fighting the Germans today," Harry whispered as he led the horse out of the stall. He handed the reins to Chef while he took off his coveralls. Underneath, his riding breeches were spotless. He straightened his tie, slipped on his jacket, and slicked back his hair to ready it for his black velvet cap. One of the grooms came over with a cloth to shine the last of the dust off Harry's boots.

No doubt, many spectators would discount the pair: the gelding was so clearly a grade horse; the rider lacked both the perfectly tailored custom-made clothes and the studied air of upper-class ease affected by most of the other riders.

But nobody who had been following the circuit all summer was quite so ready to write them off. Maybe at ringside they looked like a couple of country bumpkins, but in the ring, magic happened: the horse seemed almost to turn into a different animal and the rider was magnetic to watch, holding the crowds spellbound.

There were two main series of classes during this show. In the Fédération Equestre Internationale (FEI) fault-and-out classes, horses would be judged on speed and touching the fence would not count—only a knocked-down pole or a refused fence incurred a penalty. The fences were high and a rider was rewarded for keeping the horse tightly leashed and making turns in the air and short approaches to fences. At Piping Rock, the bigger challenge was the second group of classes, the Blitz Memorial Series. In these, even the lightest brush of hoof to railing would be penalized. Miss Sears's Ksar d'Esprit would compete in the FEI series, and the big German horse, Diamant, would go for the Blitz trophy. Neither horse would be overly taxed.

Harry had entered Snowman in both series. The big gray would not have the opportunity to rest as much in between classes—but Harry had no choice. The only way to cover the cost of the horse show was to win prize money, and with competition this stiff, there were no guarantees. Harry tried to make up for the extra jumping in competition by jumping his horse less outside of the shows, a trade-off that most of the other trainers weren't willing to make. Harry knew that Snowman was a strong horse, his muscles honed by pulling a plow, and he felt reassured that in between shows his hardest job was walking around with children on his back.

The jumper classes on the weekend afternoons usually drew the big crowds, especially for the stakes classes. So for this first jumper class, the stands were sparsely populated, although there were plenty of people in the press box. Harry picked out Marie Lafrenz there. Eleo Sears was also easy to spot—perched in the bleachers near the front, she kept her ice-blue eyes on the ring as coteries of people stopped by to pay their respects and welcome her home from Europe.

The FEI class was run on the rules normally used in international shows, where performance was judged both on ability to clear the fences and on the horse's time. These international rules favored a different kind of horse—one that could accelerate quickly, turn sharply, and gain enough momentum to clear both height and width in spite of only a short distance to prepare. Harry knew that he would have to cut corners to get a fast enough time to win. With his relaxed manner and long, lanky stride, Snowman was not a natural for classes run on FEI rules.

The course was intimidating: the all-white fences glared in the sun, and the turf footing was sometimes slippery—most horses were accustomed to jumping in dirt rings. The last jump was a big aiken just twenty-four feet beyond the previous fence. That combination would be a tight in-and-out, especially difficult since horses would be headed toward the out-gate, which led in the direction of the stables, making them more prone to want to speed ahead.

Many horses were dropping a foot on the last fence, bringing a pole down; others were refusing. The first class on the first day was always a tough one—horses, typically skittish to new sights, had a lot to take in here, with the hubbub of spectators flanking the ring in their sports cars and convertibles.

When Bill Steinkraus entered the ring on Ksar d'Esprit, it was hard to miss the harmony between man and horse. Steinkraus sat in the saddle with classical elegance, and the picture he made on Ksar d'Esprit was one of a polished equestrian. Steinkraus sailed around the course with no faults, looking every bit the veteran Olympian he was.

When Harry entered the ring on Snowman, he knew that he would have to shave the approaches close. Snowman liked to jump clean, but he had not been bred for racing, and was not as naturally fast as some of the other horses. The only way to save time was for the rider to turn his horse in the air, with a guiding hand and a subtle change in his weight over the fences. This was a risky strategy because if the weight shift was too abrupt, the horse might flatten his arc and drop a hind leg.

Harry guided the horse through the tight turns, and Snowman followed Harry's lead, but he just wasn't sharp. Over the second-to-last fence he dropped a hind leg, knocking a pole from its cup.

Exiting the ring, Harry saw his children's disappointed faces. After so many wins in a row, it was hard to watch the big gray get crushed by a horse who was so much better known and finely bred. But Harry lost no time thinking about his defeat. He needed to get Snowman cooled down and comfortable, because the Blitz Memorial series started in the afternoon. At least they would not be competing against Ksar d'Esprit in those classes, though there was no escaping Miss Sears's other formidable entry, Diamant.

The rest of the morning flew by, and before long it was time to start the routine again: grooming, saddling, and bridling.

The sun shone down on the show grounds and by midafternoon, a greater number of spectators were out. Festive red, white, and blue bunting festooned the busy stands around the arena. Snowman would have the slight advantage of having already been in the ring, even if his first performance of the day had been lackluster.

Harry headed out to the schooling area and gave a nod to his competitors. The glossy brown Diamant thundered across the schooling ring impressively—he was a big horse and you could see his Teutonic breeding in his powerful haunches and heavy bones. When the veteran gelding entered the ring with Frank Chapot on board, there was no sign of skittishness. This horse, who had competed in London and Germany, in venues that regularly drew crowds of ten thousand or more, would not have been distracted by the size of Piping Rock's stands or crowds. With the precision of a German clock, the pair turned in an effortless perfect round.

Snowman was up. Reins loose, Harry crouched low over the horse as he urged him into a gallop toward the big white triple bar, each pole a stair step above the one in front of it. The poles appeared to float in the air, making it hard for both horse and rider to judge their distance on the approach, and since the fence had both a height and a spread element, arriving at just the right spot for takeoff was paramount. Several horses had already misjudged, either taking off a stride early and bringing down the back pole or realizing their misjudgment and throwing in a tight extra stride but then, unable to snap the knees up quickly enough, plowing through the first pole. As Snowman sailed over the big jump, his knees were tucked up so that he had at least a foot to spare. Harry's face disappeared into the horse's neck, which was outstretched, making him look like Pegasus in flight. At the end of the first round, two horses had gone clean: the massive German import and the gray plow horse.

The jump crew raised the fences and tamped down divots with their feet. Harry waved at his children, then turned his focus back to the task at hand. He looked over the course, reminding himself of the hazards at the last in-and-out, deciding where he would turn, and how many strides he should allow on the approach. He galloped through the course in his mind, visualizing each fence clearly.

Diamant was to jump first, and the crowd quieted as he entered the ring. He was so impressive looking. Chapot made a small circle at a controlled canter, then headed toward the first fence. Where other horses had turned a head to look at the crowds and the flapping bunting along the side, this horse might as well have had blinders on. He was all business as he pounded down to the first fence. At the sidelines, Miss Sears leaned forward slightly. It was all over in a minute. Diamant was clear, with what appeared to be little effort on his part. This horse was unstoppable.

As Harry and Snowman trotted into the ring, the contrast was inescapable. Harry grinned again at the children perched on the fence, then smiled at the crowd; his horse, seeming to sense that this was a performance, turned his gaze there, too. The spectators responded with a smattering of enthusiastic applause, then fell silent. This was a challenging course. Would this clunky horse really be up to the task? Some in the stands had no doubt read of his earlier exploits, but many others probably considered his arrival in the jump-off a fluke.

Harry held his reins loosely and seemed to be guiding the horse more from sympathy than any obvious form of control. Careful observers noticed that he whispered something to his mount and that periodically one of the horse's ears would flick back: he was listening. Chapot had held in Diamant like a heavy-caliber cannon ready to fire, but Harry on Snowman was more reminiscent of a Native American galloping bareback across an open plain—the means of communication between horse and man were subtle, though there was no mistaking the vibrating wire that seemed to move between them. As the horse bore down on the first fence, a big post-and-rail more than five and a half feet straight up, the crowd was attentive. The rider crouched lower, and his hands moved forward, sliding up the horse's crest, making sure that the reins were loose.

The horse lengthened his neck—one stride, two, three—then drew his haunches underneath him. Harry seemed almost to disappear over the fence, his lithe frame so lightly balanced that it was hard to tell where man ended and horse began. In a flash, the gray landed with a thump. Harry's eyes brought the line of the next fence into sight and then raised up above it. Like all good riders, he looked off in the distance beyond the fence, not at the ground in front of the fence or the ground behind it.

After he had sailed over the last fence, there was a hush, as though nobody could quite believe their eyes. Then came the sharp rat-a-tat of applause. Snowman was clean.

It was time for a second jump-off, the little gray David facing off against the mighty German Goliath.

Miss Sears's ice-blue eyes watched intently from under her white fedora. A sportsman to the core, she was known to enjoy a good challenge, and no one could deny that this little nobody of a horse was allowing her prize horse to show off his skill. The white-clad fence crew tended to the grass and raised the fences once more. The bigger horse, who stood over seventeen hands tall, now had a clear advantage. Few jumper classes went to a third round of jump-offs. This class had become a grueling show of stamina. Each time a horse jumped a single fence, he was hefting twelve hundred pounds into the air. It was a one-on-one showdown, and now even the lowest fence was up over five and a half feet.

Electric excitement coursed through the air. People gathered as word circulated among the spectators that the eighty-dollar horse was still in the running. Chapot and Diamant had both performed in front of Olympic crowds—both had represented their countries, galloping under their country's flags. Anyone with a passing knowledge of horseflesh would bet on the German invader. But a feeling of excitement was coalescing around the underdog horse and his smiling rider. As for Harry—well, he'd seen German invaders before. And frankly, now as before, he was not impressed.

In this round, Snowman's turn came up first, and as he entered the arena, the well-mannered crowd again let out a smattering of applause. Still, it was not clear which horse was the favorite—Piping Rock took a dim view of outsiders, and Eleo Sears was horse show royalty. A poll of the crowd that day, no doubt, would have elicited mixed reactions. Wendy Plumb, one of Harry's pupils from Knox, was competing at the show in the junior division. She was startled to see their lesson horse in the show ring going head-to-head against one of the most impressive jumpers not just in the United States, but the world.

But Snowman always had a look in his eye that said he would do anything for Harry. And Harry, for his part, seemed to be having a marvelous time. As the crowd watched with growing pleasure, Snowman sailed around the course, making it look easy. Over the last hurdle, Harry let go of the reins entirely, a spectacular sight over a nearly six-foot fence. Snowman had made a third clean round. Now it was up to Diamant to match the gray's performance.

And match it he did. Galloping like a contained ball of fury, he rounded the course with panache. With his approach to each looming fence, the crowd fell silent, and as his hooves thundered down, leaving another clean jump behind him, the crowd took a collective gasp. As Chapot bore down on the last fence he looked as if he was almost home free—but not quite. On the big triple bar that had worried Harry, Diamant got sloppy and just nicked the pole with his hind leg. The white pole teetered, then fell. The crowd paused in silence for a moment before erupting. The eighty-dollar wonder horse had beaten the champion.

As Snowman paraded into the ring, the crowd went wild, clapping and cheering in a manner more befitting a baseball game than the manicured lawns of Piping Rock. Up in the press box, Marie Lafrenz tapped away on her typewriter.

The next day, the sports pages were abuzz with the story. As always, New York loved an underdog—in Snowman, they had found an underhorse. And Harry, the riding master, had acquired a new nickname too: the Flying Dutchman. The "eighty-dollar wonder horse" suddenly had a lot of new fans, but others were putting their money on the "European invader." Word was getting around about the plow horse who had beaten Eleo Sears's best Olympic prospect, and a parade of reporters with notebooks and pencils came around to talk to Harry. He was happy to answer questions as long as they didn't interfere with his work.

On Friday night, a new blue ribbon hung on the line next to Snowman's stall, but the horse seemed unimpressed. Harry tried to stay focused. To win the Blitz Memorial, he would have to have the highest average over the course of the three days.

On Saturday, the show's second day, the weather was hot, the skies were blue, and spectators flocked to the club grounds. Members and their guests sat in boxes or tailgated in their reserved parking spaces, and even ordinary folk were allowed onto the grounds to watch if they paid for a ticket. Harry was leading in the Blitz Memorial Gold Challenge, and he had scored an additional blue ribbon in the morning FEI class against Adolph Mogavero on Sonora. Now the crowd had gathered for the main event: the Blitz.

In the schooling ring, the German horse again looked unstoppable. Not wanting to tire his horse, Harry barely had Snowy jump at all, just took a few turns around the ring to loosen the gray's legs. He could not help but notice Chapot schooling Diamant, nor the determined expression on the sportsman's face.

Today's course looked intimidating. There were more fences, and they were higher. Harry surveyed the jumps, imagining his approach to each one. The series of obstacles played like a movie in his head. He could feel the rhythm of his horse's gallop even when he was not riding him. The aiken and triple bar both would pose challenges, though Snowman had managed them fine yesterday. Today, there was a brush-wall-gate jump that might be problematic. The three elements used to construct the jump would make it hard for the horse to correctly gauge both the depth and the height of the jump. Unlike touching a pole, making contact with the brush brought no faults, but the hidden pole behind the brush was going to be harder to avoid.

Diamant had been resting since the day before, while Harry and Snowman had done two additional time classes. And of course they were not the only two horses in the class. The seven-year-old mare First Chance—ridden by Adolph Mogavero, Harry's chief competitor at Fairfield—could hold her own in any competition.

Harry watched as the class progressed, keeping Snowman limber by walking him around in the schooling area. Already several horses had been eliminated at the big brush-wall-gate, and Harry knew that fence would be his toughest challenge. When Diamant came into the ring, Harry rode over to watch. The horse was jumping well, but when he reached the brush-wall-gate, he tapped the rail with a front foot, giving him one fault. Harry stroked Snowman's neck. At all costs, Harry wanted to avoid a jump-off, which would just fatigue his horse more.

The only way to beat Diamant without a jump-off would be to clear the first round with no faults. There was no margin for error.

Despite the pressure, Harry entered the ring on a loose rein. Past the grandstand, Snowman pricked up his ears and glanced at the spectators, then turned to catch sight of the de Leyer children. Harry cued Snowman to gallop and headed toward the first fence. On the approach to the brush-wall-gate fence, Harry saw the problem. From the horse's perspective, the fence was a hanging gate with a brush box behind it. The white pole hanging behind the brush box turned the fence into a spread, but the horse would not perceive that. Snowman had always excelled at high and narrow fences. He had a short arc and tucked his knees up tight because he had taught himself how to jump out of paddocks, needing to clear wires suspended in the air above the top rails. He was a master at vertical height, but spread fences still sometimes caught him by surprise. *Steady, steady,* Harry thought, up in a half seat, his hands sensing the power of the horse underneath him, gathering up, getting ready. Harry waited for the horse, trusted in him. "You can do it, boy," he whispered.

Snowman collected his stride and sank back on his haunches, ready to clear the tippy top of the brush, not knowing that he would not be penalized for brushing through the soft foliage. But even on takeoff, Harry could tell something was not right. The horse had not seen the hidden white pole. His arc was too tight. He rapped the heavy wooden pole hard with both legs, flipping it to the side, then faltered on the landing and took a jagged step. Four faults.

Harry reached over and patted his horse on the neck. "It's okay, boy," he whispered. In a split-second calculation, Harry realized they were already out of the ribbons and decided it would be better to pull up. Let the horse go back to his stall and rest, rather than finish out the course just to soothe Harry's pride.

The crowd sat in stunned silence.

Harry saluted to the judge and then, patting his horse on the neck, trotted toward the out-gate. The gate man swung the gate open and the pair left the ring. Snowman was eliminated. Diamant would hold his lead to win the class.

The children were crushed, but Harry took the opportunity to make the loss into a lesson. Their horse was up against the toughest competition in America—perhaps in the world. He had jumped bravely yesterday, going to a third-round jump-off. And had won the FEI time class in the morning, even though speed was not his natural style.

Winning was never more important than fostering a sense of trust between horse and man. Harry knew that tomorrow was another day. Diamant was ahead on points now; he had a first and a second, and Harry had only a first. The only way for Snowman to take home the Blitz prize would be to win the championship class, though the fences would be higher, the pressure even more intense. The mood in the barn that evening was quiet, but Harry went about his chores with his usual methodical care.

Predictably, Diamant's name was emblazoned across the sports page headlines in the morning, the excitement of the underdog's upset forgotten when he'd been eliminated on the second day. No one expected a comeback from Snowman.

The final class of the Blitz Memorial Gold Challenge was held on Sunday afternoon, scheduled to take advantage of a capacity weekend crowd. Diamant now held a commanding lead. Harry's horse may still have been a sentimental favorite, but after Snowman's performance the day before, his fans had little hope that Snowman would rise to the challenge, especially since this would be the toughest course of all.

It had been a great summer, a season of glorious triumphs. Today was the last day before the demands of the school year started again. Harry ran the body brush over Snowman's coat, working hard to bring up the maximum shine. He looked deeply into the horse's dark eyes. This horse had his own wisdom, and even though Harry had seen the hurt in his children's eyes, he still thought he had made the right decision to pull up yesterday. Take care of your horse and he'll take care of you. Harry firmly believed that.

With the most important class of the season carrying a prize big enough to help them buy a new farm, Harry would put his beliefs to the test. He slid the saddle onto the horse's bare back. If Snowy took the prize today, the first thing Harry would do would be to order a soft sheepskin pad from the Miller Harness Company catalog to protect his beloved horse's back.

Johanna and the children anxiously hovered around. Marty threw his arms around one of the horse's big legs while Harriet and Chef each whispered their own version of good-luck wishes.

Harry swung up into the saddle, taking care to settle lightly on Snowy's back. Jim Troutwell ran a rag over Harry's boots and offered up a smile.

"Don't let the German horse get the better of you," he said.

Harry walked toward the schooling area. Chapot and Diamant were already there, schooling over a big oxer under Miss Sears's watchful eye.

No matter. Snowman was rested and fresh, and he'd always risen to the challenge before. Harry was ready.

The stands were full as the fifty-third Piping Rock Show drew to its close. The table that held the silver trophies, crowded on Friday, was now empty but for the big gold Blitz cup, winking in the September sun. During the past three days, many familiar names had paraded through the winner's circle. But the final class of the Blitz Memorial Gold Challenge had kept the spectators from packing up and going home. It was such a challenging course that even the best horses—First Chance and Andante—were getting faults. Harry watched the other performances, seeing where the pitfalls lay. Thankfully, the brush-wall-gate obstacle was not there, but the floating triple bar, the aiken, and the parallel bars all presented major challenges of their own.

In this class, Snowman would go before Diamant. He would have to perform at his very best, not knowing how the other horse would fare.

Harry heard the announcer call his name over the PA; he was on deck, up next. Snowman stood still on a loose rein, his ears lopped to each side in his trademark relaxed pose. Harry surveyed the crowds, catching sight of Eleo Sears and Johanna, his children, and others he knew who were awaiting his turn. It was a hot day, the last gasp of summer, and Harry was uncomfortably warm under his hunt coat. But the sun was nothing to him. Better to be sitting here, broiling in a woolen coat, than to be bent over in a tobacco field.

"Snowman, owned by Mr. and Mrs. Harry de Leyer, ridden by Harry de Leyer," said the announcer, summoning the pair into the ring. Harry slid his hands up the laced reins and squeezed his calves gently around the horse's barrel.

"This is it, Teddy Bear," he whispered to the horse, and one gray ear flicked back, attuned to his master's voice.

Snowman walked into the ring, and Harry gave him a chance to look up at the crowd. *Let's make it a good one,* he thought, and then all thought disappeared. At a controlled gallop, Harry headed toward the first fence, and he all but vanished into the flow—hoofbeats, fast, shifting turns where the horse made flying lead changes, *up and over,* thump, thump, *up and over.* With each fence the crowd seemed to hold its collective breath.

It was over in a moment. Only then did Harry realize they had done it. Snowman had gone clean. Now he was the horse to beat.

Maybe living through a war makes a man philosophical, but Harry figured that he and his horse had done all they could do. He could control how well he rode and how well he cared for his horse, but he could not control what others did, and so he kept Snowman moving in the schooling ring so that he would not stiffen up. Harry watched the big brown horse Diamant head into the main ring, but only out of the corner of his eye. However, as the horse approached the first jump, Harry stopped to watch. He was as tightly coiled and precise as a German-engineered car—a marvel of machinery; he made the American horses look like cow ponies by comparison. It was hard to believe anyone could beat this horse.

Chapot rounded the course with care, and the horse leapt over each fence with the same methodical jumping style. Finally, they headed toward the last fence. Harry knew how crucial it was to keep a horse together on the last fence of the last class of the last day of the show— but especially in a big-money class that promised a huge gold cup as the prize. Chapot let Diamant out a hair. The horse bore down on the final fence just a little faster than before, just a shade, showing his tremendous impulsion. He sank down on his hocks, then sprang up, his hindquarters shooting off like well-oiled pistons. But before it had actually happened, before the crowd knew, before the press had finished mentally composing the "DIAMANT TRIUMPHS" headline, Diamant flattened his arc just a bit too much, and one hind foot lightly brushed the back pole. The pole teetered in place but held.

One half fault, for a hind touch.

Harry felt the big meaty hand of Jim Troutwell clap him on the back, almost knocking out his breath.

A few minutes later, Harry stood on the grass in the center of the ring, holding Snowman's bridle with one hand and patting the horse on the neck with the other. He paused to smile at Johanna and wave to the children, but then he turned his mind back to the business at hand. He could almost hear the murmur in the crowd: *Who is that? Is that the one they call the Flying Dutchman? Have you ever heard of him? I heard he bought that horse for only eighty dollars.*

Snowman blinked sleepily as the cameras flashed around him. Harry cradled the big gold cup in his arms, then raised it up for his horse to take a sniff. While they pinned a tricolor rosette to his bridle, Snowman stood quietly, as though wondering what all the fuss was about.

As the summer of 1958 drew to a close, the Soviet Sputnik missile was orbiting the earth, and the possibility of change seemed to vibrate in the air. But at the Piping Rock Club, horse show mothers gathered up their charges as they talked about golf, tennis, and the upcoming fall fox-hunting season. They were comparing notes on their summers in Maine or Europe and getting ready to send children back to boarding schools, or Chapin or Spence in New York. They were discussing the girls who would make their debuts later in the fall, and they were talking about meeting again when they would officially mark the start of the social season in the boxes of the National Horse Show, just as their families had been doing for the last seventy-five years. And they murmured to one another about the handsome young Dutchman and his astonishing gray horse who had snatched the gold cup from Miss Sears. Perhaps they would see him again at the National.

Back at the de Leyer stables, Harry was dressed in coveralls again. He and Jim Troutwell were packing up, hefting the tack boxes and hay bales into the van. Snowman had his shipping bandages and blanket on. He was ready for a ride home and a well-earned rest. But on the front seat of the station wagon, along with an empty lunch hamper, sat a tricolor ribbon. And in the clubhouse of the Piping Rock Club, the big gold Blitz Memorial trophy waited to be sent out to the engraver, then put back on display.

Next year, when the fifty-fourth horse show started, that gold trophy would be engraved with the name of a newcomer, a Dutch immigrant named Harry de Leyer, and his slaughterhouse-refugee horse, Snowman.

18

The Indoor Circuit

St. James, Long Island, Fall 1958

It was back to the routine at the Knox School, and even though the giddy summer had passed in a flash and the big gray horse had returned a champion, there was no sign that Mrs. Phinney and Miss Wood were impressed. Education was a serious business and whatever horse show frippery Harry may have indulged in on his off time was of little interest to them.

If they had seen the pictures or read the headlines, they gave no sign. Snowman returned to his stall in the semicircular stable and seemed perfectly content to carry the girls in their lessons. The days continued balmy and sunny through the first few weeks of September, and Harry enjoyed his teaching schedule even though the girls also gave no notice of Snowman's summer triumphs. They had all gone off to their vacation activities and had most likely given no thought to their school horses and where they had been.

Harry put Snowman right back into the lesson lineup. The horse needed to earn his keep, and the Knox ladies had always approved of him because he was quiet and never gave the children any trouble. More than once, a girl had come back from the barn, smiling and thrilled by some new accomplishment—a girl who had never trotted or cantered before, a girl who had been too timid to jump. Snowman's manner was so unassuming, and Harry was so encouraging, that the girls always felt that the triumph was all their own.

At night, at home with Johanna, Harry plotted out the fall. There were a few more local weekend shows he could go to—but the rest of the season looked hopeless.

The horses in contention for the big year-end prizes would spend the fall campaigning, from the Pennsylvania National at Harrisburg down to Washington, D.C., where a brand-new international show was promising to make a big splash. Then it was on to Madison Square Garden. Horses would be racking up points faster than ever at these weeklong shows. In a single show, a horse that did well could match the points earned over the entire summer season.

Harry looked bleakly at the calendar: a day to drive to Harrisburg, another day to drive back, and seven days of show. The same thing for Washington. He and Johanna talked it over. Snowman and Harry had already qualified for the Garden. If only one or two of his students could qualify for the junior division, then the Knox headmistresses would have to let him go. But the Pennsylvania National and the Washington International were out of the question. Even if Harry and Snowman won every class they entered, he could not earn enough prize money to support the horses and his family. He needed his job at Knox; that was an incontrovertible fact of his life. And the truth was, he was grateful to have the job, grateful that the swank school had taken a chance on someone like him—an immigrant who was just learning English and who had no social connections.

Maybe somebody else in his position would have felt thwarted—here he was on the cusp of an unthinkable triumph and he had to fold his hand. But Harry was a teacher. He stood in the sun in the middle of the arena on hot days. He stood in the courtyard getting wet when it rained. Day in, day out, Harry was there with his students, watching them, analyzing their riding styles, and sharing his wisdom. And Snowman was a teacher, too. Fat girls and timid girls, shy girls and stiff girls—any girl, whoever needed him, climbed aboard the big gray teddy bear and grew braver.

"Grab the mane!" Harry hollered. "Because that's what the good Lord put it there for." One after another, the girls grabbed Snowy's thick white mane to anchor them over the fences. One after another, the girls gained confidence, fell in love with the horse, and brought him extra carrots and apples, tucked into their pockets.

Harry was proud of his girls. He loved to hold them to high standards, and to ask them to do things that they did not know they could accomplish until they were done. The girls gave a little extra for their young instructor because they sensed that he believed in them—sometimes more than they believed in themselves.

Back at the de Leyer house, Johanna had started a scrapbook with clippings of Snowman's exploits, and they had placed the trophies and hung ribbons all around the tidy living room.

At Knox, in the rain and the sun, Harry put away the glorious quest of summer and focused on the present, just as he had always done. He planned a schedule of local shows and thought about his stellar pupils—the ones who might be able to ride at the Garden.

Sure, in the mornings, up early, working alongside Jim Troutwell, cleaning stalls, he thought about that PHA championship. When was the last time a horse in the lead for the trophy had dropped out of the competition? Probably never.

Luckily, Harry had no time to dwell on that question. There were back-to-back junior shows for the next two weekends, and Snowman came along, carrying his students around the courses.

Harry let Bonnie ride Snowman in the junior jumpers and she got a little cocky, thinking he was a piece of cake to ride. Instead, he fooled her, ducking out from the side of a fence rather than jumping. From the sidelines, Harry had to chuckle at his four-legged teacher. Now sixteen, Bonnie was one of his most gifted students—one he could trust with the green and challenging horses. She had taken old Teddy Bear for granted—and he had been too smart for her.

Harry saw the tears of humiliation brimming in her eyes when she rode out of the ring, but he knew she had learned a lesson, albeit a hard one: don't ever take a horse for granted, especially not a horse like Snowman. He would treat the smallest child gently, but the horse also seemed to sense when a rider could use a challenge. Harry knew that Bonnie would be working harder than ever in the days to come, and that she would learn from her lesson.

Back at the barn, as she untacked him and settled him in for the night, Harry felt for the girl, but said nothing. She would persevere and go on to win on other days.

Harry could see that Snowman was happy, and he suffered no ill effects from carrying the lesson girls around on his back and taking them through their classes at the junior shows, but each day, when Harry headed out to the stable, he thought about the summer's triumphs, and of Snowman's performance against the toast of Europe. It felt wrong. The horse had been put on a shelf before he'd had a chance to show the world what he could do. Sure, he was a hundred times better off now than he'd been as a plow horse, but he was using only a small part of his talent carrying the lesson girls around the stable. Harry remembered showing the gold Blitz trophy to the horse, and what it felt like to parade him around that swank arena at Piping Rock knowing that he was second to none.

By the end of September, Harry had resolved to do something. Dave Kelley had ridden Snowman to a win at the Smithtown Horse Show, beating his own Andante in the process. Harry knew that there were not many men who would do that—but Dave was not an ordinary man. Dave was beloved on the horse show circuit: a true sportsman, a talented rider, and a straight shooter, a man to be trusted. That weekend, at the Huntington Junior Show, Harry proposed a plan.

Snowman deserved a chance to see what he could do. Harry would stay home and tend to his duties, and Snowman would go with Dave to the Washington International Horse Show—the last big contest before the Garden.

October 10–15, 1958, was just another ordinary week at the Knox School, but the barn seemed empty with Snowman gone. Dave Kelley had loaded the horse into the van and taken him to Washington, D.C. The de Leyers would have to follow the show's progress the same way everyone else did: in the newspapers.

The Washington International Horse Show was an upstart on the horse show scene, and its founding that year showed how important horse showing had become to the social hierarchy. New York was the traditional center of the East Coast establishment, but with the Cold War in full swing, Washington was rising in importance, with the growing government bureaucracy centered around the nation's capital. The late 1950s was the era of the unbeatable New York Yankees, but in October 1958, *Damn Yankees,* about a Washingtonian who sold his soul to the devil in order to help the Washington Senators beat the Yankees, opened in movie theaters, perhaps reflecting the national capital's desire to rival New York in other areas. That same month the Washington International Horse Show made its first appearance on the national stage. Hosting a great horse show was starting to be an important aspect of a city's civic pride.

The show opened on October 10 at the spacious and well-appointed National Guard Armory. Two international teams, Germany and Mexico, were on the program. While the United States Equestrian Team was not "officially represented," three members of the team—Sandra Phipps, Frank Chapot, and Jeb Wofford—were competing for the United States. The Germans had brought a powerhouse lineup that included the 1958 European champion (and Diamant's former rider) Fritz Thiedemann and Hans Günter Winkler, the 1956 Olympic gold medalist.

As usual, the international division was reserved for members of the amateur equestrian teams. Dave would be competing in the open jumper division with Snowman.

The Washington International ran like clockwork—from the skilled precision of the jump crew to the cleanliness of the stabling and grounds, the city put on a tip-top performance, as though to challenge the old guard of New York. The stands were full every day.

But people hoping to see the Americans triumph instead saw the Germans hammer the Americans in every international class. The U.S. team members put in a collection of hair-raising rounds—complete with knocked down fences, crashes, and falls. By the last night of the show, the team had managed to collect only two ribbons, a third and a fourth. Then, during the evening performance, Frank Chapot, riding one of Eleo Sears's horses, crashed spectacularly on the final fence— a fall so devastating that the crowd paused in horror, unsure whether anyone would walk away. Fortunately, neither horse nor rider was seriously hurt.

In the open jumper classes, Snowman and the newcomer Windsor Castle battled it out. Snowman won the first class, but lost to Windsor Castle in the second, and Windsor Castle was in the lead for the show championship. Dave called Harry to give him the news. Snowman needed to win the stakes class or he would no longer be in the lead for the American Horse Shows Association Horse of the Year award.

Windsor Castle had been campaigning since the spring—winning big at Devon and in Virginia. People were saying the seven-year-old was the most promising new horse on the circuit. A high-strung half thoroughbred, he looked more talented than Snowman—by a lot.

Back in St. James, Harry waited for Dave's nightly telephone call, with his reports of the German triumphs and the United States' dismal failures, and of the fierce competition from Windsor Castle. Harry was grateful to Dave, and yet he could not help feeling that maybe if he were there . . . the horse's familiar rider . . . but there was no use thinking about that. He had responsibilities that came before winning blue ribbons. Windsor Castle was tough competition and Dave was not making any promises.

On October 15, the show's last night, the giant gates of the armory show ring swung open. It was time for the parade of nations. The U.S. Army Marching Band played "The Caissons Go Rolling Along," and President Dwight D. Eisenhower sat, with Mamie beside him, up in the presidential box. First into the ring was the German team, carrying the German flag. The four horsemen, who together had taken every single championship ribbon in the international competition, stopped under the glowing spotlights and saluted. Next in line was the Mexican team, whose mounts, according to the *Washington Post,* "looked like rodeo ponies next to the big German horses." Perhaps, but they had still managed to collect more ribbons than the Americans.

It probably did not escape a military man like General Eisenhower that Frank Chapot sat upon Trail Guide, one of the greatest horses ever to compete for the United States Equestrian Team. The last American horse still competing to have served in the United States cavalry, Trail Guide had been bred in the army's Remount Program—the ambitious breeding program that had produced so many great horses, possibly including Snowman's sire. Trail Guide, the last remaining link to the great military jumping tradition, was the only horse that actually belonged to the United States Equestrian Team.

That night in front of the president, Frank Chapot, perhaps still sore from his horrible crash of the night before, rode Trail Guide to a triumph in the jump-off over Fritz Thiedemann of Germany—the only win of the show for the American team. Last up on the agenda was the crowd-pleasing favorite: the open jumper championship. Dave Kelley rode the big gray gelding out under the spotlights of the armory, then stopped to salute the president. The crowd was already keyed up from Trail Guide's victory.

The international competitions were thrilling, and seeing the Stars and Stripes win was always exciting, but when Snowman, the underdog favorite, entered the ring, the crowd let out a cheer. Snowman represented every little guy: everyone not sitting in a VIP seat, every worker at the armory that night—pushing a wheelbarrow or a broom—and everybody who was not born into the kind of privilege that competed in the ring that night. For the American people, the competition was about more than just the horses. After all, America was in the midst of several other competitions: capitalism versus communism, the space race. Dave knew this horse needed to win this class and he wanted to have good news when he called de Leyer at home. The pressure was intense.

There was so much to distract a horse here in the armory—the Army Marching Band; the thousands of spectators; the ring steward, clad in a bright red waistcoat, who sounded out the beginning of each class on his long brass horn known as the "yard of tin." The spotlights made a stippled pattern of golden streaks interspersed with patches of darkness—not an easy place to ride a jumper course.

But Dave had a job to do, and Snowman seemed to sense it. As the honest gelding soared brilliantly over each fence under the gleaming spotlights, he captivated the crowd. Like Trail Guide, Snowman's dignity had nothing to do with class or breeding, and everything to do with heart. None of the other horses—not Windsor Castle, not First Chance—could match the gray horse's performance that night. In the last class of the night, with the president of the United States of America in attendance, Snowman brought home the championship.

Snowman was now assured of the leading spot for Horse of the Year going into the National. The rest of the horses on the circuit would go straight from Washington up to Harrisburg for another week of chances at the Pennsylvania National. Only Snowman would miss the show, returning home to the de Leyers' and the lessons at Knox.

The culminating event of the last night of the show was the Parade of Champions. Into the ring came the show's top performers—the best ponies and roadsters, hunters and jumpers, paraded around the ring and in front of the presidential box. The horses lined up in order, each gleaming blue-blooded champion seemingly more beautiful than the last. Snowman, the ex–plow horse, was the final horse to enter.

He walked around the ring, head low, pace relaxed, not spooking at the flashing lights or loud music or cheers of the crowds, but turning to look at the stands as though to acknowledge his fans. He might have been mistaken for a fish out of water—a rube who had stumbled by accident into a high-society party—were it not for the tricolor that hung from his bridle, marking him as a champion. Dave was not the showman Harry was, but he waved to the crowd as they paraded by, a crowd whose applause turned to cheers as the announcer referred to Snowman as the eighty-dollar wonder horse.

When Dave Kelley called St. James long-distance that night, the de Leyer clan, clustered near the phone waiting for news, let out whoops of delight. Winner of the stakes and reserve champion of the show? At the Washington International?

If only they had been able to go along, no doubt he would have been champion.

Johanna quieted the children and got them tucked into bed, but Harry was too elated to sleep. He remembered the honor of parading in front of the queen of Holland as the country celebrated her return from exile in London. Now his horse had paraded in front of the president of his new country. He regretted only that he had not been in the armory to share that moment with his big gray companion. That night, Harry vowed to himself that someday he himself would ride for the president on Snowman.

19

The Diamond Jubilee

New York City, November 1958

In Manhattan, you could always tell when it was time for the National Horse Show. In the first week of November, the *New Yorker* sported a horse-show-themed cover. Maids bustled along Fifth Avenue, opening townhomes as society people closed up their Long Island estates to spend the winter "in town." The *Herald Tribune* devoted half-page spreads to photographs of men in black tie and women wearing evening gowns. Newspaper society columns carried daily talk of the parties, relating who was going where with whom in exhaustive laundry lists of families—Knickerbocker, Whitney, Vanderbilt, Morgan—whose names read like American royalty.

But this year, the excitement was ratcheted up an extra notch. For this was no ordinary year at the National Horse Show—this was the seventy-fifth year, the Diamond Jubilee.

The show, which had started as a way for the upper crust to display their fine carriage horses, had improbably survived and thrived into the automobile era. The National truly was a national event. Competitors came from near and far—the finest roasters (high-stepping horses who pulled light carriages) hailed from the Midwest, the saddlebreds and walking horses came from the South, and the top riders from the West Coast made the pilgrimage every year. Air travel for horses was rare and mostly reserved for transatlantic trips. Most people vanned their horses to New York, even making the weeklong drive from California, though

Mrs. Louella Combs, the perpetual champion in the roadster divisions, brought her fine hackneys from St. Louis via private train coach.

Everyone in the horse world whom Harry knew would be there—Mickey Walsh and Captain Littauer, even Colonel John Russell, whom he'd met for the first time in Amsterdam. So would all of the professionals he admired and who had mentored him: Dave Kelley, Cappy Smith, and Joe Green, as well as his toughest competitors, Adolph Mogavero and Al Fiore.

The show lasted eight days, always opening on Election Day, a Tuesday. Classes ran all day and evening, with so many entries that competitors were winnowed down in the morning qualifying rounds. Only the top horses would be selected to perform in the nighttime events. After a grueling summer and fall of trailering and debarking, settling in to unfamiliar makeshift stables, competing in different arenas and over varying terrain, now it was time for the horse show that would task the strength and endurance of the best of them. This was more than a test of skill or breeding—though both were important. In this contest, the eight-day trial would become a test of spirit—of the quality horsemen call "bottom," and that spectators instinctively recognize as heart.

Some of the big barns, including Ox Ridge and Duffy Stables, came with twenty or more horses and a small army of grooms, but there were always a few riders who came with just one horse: Jimmy Wiebe, the saddlemaker, had brought his horse, the Stitcher. James Crawford, of Kingswood, Missouri, wanted to be there so badly that he had put every penny into the entry fee—not leaving enough money for a hotel room. He planned to bed down in the stall next to his horse. Anyone who considered himself a horseman and could find some way to get there was there.

To the press and the public, it was the National—to horsemen, it was called "the Garden." As Esther R. "Boots" Parker said in a history of the National Horse Show, "This was the world where a single rub will knock you out of the ribbons, and a marginally missed distance would send you back to the barn . . . Any ribbon from the Garden was worth its weight in blood, sweat and tears." Some horsemen even referred to it as the start of the horseman's New Year. It was the crowning event of every rider's calendar.

Harry had two students competing on their own horses in the junior classes, and he had brought along the flighty mare Night Arrest. Representing Mr. and Mrs. Harry de Leyer, there was just one horse: Snowman. Harry was itching to get back into the ring on him. He had been forced to sit at home, getting news from the shows at Washington and Harrisburg only secondhand.

But those shows were over. What mattered now was that Harry and Snowman were registered entrants in the National Horse Show. The National had its own magic. Every horseman believed it. Unexpected things happened: favorites faded; new champions were born in one thundering round under the spotlights.

The Garden. Harry remembered the year before, his improbable fourth-place ribbon with Sinjon, and the pain of leaving the horse behind.

Ach, no use in thinking about that.

Coming into the show, everyone thought First Chance would be the horse to beat. No one was thinking about Snowman, who had sat out the Pennsylvania National, the second biggest show of the year. Harry aimed to prove everyone wrong, but it wouldn't be easy.

On the morning of November 2, 1958, Harry awoke at three A.M. after having barely slept. He had been out at the barn late getting the horses ready, and now he had to prepare for the trip to Manhattan. Long before dawn, he tossed fresh hay into Snowman's feeder, straightened his blanket, and gathered up the thick cotton batting and rolls of wool flannel that he used to bandage the horse's legs to protect them from injury in the horse trailer. The ride into the city, with its jarring potholes, tight turns, and starts and stops, would be harder on a horse than the usual journeys over country roads.

Snowy stood still while Harry crouched beside him, the stall illuminated only by the single bulb that hung under the eaves. It was cold, and Harry's fingers were stiff but deft, having done these preparations hundreds of times before.

The horse must have known the routine by now, must have sensed that something was going on by the bustle of preparation in the predawn light, but he stood patiently as always, munching on hay, while Harry bandaged him. The barn was quiet except for the rustling of the horses in the other stalls and the sound of Harry's dogs sniffing around outside.

As he contemplated his handiwork on the bandages, straightening them up and inserting a finger under the batting to make sure they were just the right tightness—not snug enough to cut off circulation, not loose enough to fall off—Harry knew that some competitions were lost in the trailer on the way to the show, from a lack of care in preparation. He probably had a little edge on his competitors: other owners were snug in their beds now—maybe sleeping off hangovers from the last round of parties—and they would never know if a slipshod groom didn't get the bandages quite right. Their horse could come up lame and the owner would have no idea why.

Harry looked at his hands: deeply callused and already gnarled like an old man's from a couple of broken fingers. These same hands had grabbed hold of Snowy's mane when it was long and tangled and ratted. These hands had doctored the gray's wounds, and carried hay for him and measured grain. These hands had groomed the horse and saddled him, rubbed liniment into his legs and iced him through the night when he got hurt. Jumping a horse was more than stepping into expensive riding clothes. For Harry, competing at the Garden was more than sitting in a fancy tackroom fitted out like a gentleman's club and waiting for the groom to bring the horse around.

Each time he set out to ride in a show, he reminded himself that he knew this horse as well as he knew his own children. He had tended to him in sickness and in health like he did his own family. He had ridden the horse in shows but also down to the beach and over the hunting fields, and he had watched him carry girls and the children. Other owners did not do that. Other riders had helpers do the dirty work for them. But Harry did not wish that life for himself. That deep-down understanding—that bond between him and his horse—was about much more than winning ribbons. Harry believed that it was his secret weapon.

Harry looked Snowy over once more, satisfied that the horse was ready. He scratched the horse's withers, and was rewarded with Snowy's trademark smile. The horse looked him in the eye, and Harry felt that current pass between them—his Teddy Bear, his friend. Come what may, they would give it their best shot. They were a team. Harry grasped the lead rope with his callused hands and the horse followed willingly. Nobody could predict what challenges lay in store, but one thing Harry knew for sure: this horse had bottom.

It was still dark as Harry pulled onto Moriches Road, and the surrounding farms were quiet. The children were still asleep. They would come later with Johanna to watch. The trip to the city took several hours. The country roads in Suffolk County turned into highways in Nassau County, and then the skyline rose up in front of them as he and Jim Troutwell drove the big rig toward the Queens Midtown Tunnel. Two hours after leaving the peaceful hamlet of St. James, Harry drove the horse van across Thirty-fourth Street and up Eighth Avenue, the skyscrapers of Manhattan towering around them. Car horns honked and yellow taxis sped by, cutting in and out of traffic. They had entered a whole new world.

Among the stodgy denizens of the National Horse Show Committee, there were those who claimed that the show had reached its apogee in the year 1898—the height of the Gilded Age, the same era that had produced the mansions and way of life that surrounded Harry's home on Long Island. Every year thereafter, some old codger was sure to lament that the National was not quite the show that she used to be, the implication being that someone had let the riffraff in.

Until 1925, the show had been held in a beaux arts palace at Twenty-sixth Street and Madison Avenue in Manhattan, now referred to as Madison Square Garden II. The elaborate building, designed by McKim, Mead and White and considered a marvel of its time, contained a summer garden, an arena for the horses, and an indoor restaurant. A bronze statue of Diana soared from the rooftop. Inside, blue bloods—both horses and people—pranced. Around the arena swooped a flower-banked twenty-foot-wide promenade where top-hatted gentlemen escorted evening-gowned ladies, while young boys tried to make a buck pointing out celebrities to out-of-town visitors.

Garden II, like many large Victorian structures, had not been built to last. It succumbed to the wrecker's ball in 1927. But the committee to preserve the horse show quickly grabbed a toehold in a new venue. In 1928, the horse show moved to a building that inspired both devotion and loathing. Built in 1925 and known as "the house that Tex built" after Tex Rickard, a boxing promoter and the owner of the New York Rangers, the third building known as Madison Square Garden was not on Madison Square but on Forty-ninth Street between Seventh and Eighth avenues. From the outside, Madison Square Garden squatted angularly, a water tower awkwardly poised on the roof. The design did not naturally suit itself to an equine affair, and there were always a few old-timers who complained. But by 1958, during this distinctive week, the building itself seemed wrapped in a special mystique. As the horse trailers pulled up along Seventh Avenue, an unmistakable aura of grandeur buzzed in the air.

For all of the glory upstairs in the Garden, the basement was a sorry excuse for a stabling area. The ventilation was famously poor, and made worse by people who ignored the no-smoking rule. Horses were prone to respiratory infections, which spread like wildfire in the enclosed space. Grooms from the Mexican team cooked in their stalls, filling the aisles with the odor of sizzling tortillas. In order to allow a horse to stretch his legs, you had to walk him up on the street, but as hot and stuffy as it was in the basement, the air outside in the streets of Manhattan was cold, and the contrast could stiffen muscles and make a horse's cold grow worse.

Harry was stabled in a corner, in a few box stalls that were off the beaten path. Like everything at the Garden, there was a hierarchy. The best stabling, the best boxes, the best parties, the best order to ride in the competitions, were all distributed with an eye to social standing and status.

The upstairs-downstairs mentality—still so prevalent among the East Coast upper class—was much in force at the Garden. Despite the egalitarian notions that were supposed to characterize a democratic society, the American horseman had, from the get-go, in the words of Kurth Sprague, who wrote the definitive history of the National Horse Show, "patterned himself on an Anglo-Saxon model whose exemplar was the upper-class English country gentleman." Even in the late 1950s, at the National this mentality still prevailed.

American society was in the midst of important changes. It was becoming clear that the grand estates, like Eleo Sears's Prides Crossing and Rock Edge, were relics of another age. There was a series of articles in the *New York Times* in 1957 about how society in four American cities—New York, Philadelphia, Boston, and Washington—was starting to modernize. Social institutions that the horsey set had taken for granted were evolving as new people with new money increasingly had more power and influence.

Many of the great "old money" families had fortunes so large that they had been relatively unaffected by the financial turmoil of the 1930s. But as the 1950s drew to a close, there was a new focus on merit and equal opportunity. Yet here, at the National Horse Show, the world remained comfortably and familiarly stratified. The working folk sat up in the bleachers; the fine folk came and went in chauffeured Bentleys and clustered in the boxes along the promenade. Down in the basement, an army of grooms, mostly African-American, tended to the horses. In those days, Sprague notes, "every decent stable had a tack man," whose only job was to polish the leather and brass, and stable workers for the Mexican team, tasked with keeping the horses spotless, "did not use a pitchfork to clean the stables, but did it by hand."

A series of photographs in *Life* magazine painted the scene downstairs. A man clad in custom-made riding clothes sits on a canvas director's chair in a tackroom that has been gussied up to look like the drawing room of a country manor. In the next pictures, an African-American groom fusses over the horse, removing the neat bandage from the dapple gray's braided tail, picking his hooves, and tucking the rider's white gloves up under the saddle billets; meanwhile, the rider seated in the spotless tackroom pulls on his boots. In the final picture, the rider, astride his immaculate horse, parades across the arena wearing a silk top hat, his expression one of hauteur. The groom will stay behind downstairs, waiting until the rider returns. After handing over the reins, the rider will head out for a night on the town.

This was the life at the National Horse Show. Sometimes the owners made their way down the steep ramp to the stabling area, wanting to show off their mounts to their important guests. The grooms stayed downstairs, lovingly tending to the horses, carrying water, cleaning stalls, polishing boots and tack, and often sleeping in the stalls alongside a skittish horse that needed a companion.

Ring stewards dressed in red waistcoats and gray top hats bowed to the winners with a precise degree of shading that indicated the social

In a tackroom in the basement stables, a competitor looks over his equipment before his class begins. Outside the tackroom, a groom is preparing his horse for the competition.

standing of the competitor. Down in one of the tunnels was the Turf and Tack Club, where competitors and show committee members gathered for cocktails. After the show each night, a never-ending circle of dinner parties followed. Out the back door, on Fiftieth Street, the Belvedere Hotel was rumored to be the site of frequent illicit assignations. Until the early 1950s, the exhibitors stayed at the Waldorf-Astoria, but by the late 1950s, the hotel of choice was the Astor, along the strip of Broadway known as "the Great White Way." The Astor, with its elaborate roof gardens and grand anterooms, filled an entire block on the west side of Broadway between Forty-fourth and Forty-fifth streets; it was constructed of red brick and limestone with a green slate mansard roof. Designed as a successor to the Waldorf-Astoria, the hotel had been built in 1905, another edifice of the Gilded Age. Akin to the rest of the world so deeply admired by the horse show crowd, the Astor was "the epitome of an age that was soon to end."

Nobody was thinking about change, but change, nonetheless, was coming. You saw it in the exuberance of the ticket-holding crowds who thronged through the doors, drawn in by a love for horses, by the spectacle of beauty and youth, and by the drumbeat of danger that thrummed in the background, as horses whirled around the jumper courses. The crowd was eager for spectacle and for excitement, and nowhere was the thrill more palpable than in the open jumper classes, where horses and riders battled for their victories at breakneck speed, seven feet above the ground.

Down in his part of the stabling area, Harry was settling in his horse, coveralls on, working alongside Jim and Joe. Harry's compact frame looked tiny in comparison, and owners walking by would have no doubt mistaken him for one of the hired hands. From the way he interacted with Jim and Joe, it was clear that they were friends and equals.

A nattily turned out competitor parades through the ring in a Life *magazine article about the National Horse Show.*

Johanna and Harriet had pinned up all of Snowman's ribbons next to his stall—an impressive display. People were curious about the gray gelding. His story had been splashed all over the papers in the last few days, and the *World-Telegram and Sun* had run a cartoon drawn by the famous sports cartoonist Willard Mullin. Mullin was best known for creating a character known as the Brooklyn Bum, an everyman Brooklyn

Dodgers fan. The Brooklyn Dodgers were gone, but Mullin still had a fondness for underdogs. Mullin's cartoon recounted, in graphic form, the story of Snowman's rescue from the slaughterhouse, both his and Harry's humble origins, and his triumph over the past few months leading to the National.

For New Yorkers riding the subway and reading the paper folded to the sports page, Snowman was a favorite to watch. Spectators came by to get a peek at the horse, admiring the ribbons and the friendly manner with which Snowman greeted everyone. He never seemed to mind a pat on the nose from the array of passing children, and Harry did not mind, either. The whole family smiled and said hello, and the horse seemed to bask in the attention.

Hotheaded Night Arrest was a different story. She had been skittish and unpredictable just being unloaded from the trailer, not reacting well to the unfamiliar sooty city air and clanging sounds of Seventh Avenue. She was restless in her stall, even with Snowy's calming presence next door. When Harry took her out for exercise in the cramped warm-up area, he had his hands full. He had no idea how she would react to the spectacle upstairs, but this was not a good sign.

People spent hours, days, and years training for this show, spending huge sums of money. Owners like Eleo Sears could afford to pamper their horses, and those who worked with her said that they had only to mention wanting something for the horses—a feed supplement, grooming tool, or special piece of tack—and soon it would arrive by the cartonful, no matter the cost. A win at the Garden represented one of the few things that the rich folk could not buy outright. Every aspect of the week at the National was a competition: a contest over the best help, the finest tack, the best-organized stables, the newest chic trainer everyone wanted, the best invitations, and the most gossiped about *affaires d'amour*. The National brought many opportunities for social triumphs, but none equaled the sheer delight of a blue ribbon won fair and square in the horse show ring—a thrill money could not buy.

The children had made a sign, and Harry tacked it on Snowman's stall door with pride. Compared to the big stables, Hollandia was a simple mom-and-pop shop, a place where wooden shoes lined up in the corner and the owner was a jack-of-all-trades, handling a jumper course or a

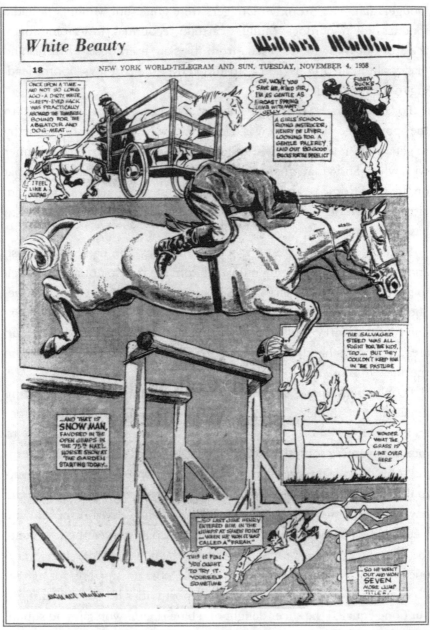

Willard Mullin's cartoon about Snowman's rags-to-riches story appeared in the World-Telegram and Sun *on the eve of the 1958 National Horse Show.*

pitchfork with equal aplomb. He did nothing to try to impress people. He cared about only one test: the one that started upstairs in the ring.

The only one that mattered.

The opening ceremonies started at eleven o'clock sharp on Tuesday, November 4, and Johanna arrived with the children with plenty of time to spare. The entrance to the Garden was flanked by Cosby's Sporting Goods on one side and Nedick's cafeteria on the other. At Nedick's, customers sat at the counter on whirl-around stools sipping the chain's famous sticky-sweet orange drink and eating hot dogs or grilled cheese sandwiches. Over the Garden's entrance hung a vast theater-style marquee, lettered with its famous abbreviation: MADISON SQ GARDEN. This year, the marquee blazed with an additional abbreviated announcement: DIMND JBLEE. All around was the din and blare of midtown Manhattan, unlike anything the de Leyer children had ever seen.

Through the doors into the grand lobby, one entered another world. People milled around wearing outfits more befitting a society ball than a venue best known for hosting prizefights and the Barnum & Bailey Circus. Beautiful people disembarked from chauffeured Rolls-Royces wearing, as Kurth Sprague noted, "melton and mink, top hats and tweeds, long evening dresses from Ciel Chapman, and chic long riding coats and flared britches from Hertz or Nardi, cordovan cuffed hunting boots and black patent-leather evening pumps, and white tie and wide-waled corduroy." The press was always out in full force—society and fashion magazines jostling elbows with an assortment of sports columnists come to cover the show for one of New York's dozen daily newspapers.

The first tier of seats were the ringside boxes, so coveted and closely held that acquiring access to one was a social triumph. Behind the boxes, the seats rose up in three sharp tiers, jamming the maximum seating space into an area only two hundred feet wide. At the time, the Garden was the largest covered venue in the world, able to accommodate more than twenty thousand spectators. Through the turnstile, manned by ticket collectors in tuxedos, ticket bearers wearing their Sunday best rubbed shoulders with the box holders in their evening finery. Around the promenade, hot dog vendors, program salesmen, and souvenir vendors tried to catch the attention of the ordinary folk who passed by the

The Royal Canadian Mounted Police parade through the arena at Madison Square Garden while the audience, in evening wear, watches from the sidelines.

ringside boxes to reach the cheap seats, known as "heaven," up under the eaves. A thick canopy of cigarette smoke always hung in a blue cloud just below the covered rooftop.

Families clutching programs purchased for an expensive $1.50 sat high up above the ring with a good view of the spectacle, both horse and human. Inside the pages of the program were pictures of the trophies to be won, and lists of members of the international teams, as well as of all the classes and participants. The air pulsed with an intoxicating mix of danger and allure, pageantry and sophistication. In addition to the competitions, the program was packed with exhibitions: the Royal Canadian Mounted Police, the Budweiser Clydesdales, displays of rodeo tricks and roping, a dressage demonstration by television personality Arthur Godfrey, and the glitz and glitter of the Latin American teams, whose gold-braided white military jackets and charging riding styles always spiced up the international events.

For a child up in the stands, it was all a wonderland. Even for the de Leyer children—Chef, now seven, Harriet, five, Marty, four, William, three, and the baby, Harry junior, eighteen months, who had grown used to watching their father perform in the horse show ring—the crowds, the spectacle, and the spotlights of Madison Square Garden made the entire experience seem new. As always, they were dressed up, slicked down, and perfectly behaved under Johanna's watchful eye, but for the next eight nights, they would be allowed to stay up late in the stands and watch. This was the most exciting week of their lives.

Eager to watch the opening ceremonies, crowds packed the stands. Just as in Washington, the U.S. Army Marching Band played a rousing Sousa march for the parade of the international teams. With all of the dazzle of the Diamond Jubilee, the stands were filled to capacity—a bigger crowd than ever, and a more boisterous one. Unlike the decorous society crowd that showed up at places like Piping Rock, this was mostly a New York crowd, clapping, stomping, cheering, and catcalling as they saw fit.

The international teams paraded in, each stopping in the center of the arena under a ring of spotlights as the Army Marching Band played its country's national anthem. Every time he saw the parade of nations, Harry could not help but feel some mixed emotions: sadness that his native country of Holland was not represented, an underlying sense of dismay at the presence of the German team, and a pride in the team of his adopted homeland, the United States of America, tinged with just a shadow of regret that as a professional, he would never be able to carry his adopted homeland's flag into the ring.

The Cuban team paraded into the ring to the stirring trumpet blasts of "La Bayamesa," flanked by the blue, red, and white of the Cuban flag. Suddenly the crowd erupted, spewing forth a group of men who stormed down from the stands into the ring, shouting protests against the Cuban team and trying to grab the Cuban flag and disrupt the Army Marching Band from playing the anthem. In a flash, the arena was filled with the "Irish Mafia," the dedicated network of ring stewards and groundskeepers who informally policed the show. A moment later, brass-buttoned, billy-club-toting members of the NYPD escorted the rabble-rousers out of the stadium, and the show continued. Some in the crowd hooted and heckled as though this were one of the prizefights the Garden was famous for hosting. It was unclear whether the noisy spectators were supporting the hecklers or the police who quelled the protest.

World politics erupting in as sheltered a venue as the National Horse Show seemed unthinkable, and the front-tier crowd seemed embarrassed by the spectacle. The horse show was unaccustomed to being the center of a nonequine matter. Just seven weeks later, on January 1, 1959, Castro would overthrow the Batista government and set up Communist rule in Cuba. But that night, the horse show crowd did not seem to know what to make of the unexpected intrusion of politics from a foreign land.

By 1958, it was getting harder and harder to shut the gates around this bastion of privilege. Cracks were appearing in the venerable seventy-five-year-old institution. The people in the stands did not know it then, but the National Horse Show would never again be quite as sheltered from the world at large.

The world was pushing at the edges of the horse show, and the audience was opening up to a new breed of fans. As one journalist put it, "The crowd seemed to have inherited a lot of Dodger fans." The Brooklyn Dodgers no longer existed; Roy Campanella, their beloved catcher, was in a wheelchair; and the excitement of the Subway Series that had pitted the Yankees against the Dodgers was no more. But nothing said New York like the National Horse Show. In 1958, the spectators seemed different. They were noisy and boisterous, clapping and whooping from the stands. And in 1958, they were in love with an upstart gray horse and his brash, smiling rider. Even in the noise and din of the Diamond Jubilee, there was a little magic.

As the program continued, the heckling crowd gradually settled down. After the international parade of teams, the Canadian Mounties, brilliantly clad in red coats and riding all-black horses, came in to show off their precision quadrille. Johanna was far too strict to allow her children to join in the general mayhem of the crowd, but they sat quietly on the edges of their seats, drinking in every sight and sound of the thrilling spectacle. Still, they were eager for the jumper contests to begin. In the center of that ring, horses and riders morphed into movie stars and royalty. At ringside, in the press box, the "lady reporters," Marie Lafrenz and Alice Higgins, of *Sports Illustrated,* jockeyed for space as they rat-a-tatted away on their manual typewriters.

The announcer, Otis Trowbridge, was famous for mumbling and mispronouncing riders' names; spectators had to wait patiently since the order of competitors was not listed in the program but, rather, determined by the gatekeeper on an ad hoc basis as each class proceeded.

There was an open spot in the arena wall, called "the gap," where the trophies were kept, along with a red carpet, a small blue table, and a potted palm. At the close of each class, for the presentation of the trophy, the red carpet was unfurled, the table carried out, and the palm and silver trophy set upon it. The red carpet appeared to honor the horses, but in reality, it was there to protect the shoes of the important society ladies, who could not walk through the thick dirt in their dyed-to-match evening pumps. Throughout the show, the silver winked from the shadows of "the gap," the embodiment of promise.

The ringmaster, Honey Craven, wore a royal red waistcoat and a gray silk top hat modeled, as tradition dictated, on the costume of the English Royal Guard. Each class was announced by the call of a long brass English hunting horn. His thin, clear piping on the horn, signaling the start of each new class, brought every competitor to full attention.

Snowman's first test would be a rematch against Diamant in a fault-and-out class. The combination of timed courses and big spreads always bedeviled the big gray, while Diamant, the German horse, excelled at this kind of class, since in Europe all of them were run this way. Of course, Miss Sears was watching Diamant from her usual private box along the promenade. Her horses had been winning at the Garden for decades. Snowman was here on his first improbable trip.

Horses and riders milled around, unsure when they would be called. Even the most seasoned competitors looked tense, the horses jigging in place, chomping on their bits. The air vibrated with coiled-up energy waiting to be released.

Diamant went early and, true to form, took no notice of the lights or the crowd. He rounded the course with no faults, finishing with a fast time that would be the one to beat. In order to compete, Harry would need to cut the tight corners even tighter.

Harry sat astride Snowman, trying to block out the confusion around him. He visualized the course in his mind's eye, imagining each turn, trajectory, and approach. Show jumping resembles sports like diving and ice-skating: years of training, honing skills and fostering endurance, are sandwiched into a few brief high-risk moments in the spotlight. Every move must be so ingrained, so practiced, so much like breathing that no thought is necessary. Like ice-skaters, who sometimes, upon finishing a flawless round, look momentarily surprised, in high-stakes jumper competitions, after years of training—of sacrifice and striving—moments in the ring pass so quickly that the rider and horse barely register what has happened until they are through.

Now it was Harry and Snowman's moment.

The gate man called out Harry's number. The big gates swung open, revealing the ring, the crowds, the flags, and the huge fences.

Harry whispered a word of encouragement and saw Snowy's ear flick back. He patted his neck and urged him forward. The Flying Dutchman and his plow horse were lit up in the glaring center-stage lights of Madison Square Garden.

Harry sensed his horse's mood, reading the horse's signals through his seat bones, thighs, calves, and hands. Snowman was listening, but with a slight undercurrent of distraction. Harry kept the reins loose, telegraphing trust to his horse. Another pat on the neck, then a cluck. Snowman picked up a canter and Harry rose up out of the saddle, leaning forward. "Go boy, go," he whispered. Noise bounced from the walls of the cavernous Garden, but Harry saw an ear flick back. The horse was listening.

Then all was flying color and spinning motion. The pair flew around the tight turns of the course until they were heading toward the last fence, a big spread. Harry felt the horse's gathering approach, measured the length of his stride, slipped his hands up the crest so that the horse elongated his neck. A striped pattern of light from the spotlights fell across the approach, making the distance hard to judge. On the takeoff, Harry sensed a slight miscue, and sure enough the horse rapped the fence hard with a hind leg.

The pole teetered. Then fell.

The crowd groaned.

Looking unperturbed, Harry dropped his reins and leaned over to pat Snowy with both hands. Snowman had failed to beat Diamant's clear round, handing the blue to the German horse. Second place would be decided on time, and when Snowman's time came up on the clock, the crowd erupted in applause. The plow horse had finished the class in second place.

In the winner's circle in the center of the ring, cameras flashed, lighting up the winking silver trophy. Eleo Sears accepted it with a gallant air, her weathered, angular face a familiar sight in the ring. When Harry's name was called, he took the red ribbon and waved to the crowd. Second place at the National Horse Show.

The Diamond Jubilee was off to a glorious start.

Next to Snowman's stall, the children added the silken red ribbon, protesting their certainty that Snowman would win first place in the next class. Nobody could convince them that their horse deserved any less than the blue.

The next night was the first of the open jumping classes, where any touch or rub against a fence counted against a horse. Diamant did not compete in touch classes, but the competition would still be tough. The morning elimination round had winnowed down the pack. Only the top contenders would jump in the nighttime round. Every horse that had been chasing points all fall was entered, and every horse that completed a round in the ring tonight had a shot at winning. At the Garden, there were no heirs apparent: one false step, one missed turn or misjudged distance, could put a champion out of the running. Every year, new heroes were born and a few seasoned competitors turned into also-rans.

Harry was riding both Night Arrest and Snowman tonight. The mare was fidgety and could not seem to get used to the surroundings. Harry took her to the tiny schooling area, wedged between the ramp to the arena gate and the edge of the stalls. Competitors swapped stories about the best way to sharpen a horse within the Garden's cramped confines. Trainers set up jumps in the barn aisles, sharing space with grooms priming horses for their moment under the spotlights. The trainer Cappy Smith was said to use the "three-stall method," jumping his horses from one stall into the next, making a perfect one-stride in-and-out. Riders looked for opportunities to pole their horses, sometimes arming grooms with broomsticks to rap the horses' legs on the way up the ramp to the ring, timing these blows to the moment when an ASPCA representative had ducked around a corner.

Harry rode Night Arrest around the cramped schooling space, trying to transmit calm to the horse. If she was already this nervous in the schooling area, Harry wondered, how would she react to the grand spectacle in the ring? He did not know how long it would be until his horse was called. The gatekeeper, who worked for Eleo Sears in the off-season, was known for playing favorites and being influenced by tips. Like everything else at the National, there was a quasi-invisible pecking order, based on status, position, and wealth.

The ramp up to the ring was spread with sawdust and hollow underneath—wooden slats, like frets on a guitar keyboard, anchored the horses' hooves. More than one horse had been disqualified before ever entering the ring because the rider could not coax the horse up the ramp, and grooms stood at the ready behind, in case a horse needed encouragement in the form of a well-timed flick of a whip.

Night Arrest jigged up the ramp without prodding, barely contained underneath Harry's steadying hands. Up at the gate, there was nowhere to circle, just a narrow alleyway. He tried to keep her moving. She was nervous and skittish as a cat—each time the crowd burst out into raucous applause, she spooked and pranced in place.

When the big gate swung open, she shot through it like a stone from a catapult. Harry squeezed the reins and settled his weight deeper in the saddle, but she was not listening well. As he headed toward the first fence, Harry knew he had his work cut out for him. She made it over the initial few fences without mishap, but as he cantered toward the big oxer, a post-and-rail spread fence, she started to come apart. Right before the jump, she threw in an extra stride, leaving her off-kilter on the takeoff.

Before the horse even left the ground, he knew that she would not be able to clear the hurdle. He braced himself. Her front feet flew through the barrier, crashing in a tangle of flying poles. On the landing, she stumbled, about to fall; Harry let his body go soft, preferring to get thrown rather than risk staying with a horse who might tumble on top of him. But in a disastrous turn of events, his foot caught in the stirrup.

As the crowd groaned in horror, the Flying Dutchman pounded across the ring, one stride, two, three, dragged by his hooked foot. People watched the disaster in hushed silence—a minute more and he would be flung against the wooden barrier at the side of the ring or, worse yet, kicked in the head. But not a split second too soon, Harry managed to wrench himself free. In a flash, he stood up and patted the dirt from his breeches. Night Arrest, her sides heaving, stood near the arena wall, trumpeting hot breath through her nose, her eyes still flashing white rims of fear. Harry held out his hand, then slowly walked toward her. She snorted twice, then lowered her head to his outstretched hand. Harry reached up with his other hand and grasped the reins. She did not back away. The crowd clapped as the pair left the ring. Probably only Johanna, up in the stands, could see the way he winced when he walked. Harry rarely showed pain.

As if to taunt him, only two horses took their turns before the gate master called out, "Harry de Leyer on Snowman is in the hole." Time to get on the big gray. Putting his bruises out of his mind, Harry stuck a foot through the stirrup and swung up onto Snowman's back, settling his seat bones into the saddle. Snowman walked willingly up the ramp, his reins loose, and stood quietly at the in-gate.

The crowd clapped appreciatively as the pair entered the ring, impressed that the young man was back on another horse so soon. He looked confident enough, even though the crowd had watched him being dragged across the dirt just minutes before. To the spectators, his calm seemed preternatural.

As always, Harry gave Snowman a chance to pause and survey the crowd—a gesture that made the crowd clap and stomp in appreciation. Maybe it was the horse's story that had drawn them in, or maybe it was seeing the young man get up from his dreadful fall, but Harry felt that the crowd was behind him. Excited and nervous for the young Dutchman, they were ready to be swept along with him. Harry forced his mind to go blank as he tuned in to his horse—then there was nothing, no sound, just the feeling of talking to Snowman without words and the sense that he was guiding him around the course with his thoughts alone.

But with just two fences remaining, Harry heard the hollow knock of a hoof hitting the pole. One half fault for a hind touch. Horse and man galloped toward the final fence. If they could clear the last fence with no faults, they'd still be in the running. Snowman sank back, then leapt

upward. But Harry sensed rather than felt Snowman's rear foot knocking the pole from the fence.

Two faults.

A good round but not good enough. Adolph Mogavero took home
the blue for Oak Ridge with the flashy mare First Chance. For the first
time any of the de Leyers could remember, there was no new ribbon to
pin up next to Snowman's stall. After a season of incredible consistency,
Harry and Snowman could not seem to hit their form.

Garden magic: unevenly distributed, hard to get ahold of, unpredictable, and sometimes cruel. Year after year, horses brought strings of successes to the Garden, only to fail to be sprinkled with the magic. The
Garden had a way of forging new champions under the crucible of its
spotlights. Right now, the magic was neglecting the small, out-of-the-way
corner of the basement stables that was known as Hollandia Farms.

The children looked crestfallen, but Harry tried to reassure them. It
was a long show and there'd be many more chances. He went about his
barn tasks with the same degree of vigor as usual that night, not telling
anyone of the places all over his back where the fall had left bruises. He
spent an extra minute in Snowman's stall, whispering encouragement to
the big gray. Okay, it was a slow start, but they weren't licked yet. Over
the course of the show, there would be many more classes, culminating in the biggest challenge of all, the jumper stakes on the show's final
night. The horse with the highest number of cumulative points by the
end of the show would be champion.

The next day, suddenly, Snowman hit his stride. He flew around the
course with an effortless clean round—securing a spot in the jump-off
against First Chance. First Chance's rider, Adolph Mogavero, a former
jockey and steeplechase rider, had been winning on the show circuit for
ten years. Mogavero knew the ins and outs of Garden courses and he
was coaxing outstanding performances from the mare. But Harry felt
good about Snowman. First Chance had an advantage: only seven years
old, she had spent her entire life as a pampered show horse. Snowman
looked like a grizzled veteran in comparison—even though this was the
older horse's first outing at the National.

Mogavero and Harry waited side by side in the narrow alley adjacent to the in-gate. Behind the big white gate, the crew was raising the jumps.

First Chance would be up first. From their vantage point at the in-gate, neither rider could see the fences. As the in-gate swung open, bringing with it the musty smell of the dirt surface of the ring, Harry caught a glance of the shortened, raised course of the jump-off. The gate man ushered Mogavero and First Chance into the ring, then closed the gate behind them. Harry could not watch Mogavero's ride, but he followed the progress from the sounds: the galloping strides, the brief moment of silence over the fences, the applause that followed each clean fence. A moment later, the gate swung open again. First Chance had put in a clean round.

It was Snowman's turn. Harry turned to acknowledge the crowd, allowing his horse to do the same, then got down to business. He steadied Snowman on the approach to the first fence; after that, he dissolved into the teamwork of a ride that is working well: his body became his horse's body; his soul became his horse's soul.

In a flash, the round was over. Snowman was clean. Another round of fence raising for a second jump-off. The crowd exploded in applause.

The crew raised the jumps again, and Harry and Adolph Mogavero waited in the wings. The two horses and riders could not have looked more different. First Chance, naturally high-strung and now more keyed up than ever, jigged in place, then paced in the narrow space. Snowman stood on a loose rein, one leg cocked in a horse's typical resting pose, his ears relaxed to the sides. Harry held the rein on the buckle and waited. When the gate swung open, First Chance bolted into the ring, leaving a small eddy of wind behind her. Again, Harry listened. This time, he heard the wooden thump of a pole hitting the ground, followed by a small groan from the crowd. The gate swung open, and Adolph nodded with a friendly camaraderie.

Harry had an opening. A clean round would bring them the blue ribbon. How many clean rounds had Snowman put in over the last few months? Too many to count. But this was the Garden—not a time to count on anything. As Harry trotted Snowman into the arena, and as the horse turned to look at the stands, the crowd erupted in applause. But this was no time to pay attention to the sights and sounds. Horse and rider had to muster every ounce of concentration, every bit of training and skill, courage and heart. Twelve challenging fences, twelve chances to fault—from something as simple as a hoof rubbing against an obstacle to something as catastrophic as a crashing fall. In the high-stakes Garden classes, horses faced the highest fences late at night, when they were tired and frazzled and would normally be home in their stalls. More than once, a challenging late-night jump-off had pushed a horse past his limit. The jump crew, dressed in khakis, dark shirts, and driver's caps, clustered in the center of the ring. The ringmaster and the judge stood by, ready to take note of any mistake.

Back in St. James, by this time of night, Snowman would be hanging his head over his stall door, his belly full of hay, looking at the stars in the dark countryside sky. Instead, the gray horse was about to face a difficult and highly demanding challenge. Harry gathered up the reins, squeezed his horse around the barrel with his calves, and whispered a word of encouragement. Now or never.

Snowman stretched his neck out and bounded toward the fences with an evident joy. Up in the stands, the crowd went with him as he soared over each fence, unbound from gravity, unbound from his past and from the plow that had once weighed him down. Twelve times he flew, clearing the fences with room to spare. Twelve perfect fences. No faults. For the first time, the blue ribbon at the National Horse Show belonged to the big gray gelding, the lesson horse from the Knox School.

Returning to the center of the ring to receive his prize, Snowman ambled along behind Harry, seemingly unaware of the ruckus that surrounded his victory. Up in the stands, thousands of people—families with children, shopkeepers, police officers, and secretaries—looked down from their perch high up in "heaven," clapping wildly and uproariously cheering, smitten by the horse who seemed to fly without wings and yet was so firmly anchored to the ground. This horse knew how to steal hearts. That he had already stolen the heart of the handsome young man who rode him was apparent for all to see. Harry led the horse around the arena for a victory lap. The affection between the two could not be missed.

That night, the de Leyers hung a blue ribbon next to their horse's stall, and for the first time, a little bit of Garden magic settled over their corner of the stables.

But the show was hardly over. The open jumper competition was not one contest but a series of contests. Each day brought a new series of grueling jump-offs and tiring courses. The opportunities for mistakes were everywhere. The courses demanded that the horses perform flawlessly, time after time. The following day, First Chance pulled ahead again, beating out Snowman.

The two horses were neck and neck for the championship.

Up in "heaven," under blue clouds of cigarette smoke, munching on hot dogs doused in mustard, the ordinary folk held their breath, spellbound, every time Harry trotted into the ring. Harry smiled and waved to them after each clean round, raising his eyes up above the boxes to take in the entire crowd, and Snowman always followed suit. The competition was fierce. Every horse in the show had talent—but stamina would win in the end.

For Harry, the week passed in a blur. Caring for the horses and keeping them in show shape in the cramped basement of the Garden was almost a round-the-clock affair. The jumper classes sometimes did not start until ten P.M. The jump-offs could stretch until one or two in the morning. After each class, Harry had to get the horses hot-walked and rubbed down, fed and groomed, and then the routine started up again in the predawn hours. The world outside the Garden receded, and the smoky, dusty, cramped confines of the basement stables became the world.

One competitor referred to the week at the Garden as being akin to life aboard ship on a long cruise. But by 1958, the cruise that the Garden represented was like the voyage of the *Titanic,* a final gasp of a privileged way of life. The jubilant, chaotic, disorganized private spectacle of the rich at play would soon start on a course of changes that would come to seem inevitable, and as ordinary folk crossed paths with society swells on their way through the turnstiles, it was a giddy, marvelously unsettling moment in time. The show that had begun with the Cuban protestors bringing the world stage to what had once been a parochial affair was ending with a big dose of Garden magic.

And, like an eight-day cruise, the week that at first had seemed as if it would last forever was suddenly drawing to a close. The show's last day would feature the open jumper stakes. There were three legs to the horse show Triple Crown: the American Horse Shows Association

Horse of the Year, the Professional Horseman's Association Championship, and the National Horse Show Championship. The Horse of the Year and PHA honors were decided on points accumulated throughout the season, and Snowman had already earned enough points to secure those two prizes. Going into the last night of the National, the final leg of the Triple Crown was at stake. If Snowman won the class, he would make a clean sweep, winning show jumping's top three honors.

The last class of the show involved two rounds over an identical course, one in the afternoon of the show's last day, and one that night. Points for the two rounds would be added together to decide the champion. The only horses still in contention for show champion were Snowman and First Chance. Going into this final class, First Chance had a one-point lead.

20

"Deutschland über Alles"

New York City, November 1958

On the eve of the last night of the show, Marie Lafrenz, who had been sitting in the press box all week, playing Snowman's fairy godmother as she sent dispatches to the *Herald Tribune,* came to Harry with a proposition. Lafrenz did not content herself with pitching stories to newspapers; she had seen the power of television. But she knew that to get a horse story on the air, she needed to have an extraordinary tale to tell. Knowing that, as she put it, "a racy, dramatic presentation helped catch their attention," she pitched the story of the winning plow horse to a popular talk show on NBC: *The Tonight Show.* The usual host was Jack Paar, but tonight, a young man named Johnny Carson would be the guest host.

Harry hesitated. How was he supposed to get his horse to the NBC television studios when he had a class coming up that night? Jim Trout-well had taken the van and parked it back in St. James for the duration of the show, since it was far too expensive to pay for New York parking. Marie suggested that he hire a van, but Harry laughed and said no. If it wasn't too far, then perhaps he could just walk. Harry, leading Snow-man, and Marie Lafrenz walked east to the NBC studios in Rockefeller Plaza at Sixth Avenue and Forty-ninth Street, passing through the Broad-way theater district en route. Snowman ambled along amid the noise and confusion of midtown, much to the delight of nearby pedestrians and cabbies, who leaned out of their yellow taxis to shout encouragement and advice.

In a studio inside the GE Building, Harry and Snowman found themselves plunged into an unfamiliar world. *The Tonight Show* was broadcast live from New York and sent out on forty-six affiliate stations. The show was filmed on a soundstage—the backdrop, with Carson's desk and the chairs for his guests, was lit up by banks of big, hot klieg lights. The cameramen, wearing headphones, sat behind huge, newfangled-looking television cameras. A microphone, moving around on a long wire suspended above the stage, accidentally dipped into the picture from time to time.

Beyond the lit-up stage, a live studio audience sat in the small theater. The space was hardly suited for an animal—especially not a show horse. The studio was noisy, crowded with technicians and all manner of complicated electronics; to a man like Harry, the scene looked eerily futuristic.

Snowman waited in the wings until it was his time to appear onstage. Johnny Carson retold the story of the eighty-dollar wonder horse, and then Harry, leading Snowman, stepped out onto the cramped stage, looking around, calm as usual, his big, sleepy eyes blinking at the hot, bright lights. Harry reassured the TV host that the horse was gentle, and right there, on the tiny stage, Johnny Carson climbed up a stepladder onto Snowman's back, sitting backward, facing the horse's tail. Harry held onto Snowman's halter, but the horse went along with the stunt, seeming to almost smile at the camera. The audience erupted in delighted laughter and applause.

Harry did not realize it, but in those few minutes, the horse's fame spread far beyond the confines of the Garden and of New York City itself. People were only beginning to understand the power of television. When Snowman walked back to Eighth Avenue and Forty-ninth Street, to the basement stables, he and his young rider had been transformed into celebrities.

Television viewers across the country were now tuned in to the outcome of this contest. Snowman was holding steady in second place, though First Chance still had a one-point lead. Snowman had been performing well, throwing himself into every event, but it had been a long, grueling week. This was a championship class, so the fences were higher and the spreads greater than they had ever been. First Chance, about four years younger than Snowman, may have had a slight advantage in terms of endurance. The top twelve horses from the last day's afternoon event were invited to compete in this great stakes class—the last contest before the closing ceremonies.

Before the class, Harry gathered Johanna and the kids together. "Keep your clothes nice and don't muss them up," he told them. "If we win, we'll all go out together."

Before Snowman got his chance in the ring, Harry had to wait for the last of the international jumping contests, the Nations Cup, to finish. This competition pitted the six teams against one another over an identical course in two heats, afternoon and evening. The strong German team, which had beaten the Americans in both Washington and Pennsylvania, was dominating here in New York, too. Alice Higgins of *Sports Illustrated* had quipped at the Washington show, "The Germans were collecting everything but the tickets."

Here in New York, there had been some isolated American wins, but Hans Günter Winkler, one of the top European riders, had turned in one flawless performance after another, and the German team was cleaning up on points. Harry waited on the sidelines for the drama to play out.

The nighttime performance of the American team was disastrous. George Morris had a knockdown and a refusal. William Steinkraus, whose performance throughout the week had been the one standout for the American team, had two knockdowns. Then Hugh Wiley, on the flashy palomino Nautical, who had won the King George V Gold Cup in London back in June, had a disastrous round—a knockdown and a refusal, followed by a frightening crash. Horse and rider were fine, but a photographer managed to snap a dramatic photo of the fall, which appeared in the next edition of *Sports Illustrated*. Harry was down in the basement doing last-minute preparations—checking his stirrup leathers and irons, tucking the leather keepers into place on his bridle, adjusting the crownpiece and throat latch—as the strains of "Deutschland über Alles," the German national anthem, floated down the ramp and into his corner of the stables.

It had been eighteen years since the German occupation of his native country, but eighteen years was not nearly long enough to forget. As a

Dutch immigrant and as a professional, he was barred from representing the United States, but tonight, Harry very much wanted to win in the open jumper stakes—the one place in the show where any rider on any horse had a chance to compete.

Tonight, Harry was not representing any one particular nation—he was representing the little guy. He was riding for anyone who had ever been kicked around or neglected or underestimated. Anyone who had ever been shoved to the margins, given up on, or rendered invisible. The special bond between Harry and Snowman was the bond of survivors: a horse so beat up that nobody thought his life was worth saving, and a man who, his life destroyed by war, had had to start fresh in a country where he did not speak the language and had no capital except that of his own two hands, his love for his family, and his personal dignity.

Go ahead—play the German anthem as many times as you want! They were not licked yet! Tonight, Harry wanted to *win*—for Snowman, for his American family, for his Dutch family, for himself. This was personal. The children promised solemnly to keep their clothes neat and clean. They had no doubt that Snowy was going to triumph on this most important of nights.

A huge crowd packed the stands, waiting to see the gray plow horse and his can-do rider. Together, they represented the attitude of Harry's adopted homeland: skill, a little luck, a lot of grit, and most of all a belief that big dreams can come true. More and more people were rooting for the underdog horse with the oversized heart.

The sport of jumping is like no other. Man and horse, as they hurtle toward towering fences higher than a horse's shoulders, speak to each other in the language of feel, a deep-seated connection beyond words, beyond specific cues. A great rider tunes in to his horse so deeply that he hears only with a sense of touch, and sees only through a sense of feel. On any given round, the horse's heartbeat melds with his own, the hoofbeats becoming his own rhythm. The world around them melts away. All that remains is motion, flow, silence, and that incomparable feeling that is flight.

This was the biggest night of the biggest horse show of Harry de Leyer's life. The big plow horse had captivated all who had seen him, but that guaranteed nothing.

Twelve horses, twelve riders, twelve owners: a year of training, discipline, and sacrifices to get ready for this one night. Nerves had no place. Fatigue was no excuse. This was a time for a rider to dig deep, to ask of his horse, and to see what the horse had left to give back. The last night of the last week of the last show of the year. Tonight, this was a test of courage—of bottom.

Harry sat astride his old Teddy Bear, reins loose, the same look of un-flappable calm on his face that the spectators and competitors had seen there all week. Nobody at the show except for Johanna knew about the time that Harry, as a boy, had driven a beer wagon past Nazi checkpoints with contraband grain hidden inside one of the empty kegs. Nobody knew about the time he had found his brother Jan lying still as a stone in the field after touching a cultivator made live by a blown-down electric wire. Nobody knew that Harry de Leyer—had World War II not intervened—would probably be on the Dutch team, riding the European circuit, getting the best horses, and looking toward a berth for the 1960 Olympics. You could not read any of that on Harry's face—but you could not miss the look of steadiness. It was something shared by man and horse. These two understood endurance. Both knew you could do no better than to give it your all.

As the riders and horses circled the schooling area, as overdressed and interfering owners strutted back and forth, as grooms scurried about flicking away invisible bits of dust from their charges, Harry and Snow-man seemed above the fray. The horse was relaxed, and so was the man. They would help each other, come what may. So far, not a single horse had achieved a clean round. Any faults and the horses would enter a grueling jump-off, but a clean round would win the title.

The big gates swung open and Snowman entered the ring. As usual, Harry gave him a moment to survey the crowd—the sounds of the shouting and applause from up in the cheap seats was deafening. Harry tipped his hat to the crowd to acknowledge the support. Then the noise and the crowd, all the people in the grand hall, and even the hall itself all fell away.

There was nothing left but the sound of his horse's footsteps on the dirt, the line to the next fence, the gathering, the lift, the soar. Each approach to each fence was fluid, each takeoff sure, each landing effortless. Harry and Snowman seemed in such harmony that it was hard to tell where one stopped and the other began. Harry guided the horse through the tight turns, over the cross-bars and hanging gate, the brush box and the big wall. Each fence seemed effortless; the horse appeared to float in midair, leaving room to spare.

When Snowman soared over the final fence, Harry dropped the reins and raised his arms in an exuberant hurrah. As Snowman galloped calmly over the finish, he grabbed the horse around the neck and kissed him.

Not until they were finished did he hear the crowd cheering. They had done it. There were no challengers. Snowman had clinched the championship.

Down in the stables, Johanna and the children were waiting. Johanna looked lovely in a dark blue suit with fur trim. The boys had on blue jackets and bow ties, and Harriet wore a button-up party dress with a pretty flounce.

The children were young, the arena was large, and the crowd noisy and quite frightening, but the family followed their beloved Snowman up the steep ramp, through the big white gates, and into the ring. When the crowd saw the de Leyer family, with the darling children lining up in stair-step fashion, they went even wilder than before.

It was a clean sweep. The horse show Triple Crown. Snowman was Horse of the Year, the Professional Horseman's Association Champion, and the Champion of Madison Square Garden's Diamond Jubilee. He was presented with a snow-white cooler, a big, thick woolen blanket that covered his neck to his haunches and hung down to his knees. The cooler was embroidered with the seal of the PHA and had 1958 CHAMPION emblazoned on the side. From now on, whenever Snowman went to a show, he could parade around the grounds wearing that cooler. It was an honor that all the other owners, with all their money, could not buy.

Flashbulbs popped as newsmen snapped picture after picture of the champion horse and the de Leyer family. Harry had the big engraved silver tray in his hand. Behind him stood the beloved gray horse.

Harry did not realize it then, but from that day forward, things would never be the same. That horse, whose picture was splashed all over newspapers the next day, who had been seen on television—now it was more than just Harry's children who loved him, and the girls at Knox, and the people lucky enough to be up in the stands. Snowman was the people's horse.

Every child who saw the horse's proud parade under the spotlights went home inspired.

On that November night in 1958, it started to seem as though anything was possible.

21

Famous!

New York City, 1958

No one truly knows how he will respond if struck by the blinding light of fame, unless it happens to him. Harry de Leyer arrived at Madison Square Garden in 1958 as an unknown and an underdog— appreciated by only a few serious people on the horse show circuit, his horse's name perhaps remembered in passing from a mention in the morning paper, the kind of ephemeral notice that fades almost as soon as the reader turns the page. But in one glorious, blinding week at the Garden, all that changed.

At the end of the horse show, after the jumper stakes, after the family paraded under the spotlights, after the trophies were awarded and the photos snapped and sent out over the wires, that's when the real business of the horse show began.

After the big win, the stable was abuzz with well-wishers and newspapermen, new fans and old rivals, come to pay their respects. But there was another tradition as old as the horse show itself. Around that ring, in the boxes, smoking cigars and wearing top hats, clustered some of the most powerful men in America. Men whose names were known in every American household, stamped as brand names on the products people used and printed in the society pages from New York to Palm Beach. Men who could have anything they wanted, and who were not accustomed to being turned down.

Snowman. The eighty-dollar wonder horse, the Cinderella horse, as the press was calling him, was the sports world's newest sensation. He had shown under the colors of Hollandia Farms, Harry and Johanna's small family enterprise. But now he was everyone's darling.

Just hours after the big win, while Harry was still dressed in his work clothes with a pitchfork in his hand, Bert Firestone came calling. Firestone, who had made a fortune in New York real estate, was a horseman who had competed during the show in the hunter division.

He approached Harry after the show with an offer: he wanted to buy Snowman, and Harry could name his price. Up until now, Harry had not been involved in the wheeling and dealing that went on with expensive horses—horses like Diamant, whose prices were speculated on in hushed conversation. The last time he had sold Snowman, the price tag had been $160 dollars. Now the horse's prize money had paid for his purchase price many times over.

Bert Firestone was a big man with broad shoulders and a round face. He looked Harry in the eye—and he saw the hesitation there.

"Thirty-five thousand dollars," he said. "I'll pay for him right now. Take him home with me."

Thirty-five thousand dollars! Enough to buy a new farm outright. Ten times more money than Harry earned in a year. A horse was lucky if he won several hundred dollars at a horse show, minus the expenses of caring for him throughout the year. Even a prizewinning jumper barely earned his upkeep.

But for many of the champions' owners, thirty-five thousand dollars was play money—the sort of money these men spent on their yachts and their Rolls-Royce automobiles.

Bert Firestone was a nice fellow—not a bully, not one to throw his weight around. He waited, smiling, with an expectant look on his face.

Harry was thinking. He still remembered leaving the Garden the year before with an empty horse van behind him. He remembered watching Sinjon walk away from him into the shadowy basement stabling.

Harry shook his head. Not for all the money in the world. Not even for life-changing money, like the kind Firestone was talking about. Snowman had earned his place in the family. Harry had promised never to let him go. He had been foolish enough to sell him once. But the horse had known better, and had come back. Harry was not going to make the same mistake twice. Bert had a check in his hand. He held it up for Harry to look at.

"The check is signed. You can fill in the amount."

Bert extended his hand, as though expecting a shake. He was reading Harry's hesitation as hard bargaining, which was the furthest thing from the truth.

Harry shook his head slowly. Even with so astronomical a sum, he knew he did not have to ask Johanna. There are things a man cannot put a price on.

"He's not for sale," Harry said. "My children love him."

Harry saw that Firestone was starting to understand. The businessman was not only a rider, but would later prove his sound instinct as a judge of horseflesh when he picked out the filly Genuine Risk, an eventual Kentucky Derby winner, from a yearling sale. Harry knew that if he was going to sell the horse, he'd want to sell him to someone like that.

Firestone repeated his offer: "But I want you to know, there's a blank check with your name on it. You fill in the price, I'll pay it."

Harry smiled. "Well, I'm not planning to sell him, but if I ever do, I promise I'll come to you first."

The two men shook hands, and as the magnate walked away, leaving Harry to his work, Harry turned and looked at his plow horse without a single trace of regret.

The morning after the win, the newspapers told and retold the story of Snowman's rags-to-riches triumph. The *Chicago Tribune* related the story of the "sad-eyed horse" in an article titled "DOOMED HORSE LEAPS FROM KILL PEN TO FAME." The *Schenectady News* crowed that the horse had been "saved from execution." Reporters, photographers, and television crews all wanted to talk to Harry. They had to follow him around the barn while he was working in order to get some of his time. But his horse seemed to enjoy performing in front of the camera. One reporter noted that "Snowman paws the ground, arches his neck, to see if the boys are really catching his best qualities." Harry and Snowman seemed to capture the pull-yourself-up-by-your-bootstraps approach Americans admired, especially now, with the Cold War threatening those very values. The *Tribune* even ran a picture of Snowman, the "eighty-dollar jumping wonder," next to a Russian racehorse who was soon to compete in an American race, with the caption "Will Russians reverse capitalist rags-to-riches story?" Perhaps the Russians were winning the space race, but Snowman seemed to fly without wings.

You would not have known, spending time with the de Leyers, that they now had in their stable one of the best-loved horses in the country. At home, life continued unchanged. As usual, the family did everything together, from barn work and chores to meals and riding. And Snowman, back in his stall at Knox, took up his life as a lesson horse again.

After the Garden, the season went on hiatus through the winter months, but Harry was as busy as ever with the schoolgirls. He kept them riding straight through the depth of winter, bundled up in woolen jackets, heavy scarves, and thick mittens. And when he set them aboard the big gray, Harry raised the jumps a bit higher than they were used to, cheering them on and reminding them to grab Snowy's thick mane to help them keep their balance.

In March, he put his student Bonnie Cornelius on Snowman and sent her through the jumping chute in the covered alley in the stable courtyard. Perhaps remembering her disappointing performance on the horse the previous year, this time Bonnie flew over the fences without the slightest difficulty. At the end of the lesson, Harry had raised the highest fence up to five feet, six inches—the height of fences in an open jumper class. Snowman and Bonnie sailed over it with ease, a moment she still remembers: the gathering rush of the takeoff, the heady instant suspended high in the air, and the long, long distance back to the ground. Encouraging and tenacious, the two-legged teacher and the four-legged teacher worked together to bring out the best in everyone.

The older children were in school, the foxhunting season had ended, and life returned to its usual rhythms. The family would soon move from the chicken farm into a slightly larger farm on the corner of Edgewood Avenue, a quiet street a little closer to the center of St. James. The house was smaller, but the barn was a little bigger, with more room for the horses. Johanna got busy trying to get the house ready for her family.

As spring drew near, Harry made plans to take Snowman out on the circuit again—maybe they could even repeat the performance of the year before.

But even if life had returned to normal, signs abounded that things were not the same.

At the stable, reporters came around, asking to see the wonder horse. An equine vitamin company offered Harry's horses a free supply of supplements, and put a now-familiar picture of Snowman soaring over a fence in an advertisement.

The headmistresses of the Knox School, who had at first seemed uninterested in the young riding master's successes, began to sing a different tune. It seemed that everyone wanted his daughter to train with the man who had won a national championship. The phone in the admissions office was ringing off the hook, and the school was establishing a terrific reputation as a wonderful place for horse-minded girls. Harry was happy with his job, and his bosses were happy with him.

One day, a 1958 Cadillac pulled up in front of the school, and three men wearing sunglasses and fancy suits got out. One was an actor named Edmon Ryan, currently the star of a hit Broadway comedy; next was Ryan's agent, Robert Lantz; the third was the Broadway financier Tom Orchard. None of them was comfortable around a stable. They were not horse people, but smooth talkers who were tossing around big numbers, numbers with six figures in them. They came with a pitch: this horse, they said, belonged in the movies.

Harry was polite to the visitors, but he didn't put much stock in the conversation. He wasn't sure how to read these men. He said he would discuss it with his wife and get back to them.

Harry and Johanna talked it over. Both of them had seen the way children lined up to see the horse, the way his story seemed to inspire people and give them hope. But Harry kept feeling that there was a catch somewhere, if he could just figure out what it was. He was straightforward and he liked people to be the same. With these fast-talking Hollywood types, it was hard to tell what they really had in mind.

Harry dragged his heels but finally agreed to it; the movie people had told him that Snowman could be an ambassador for the sport. But they were talking about filming the movie in Los Angeles. Harry could not let Snowman go to California—he was busy with his students, and gearing up for the fall season.

The movie people offered to substitute another horse, but Harry said no, and if other horses were going to play Snowy as a foal or as a plow horse, Harry wanted to see them himself, so that he could make sure the stand-ins looked right. There was nothing worse than a horse movie in which it was obvious that the people who made it knew nothing about horses.

But the movie people did not seem to understand his demands or why they were important to him. Any whitish horse would do, they insisted, making vaguely menacing statements about why he had better agree. Maybe they weren't used to people disagreeing with them. Most everyone was just so flattered when Hollywood came calling.

But this Hollywood trio was about to come face-to-face with Harry de Leyer's famous stubbornness. No horse could play Snowman in the movie unless he vetted it first.

Finally, an agreement was hammered out. Harry would take Snowy to Baltimore to film the jumping scenes, and if another horse would appear as Snowy in the movie, Harry would get a chance to approve.

Soon it was March, and the show season opened again—and this time it was clear from the start: Snowman was unstoppable. As the drumbeat started building up to the National Horse Show, once again Harry and Snowman held the lead for the Horse of the Year trophy. Once again, spectators lined up to watch his thrilling performances. Now everybody wanted a piece of this horse.

Snowman had brought so much interest to show jumping that the prices of other horses were going up. Snowman was not for sale, but another rising star, Windsor Castle, Snowman's big rival at last year's Washington show, had sold after a win at Devon to Si Jayne and Howard Marzano, a pair of investors from Chicago, for $25,000. In June, when Harry and Snowman returned to Fairfield, the *Hartford Courant* blared, "$80 WONDER HORSE WORTH $25,000." Suddenly, the price of show jumpers was garnering the kind of attention that had previously been reserved for racehorses. That weekend, Snowman took home the championship, beating Windsor Castle for first place.

That summer bad news came from back home in Holland. Harry's mother was suffering from cancer. It was time for the family to make a visit—and, in an incredible stroke of good fortune, Snowman was invited to do an overseas tour of exhibitions. Nine years after arriving in the United States as immigrants, Harry and Johanna were bringing the whole family—four-legged and two-legged—for a visit back home.

Snowman rode abroad in style in a specially equipped turboprop plane, just like the ones that ferried the Olympic horses to and from Europe. Their departure was filmed by a crew from MGM, which captured the moment when Snowman walked up the ramp to the waiting aircraft. Harry rode with Snowman and brought five-year-old Marty along on the plane. The crossing took eighteen hours, with a stop for refueling. Many horses are frightened on airplanes and have to be tranquilized, but Snowman took the trip in stride. Along with the other children, Johanna made the journey in relative comfort on a passenger airline.

For the rest of his life, Harry would remember the moment he walked with Marty and Snowman across the tarmac in Amsterdam. It had been less than a decade since he and Johanna had left home on the SS *Volendam,* his beloved mare Petra left behind, his hopes and aspirations tucked away with his saddle and boots in the solitary crate that had contained all of their worldly possessions. Striding across the tarmac today, holding Snowman's lead rope in his hand, with his young son walking beside him, he was returning a champion.

In St. Oedenrode, the de Leyer farm still looked the same—the high, peaked red roofs and stucco façade, the chickens that pecked in the stable yard, the brewery, and the fields surrounding the farm. The place looked more prosperous now, and the brewery was back to producing its popular local beer. Harry's brother Jan, who had made virtually a full recovery, was still riding horses, and was thrilled to see his brother. The town was plastered with posters announcing the arrival of the American champion. Harry and Snowman performed true to form, jumping brilliantly in several exhibitions. Snowman now had fans on both sides of the Atlantic.

But the trip was tinged with sadness. The children spent time with their grandmother, and they all knew that this first visit together would likely be the last.

Back home, Harry got a phone call from Philip Kunhardt, who introduced himself as the assistant sports editor of *Life* magazine. In the days before television had taken a firm hold, the glossy pages of *Life,* then near its peak circulation of 8.5 million, were the ultimate celebrity-making machine. Everyone who was anyone eventually showed up in those

Turned loose in the ring, Snowman jumped fences just for the fun of it.

pages, the glamorous black-and-white pictures producing the images that came to be indelibly associated with the famous. Even today, when we imagine the faces of the 1950s and early 1960s—James Dean, Marilyn Monroe, the Kennedys—it is the iconic black-and-white photos from the pages of *Life* that spring to mind. Harry was agreeable to being interviewed and photographed as long as no one interfered with his work.

When photographer George Silk arrived at the Knox School with his camera, Harry asked if he would like to watch Snowman jump fences in the paddock on his own, without a rider on his back. Silk agreed that this would be unusual, so Harry led the horse out of his stall and over to the Knox ring, which stood empty except for some jumps.

Harry slipped the halter from the horse and gave him a cluck. Always the show-off, Snowy obliged by circling the ring and heading toward one of the fences. The photographer snapped a magnificent photo at the apex of his flight: the big gray horse sailing over a jump with no bridle, no saddle, and no rider—out free in the center of the ring. This was the paddock jumper who had run home to his master.

The magazine appeared on newsstands nationwide the week of the 1959 National Horse Show. A sultry picture of Marilyn Monroe looking over her shoulder graced the cover. Inside, a long story described the "puzzling art" of abstract painter Jackson Pollock. Another article related the training regime of Russian cosmonauts. There were advertisements for sleek new GM cars with futuristic fins, and RCA TV replacement picture tubes. And there were also several pages devoted to Snowman, under the title "Old Nag's Long Jump from Plow Horse; Discarded Farm Horse Finds Unexpected Fame." Below a picture of Harry scratching Snowman's withers to elicit his trademark laugh, the caption read, "De Leyer rides the horse in all contests, but lets the horse have his way."

The blond de Leyer children, the smiling father, the old plow horse—among the puzzling abstract art and racy movie-star pictures, the new technologies and worrisome political developments, here was a scene that evoked all that was comforting and familiar.

On Election Day, 1959, the de Leyer clan was back at the Garden, but this time they arrived as celebrities. Snowman was here to defend his title. And now millions of people knew about his humble life as a plow horse, and about the family who loved him.

Down in Hollandia's corner of the basement, not much had changed—Harry still pulled on coveralls and worked alongside Jim and Joe. Johanna and the children slipped on wooden shoes and helped out with the chores. And Snowman, as usual, took the whole spectacle of the seventy-sixth annual National Horse Show in stride.

But Snowman was not the only horse in the headlines at the start of this year's competition. Windsor Castle, fresh from the open jumper victory at Harrisburg, was commanding headlines, too.

While the price of racehorses and their prize money totals had been skyrocketing, show jumpers, winners of much smaller purses, had not been as valuable. That all changed on November 6, 1959, when Windsor Castle beat back Snowman to win the first class of the National. That night, Bob Ballard of the Canadian Equestrian Team purchased Windsor Castle for the then astronomical sum of $50,000. This was the second time in less than six months that the horse had changed hands. The next morning, the *New York Times* trumpeted news of the deal: it was an unprecedented sum of money for a jumper.

His current owners, a couple of horse traders from Chicago, had no scruples about selling their horse in the middle of a show. "We have no sentimental attachment toward the horse," one of them said. "It's business."

Windsor Castle was a horse to be reckoned with. He had dominated the competition at Harrisburg that year, and despite the fact that Snowman was the sentimental favorite, most horsemen thought he had little chance to beat out the younger horse this year. People were already starting to say that Windsor Castle was the most talented horse on the jumping circuit.

The show, as it did every year, involved a series of classes spun out over the course of eight days, but the public's growing fascination with the sport of show jumping was newly apparent in the suddenly larger purses. This year the championship stakes was a sponsored class, the Chemical Corn Bank Trophy, and the sponsor had put up a $5,000 prize—an unheard-of sum that would not only cover a rider's show expenses but leave a nice dividend to bring back home.

Throughout the eight days, Snowman and Windsor Castle traded places, the horses staying close in points. The last class of the show, the $5,000 championship stakes, was the biggest prize Harry had ever competed for—in 1959, $5,000 was the average American annual salary. Harry pushed the thought of the big check out of his mind as he and Snowman waited for their turn; he concentrated only on his horse and on the task at hand.

The beloved champion's entry into the arena was greeted with a roar of approval from his legions of fans. Harry waved to the crowd, grinning broadly, then headed for the first fence. In a brilliant whirl, Snowman and Harry put in a seemingly effortless clear round, cinching the big purse and the tricolor. That final victory clinched Snowman's place: the big gray was the first horse in history to win the PHA and AHSA Horse of the Year honors two years in a row. None of the other horses— not Diamant, not First Chance, not even Windsor Castle, the $50,000 horse—had matched Snowman's cumulative points performance in 1959.

And the de Leyer family made one thing clear: their horse might be beating the high-priced competition in show jumping's competitive stratosphere—but this was *not* business. On the final night of the show, once again Harry led Snowman into the grand arena, and once again Johanna, clad in an evening dress, and the children came along to share in the glory. The boys had on blue jackets and Harriet looked fancy in a party dress. Pictures snapped, flashbulbs popped, and the crowd— especially the families up in the cheap seats—went wild. For a second year running, Snowy had stolen the show.

Next up for Harry was another television program. Harry was invited to appear on the new game show *To Tell the Truth*. In the show, the host posed questions and the panelists had to guess the person's identity. In 1959, at the close of the National Horse Show, one panelist remembered the *Life* magazine article, one had seen the story in the paper, and the third had seen the National Horse Show broadcast on TV. All three stars guessed the occupation of horse trainer Harry de Leyer.

Only nine years after landing in Hoboken with his wooden crate and his young bride, the Dutch immigrant had become a household name.

The Wind of Change

St. James, Long Island, 1960

In January 1960, the British prime minister, Harold Macmillan, gave his famous "Wind of Change" speech, in which he signaled that the long era of British colonialism was coming to an end. In July 1960, when John F. Kennedy won the U.S. Democratic Party's nomination for president, he and his beautiful young wife seemed to embody youth and change.

Busy with his duties at Knox, Harry gave little thought to world affairs. Even so, as the 1960 spring season started to roll into high gear, there could be no mistaking that the pressure was on. While not much had changed in the routine at the Knox School, with the film contract signed now, sealed and delivered to Metro-Goldwyn-Mayer Studios, there were men in suits in far-off offices who cared how the horse performed.

The girls at Knox noticed no difference in their beloved Mr. D, and Snowman still happily obliged whenever the de Leyer children wanted to take him for a ride to the beach. Harriet loved to jump on the horse with her brothers and ride bareback triple-seated down to Long Beach, St. James's sheltered harbor. Here, on the shores of the Porpoise Channel, ringed on all sides by wooded countryside that hid the big estates, gulls swooped by, and the children could alternate between digging in the sand and riding Snowman into the bay. Harriet, a daring rider of eight years old, could keep up with her brothers in all things, but when

Snowman took off into the bay and started swimming, she worried that she would not be able to haul him back. The horse just loved the water.

Harry was careful not to overjump Snowman. He was allowed to school over fences only once a week. Harry was also convinced that seawater was therapeutic for horses. Snowman was sound, but at thirteen-odd years old, his legs might not bear up well to the stress of repetitive jumping. Harry carefully watched his horse for any signs of lameness. Riviera Wonder, the great horse who had won the jumper championship in '55 and '56, had been sitting out for two years due to a sore back. Jumping put a lot of wear and tear on a horse, and Snowman had already faced more hard labor than the average horse before he'd even started his career as a jumper.

In the spring and summer, Snowman and Harry went to the familiar round of shows: Fairfield and Lakeville, and the seashore circuit of Sands Point, North Shore, and Piping Rock. Only three years had passed since Snowman had entered his first show as a junior jumper, with the timid Louie Jongacker aboard. But already, it was a new world in the show ring—more horses, more money, more competition. Show jumping was rapidly changing—from an insider affair to a big-time sport. There was a lot at stake when horses were swapping owners for astronomical sums. A valuable horse like Windsor Castle had to put up with the additional challenge of being ridden by a number of different riders over a short period of time.

Harry planned to keep going with Snowman as long as the horse still seemed to enjoy it, but not a day longer. Already, the gray had brought him blessings in the form of new business. Scarcely a day passed without another nervous mother in furs or a fat-cat dad showing up at Hollandia, wanting to know if the desirable young trainer could take his daughter or son in hand as a private student.

New students with money to spend on lessons and horses were good for business, but a kid did not need money to be able to ride at Hollandia Farms. When a new teenager showed up shyly offering to work in exchange for lessons, Harry always found a way to take him in. In the snooty environs that surrounded St. James and neighboring Smithtown, the de Leyer household was a place where everyone felt equally valued. All a young man or woman needed to survive there was a capacity for uncomplaining hard work. For a number of them, experiencing the force of Harry's personality and Johanna's gentle dignity were key formative experiences in their young lives.

School let out in June, and as usual, the Knox graduation interfered with the Devon horse show. Snowman spent the opening weekend of the 1960 season parading on the school grounds with pink ribbons in his mane.

Joseph (Chef), Harriet, and Marty riding Snowman in Long Island Sound.

On June 15, Harry headed up to Connecticut for the Fairfield show. Local newspaper headlines plastered his picture all over the sports pages, trumpeting that "the Cinderella horse," national champion and two-time defending champion at Fairfield, was coming to town. But during a preshow exhibition, over a giant fence six feet, nine inches high, Snowy's leg buckled on the landing, and he took a nasty spill. He limped away from the fence but was not seriously hurt. Even so, news of the accident headlined in the sports section of the *New York Times,* and the *Chicago Daily Tribune* screamed, "JUMPING KING SNOW MAN IS HURT IN FALL." All eyes were on Snowy. Fortunately, though the crash had looked gruesome, the rumors were worse than the reality. The following day, for the third year running, Snowman captured the title at Fairfield.

The season was going well, but by the end of the summer, Snowman was not in the lead for the PHA prize. Still, having racked up a string of firsts, seconds, and thirds, he remained one of the top contenders. Now, however, there were expectations. A *Reader's Digest* article titled "The Farm Horse That Became a Champion" brought the horse's story to millions more people. That same year, a Dutch version of the story was published. People no longer came out just to see the plow horse who could jump; they came out to see him win.

Whenever Snowman faulted or won the second- or third-place ribbon, Harry saw the look of disappointment clouding the eyes of the children watching from the bleachers, children who knew nothing about the age of the horse or the competition—which seemed to ratchet up in terms of quality of horses and riders with each passing year. Alice Higgins of *Sports Illustrated* commented, "This has been a season of plenty for horse shows, with most of the major fixtures on the tight fall circuit boasting more horses and spectators than ever before." To stay at or near the top for three years running was a spectacular feat, but now, to his list of concerns, Harry added concern for Snowman. As always, he tried his best, and week after week he put in solid performances. It was just that now, sometimes, they were not good enough.

The summer whirled by in a familiar pattern of horse shows and hamburgers, of rides and ribbons, of trophies and triumphs, and the occasional defeat. Then as the Knox year started up, the de Leyers settled down to their school-year routine. But this year would be different. In October, Harry and Snowman were going to Washington, to perform in front of the presidential box. Harry knew the competition would be fearsome. Windsor Castle had been cleaning up all over, and at this international show, the nine-year-old gelding's owner would want his expensive purchase to make a splash. There were newcomers from all over, and some of the old favorites were still going strong. Snowman had triumphed once in Washington, but Harry had not been there to see it. Now Harry's turn to ride for the president had come.

On October 10, 1960, Harry trailered Snowy to the Armory with a happy sense of anticipation. He and his horse were ready for this show.

Johanna had stayed behind with the younger children, but Chef and Harriet came along to help, along with Jim Troutwell, Harry's and Hollandia's buddy and groom.

On the way down to Washington, Chef and Harriet squirmed in the front seat of the van with excited anticipation. They were no longer ordinary competitors; they were special guests, invited to perform an exhibition before the show—their first in front of a crowd of this size. Harry and his horse loved nothing more than to perform for children and for the general public—people who might never have seen a real live jumping horse before. He and his horse were now ambassadors for this sport he loved.

While other owners were driving toward more—more money, more tension, higher stakes in every class—Harry drove along the highway with his window rolled down and the radio playing, a hamper of Johanna's famous sandwiches next to him and his kids playing hooky. They planned to have fun.

The exhibition was on the first day of the show. The grandeur of the opening ceremonies, with the U.S. Army Marching Band and the parade of international teams, was a spectator favorite and always drew a big crowd. In the afternoon, special exhibitions were planned: dancing dressage horses, cowboys on roping horses, and the world-famous jumper Snowman.

The exhibition was also time to shine for helpers Chef and Harriet. Harry entered the ring aboard Snowman. They started the show by flying over a series of high fences, leaving the crowd gasping in shocked delight as Harry tossed the reins down while arching over the fences.

In the wings, Harriet and Chef awaited their turn. At home, they had been practicing a show-stopping trick. Chef held on to the lead rope of the second horse they had brought for the occasion, Lady Gray. A flea-bitten gray like Snowman, she was a dependable field hunter and lesson horse; they looked so much alike that some people had trouble telling them apart, and the two horses were friends.

At the signal from their dad, Chef and Harriet walked into the big arena leading the gray mare behind them. The jump crew had set up a

At an exhibition, Snowman jumps over Lady Gray. Harry is in the saddle and Chef is holding Lady Gray.

big square oxer, as high as Lady Gray's withers. Harry circled Snowman around, flying over the fence and leaving the audience wondering what was going to happen next. Cued by his father, Chef led Lady Gray into the space between the two halves of the spread fence and held tight.

The children heard the spectators gasp as Harry and Snowman bore down on the fence, this time with the other horse standing smack in the way. To clear the hurdle, Snowy would have to clear the horse as well. Bravely, Chef, nine years old, stood holding Lady Gray's lead rope, watching Snowy bear down on them. One false move would result in a tragic tangle of legs and horseflesh.

There were no false moves. Just as they had practiced, the big horse, his trademark small ears pricked forward, soared over fence and horse with room to spare. It was breathtaking.

The crowd erupted in furious applause. Chef grinned shyly and fished a carrot out of his pants pocket to feed to Lady Gray. None of them, neither horse, nor child, nor Harry, had ever had even a moment's doubt.

A sport that had so recently seemed a stodgy and repetitive pastime—like parents watching their own children's ballet recitals—had become, thanks in good part to Harry and Snowman's charm, the kind of spectacle that brought crowds out in droves.

The Armory looked splendid with the tricolored bunting, presidential box, and Army Marching Band. The feel of the show was more cosmopolitan, less stuffy high-society than the Garden. It was a newcomer on the show circuit, but it was fast becoming the second most important venue after the Garden itself. Now that the fun and games of the exhibitions were over, the competition would begin. Even before the show had started, a lot of people had assumed that there would be a rivalry between Snowman and Windsor Castle. On the show's opening night, the *Washington Post* announced, "HORSE SHOW BRINGS BOTH $50,000 AND $80 ENTRANTS." The plow horse and the expensive jumper would face off in the first class.

The opening event of the evening was the fault-and-out, in which a horse would be eliminated by a single fault. Right away, it became clear that out of a huge field of open jumpers, it was going to come down to a contest between the big two: Windsor Castle and Snowman.

The pair of horses were a study in contrasts. Snowman, the gentle giant, would safely carry a small child or a beginner on his broad back. Brilliant but erratic, Windsor Castle had a firecracker temperament. When the horse was on his game, he could be unbeatable, but other times, he was a dirty stopper, or refused even to let his rider mount. Each time the horse needed to enter the ring, there was a ruckus of handlers shouting, of crops and spurs. The bay gelding could back away from the ring entrance at an astonishing speed. When the two horses competed in the same class, Harry sat—reins loose on Snowman—and watched the spectacle with amusement. He simply never rode a horse like that—or, rather, no horse he'd ridden had ever behaved like that. Not to say that Windsor Castle had been mistreated, but he had changed hands often and had experienced many riders. It was impossible to know what Snowman thought of his unruly competitor, but anyone who had ever watched the pair together could tell that Snowy loved and trusted Harry.

"Ya gotta talk Dutch to them," Harry chuckled to himself. If that were his horse, he would lie in bed puzzling it out, trying to figure out how the bay thought. Harry believed that there was a way to get along with any horse. The great grand prix rider Bernie Traurig commented that Harry "seemed like he could get on any horse, no matter how dead green, ride him for a couple of weeks, and then take him into the show ring—he had a tact with horses that was surpassed by none." So Harry watched Windsor Castle with a mixture of interest and disbelief, amazed that the horse could make the whole thing look so difficult, when in contrast, Snowman made it look so easy.

Still, once they got him into the ring, Windsor Castle was sharp and a good jumper—good enough that he often couldn't be beat, and he had a string of championships to prove it. And his owner was not taking any chances. Ballard had coaxed the wily old trainer Joe Green out of retirement to ride the horse. Green was a legend among show jumpers. In the old days, he was known to bet on his own horses, sometimes pulling up between fences during a class to offer to change the odds on his bets. Green hadn't ridden much since breaking his pelvis a few years ago at Piping Rock, the year Dave Kelley had stepped in to ride Green's horse, Belmont, in the championship. It was Green who had first sold Sinjon, and the trainer had, according to legend, lost another horse, Nautical, in a poker game—the gelding who, under Hugh Wiley, had become the first American horse ever to win the King George V Gold Cup in London. Tonight, Green had bitted the bay with a complicated scissor bit—a severe bit that gave the rider tremendous control.

That night, the first round eliminated all of the horses except for the big two. The jump-offs started, and since this was a knock-down-and-out class, the fences were raised each round and time was a factor.

Harry sat unperturbed on his horse, waiting for the jump-off to start. Sure, Windsor Castle was younger, and his half-thoroughbred breeding made him naturally better suited to competing with time as an element, but he was using up a lot of energy fighting his grooms and rider, and all of the commotion with crops and spurs and people waving their arms and shouting just might distract him from the task at hand. Green rode the horse hard, with a firm hand on the rein. It was not pretty, but it was effective.

At the end of the first jump-off, both horses were clean. The efficient jump crew quickly raised the jumps another four inches. Now even the lowest fence was five feet, nine inches. These were big fences. But the flashy bay showed no signs of tiring. He was still willing to put up a stink before each of his entrances into the ring.

Harry worried that Snowy might tire. He walked the horse around to keep his legs soft, and Jim Troutwell folded his white PHA Champion cooler over his haunches to keep him from being hit by the evening chill. Harry muttered encouragement to the horse, and as always, he saw the horse's ear flick back, a sign that he was listening. By now, Snowman knew the ropes.

Inside the arena, the crowds were overflowing, and though it was getting late, not a single spectator was heading for the parking lot.

Another round—a study in contrasts. Windsor Castle was fire, and Snowman was ice. Two clean rounds.

The jumps went up again. Every obstacle in the ring was over six feet. It was a challenging course for any horse—even a horse with fresh legs, even a young horse. Snowman would have to give it his all—and, at the same time, be fast enough to beat Windsor Castle.

Snowman went first, and Harry entered the ring for the salute. Each glance at the presidential box down at the end of the ring reminded him how far he and his horse had come. In the beginning, he had never really expected to become a champion; he'd had so much to prove—to himself, to his horse, and to the snooty horse show people who had never heard his name or believed that he could be anyone who mattered.

Now, in his adopted nation's capital, he and his eighty-dollar horse had made a name for themselves, but they were still the underdogs, the outsiders, the pair with something to prove. Harry urged his horse into a gallop and the world fell away. If this contest was going to be decided on time, then Harry would give his horse the best chance to win. He could not pick up Snowman's feet to clear the fences—that was the horse's job—but he could calculate exactly what the shortest safe path around the course was. A single stride could and would make all of the difference: if he cut it too close, the horse couldn't jump; if he cut it too long, he would lose on time.

At a gallop, the pair headed toward the first fence. And in a flash of flying turns and jumps, they were already through.

No faults. A clean round. Followed by a thunderous roar from the crowd. Harry heard it but as if in time delay. It took a moment before his time flashed up on the clock. Even if Windsor Castle went clear, Snowman had established a very competitive time to beat.

The flashy bay made a valiant effort—but it was no use. Perhaps he was tired, or rattled, or the sharp-cut corners were just too much. Perhaps all the fighting at the in-gate had taken its toll.

At the end of the third jump-off, Snowman held on to first place. Windsor Castle had knocked down a pole with his hind legs. Harry and Snowman had won the open jumper championship.

On the last night of the show, just one class remained: the President's Cup, a new trophy to be awarded for the first time this year. Harry was worried that Snowman was tired and hoped that there would be no jump-off. But again, all of the horses were eliminated except for the gray and the bay. It had been a long week, full of competitive jump-offs, and Snowman had given his all. Competing against a younger horse had taken its toll on the big gray. But Windsor Castle was unpredictable. Even tired, Snowman stood a chance to win the cup—but it would be tough. It was late and the fences were high. Harry had half a mind to bow out now, but he knew how much that would disappoint the crowds who had turned out chiefly to see Snowman compete.

In the schooling area outside the Armory arena, Green was off the horse. His grooms were working over Windsor Castle, rubbing his haunches down with liniment, obviously worried that the horse might stiffen up. Green stood in a huddle with the horse's owner, engaged in a whispered conversation. It looked as though they were plotting something, although it was not clear what kind of strategy would help. Nothing was going to change the horse's fatigue or how high the fences were.

Snowman was up first, and as Harry entered the ring, he fought off a feeling of dismay as he urged his big horse into a canter, leaning forward to give the gelding a pat on the neck. They galloped toward the big fence and Harry focused in on his horse, feeling his slight reluctance, but transmitting silently that the horse was going to manage fine. The pair rounded the course, Harry closely attuned to the familiar rhythm of approach, takeoff, landing, a few strides, and then a gathering for another takeoff. But Snowman could not quite do it—over one of the big post-and-rails his takeoff was just not strong enough, and as he landed, a pole fell into the dirt with a dull thud. Finishing his round, Harry patted Snowman, loosened his reins, and waved to the crowd as they left the arena. He wasn't too worried. Joe Green's mount might take down a pole or two as well. The class was not over yet.

But when Harry exited the arena, he was surprised by what he saw. Joe Green was standing on the ground next to Windsor Castle. Sitting astride the bay was twenty-year-old Kathy Kusner from Virginia. Tiny and petite, she was an ace rider and one of this year's sensations in the show ring. As far as Harry knew, she had never ridden Windsor Castle before, but now she was poised to ride into the ring for the final class. A single glance told Harry the whole story; barely five feet tall, Kusner probably did not weigh a hundred pounds. For a tired horse, taking away the extra forty or fifty pounds by putting a lighter rider in the saddle might make all the difference. It was a gutsy move—and Harry admired guts. He wished young Kusner luck as he watched her ride into the ring. She might have been small, but Harry had seen enough of her to know that she was a tough competitor.

Sure enough, the petite dynamo piloted the horse around with panache, and Windsor Castle finished with a clear round. From the way Joe Green was grinning, Harry figured he must have made a good jackpot by betting right on the outcome.

Windsor Castle won the President's Cup, but Snowman, winner of the stakes class, was still the show's overall champion open jumper. When it was time for the parade of champions, Harry led Snowman into the ring to the rousing sounds of the U.S. Army Marching Band and the uproarious cheers of the crowd. And as they crossed in front of the presidential box, Harry was filled with pride. He and Snowman had reached the moment they had worked toward for so long and so diligently.

It was another great triumph for Snowman, hard earned over the course of a tough week of competition. But Harry was worried. Only another few weeks until the Garden, and the repetitive jump-offs late into the night had taken a toll on the horse. Harry vowed to lay off jumping until the National, where he knew a fresh posse of horses would be waiting, eager to steal the plow horse's crown.

23

Camelot

New York City, 1960

November 8, 1960. Election Day. And this was a momentous one. Eisenhower had completed his two terms, and the Democrat John F. Kennedy was running against the Republican Richard Nixon. The seventy-seventh National Horse Show opened with its usual pageantry; the Parade of Teams, the Royal Canadian Mounted Police. The de Leyer children lined up in the stands, blue eyes lit up by excitement. As the two-time reigning champion, and recent victor at Washington, their beloved family pet was the star of this year's show.

Harry had told the children not to worry. Snowman would do his best.

By the end of that day, John F. Kennedy had been declared the winner and the era that became known as Camelot was ushered into existence. As though in celebration, the first class of the show started beautifully for Snowman, too: he brought home the blue in the first open jumper class. There seemed more wheeling and dealing than ever behind the scenes. Bigger, more astronomical sums of money changed hands. It was a new era in the horse show world, too. Corporate sponsorship had arrived. This year, for the first time, the horses would be competing for a Ford Motor Company prize. In the lobby was a gleaming Ford car. The classes had been rearranged and shortened to cater to the ticket-paying spectator, so that people could come out to watch the show and still make it home on the last train.

Harry knew that he could sell Snowman in an instant, or take up Bert Firestone on that blank check, but word had gotten around that the horse was not for sale. Harry de Leyer had not been cut from the usual cloth, and people had figured that out.

When Harry was not competing or looking after the horses, he was an avid spectator in the stands, and he loved to watch the international team competitions. The pageantry of the parade of teams, the different riding styles of the riders from different countries, the playing of the national anthems—it was a chance for Harry to watch and learn from top riders without being involved in the competition.

On November 12, Harry took a break from the routine downstairs to come up and watch the international jumping contest. There were teams from Canada, Mexico, France, and the United States, among others.

The sentimental favorite on the American team was the old horse Trail Guide, with Frank Chapot on board. Harry had a soft spot for Trail Guide, a relic of the old days, when the international team jumping had been a military affair. At twenty-one years old, Trail Guide was like an old colonel among a bunch of civilians. The year before, Harry had taken a tour through Amish Country, trying to learn something about Snowman's origins, and he'd found an old blacksmith who was pretty sure his horse had been the product of an Amish dray horse bred to an army remount sire. Harry could see the similarity between the two old troupers.

Trail Guide had been a perennial champion for the U.S. Equestrian Team: low scorer at both the '56 and the '60 Olympic games, he had put in six flawless rounds at Washington and taken home the international championship at Harrisburg. With Frank Chapot aboard, he had salvaged the American record at Washington in 1958, the year Snowman won the open jumper championship with Dave Kelley in the saddle. Now the great champion was competing in his last show.

In fact, originally, the team had planned to officially retire him at the end of this year's Garden competition, leading him out under the traditional blanket of roses. But that plan had been scrapped because American Horse Shows Association rules forbade a horse from competing in the same event in which he was retired. The decision was made to postpone the retirement. The team needed the horse to compete.

And Trail Guide had not disappointed, winning the first class for the

American team. Tonight the international teams were competing for the Good Will Challenge Trophy, a huge silver bowl. Thus far, 1960 was a banner year for the U.S. team, which had brought home the first ever team medal at the summer Olympics in Rome, second only to the jumping powerhouse Germany. Harry had followed the results from afar, reveling in his old mount Sinjon's accomplishments and proud that he'd been the first to spot the horse's potential. And after the string of defeats in '58 and '59, the American team had just triumphed at both Washington and Harrisburg. This November at the Garden, the Americans were ready to finally bring the trophy home.

Here at the Garden, the course was high, the times were swift, and the competition was intense. At the end of the first round for the Good Will Challenge, there was a four-way tie—four horses with clean rounds: Trail Guide with Frank Chapot, George Morris of the United States, Tom Gayford of Canada, and a Venezuelan horse and rider. The jump-off started: the Venezuelan knocked down two poles, but Morris had a clean round. The Canadian also put in a clean round, but his time was not as fast. When Trail Guide entered the ring, George Morris, on High Noon, had the round to beat. The pressure was on Trail Guide's rider. To win the class, he would have to go clean and fast enough to beat Morris on time.

The brave old horse flew over the first two fences, sailing over them clean. But over the third fence, a double oxer, in the blink of an eye, something went horribly wrong. He caught a foot on a rail and fell in a gruesome flipping crash, sliding into the side barrier with a sickening thud. As the crowd sat in stunned silence, Chapot got to his feet, unhurt, but the grand old horse lay uncannily still.

From the stands, Harry instantly knew that the situation was bad. Used to jumping in to help whenever there was a problem, he leapt over the barrier, following the horse show vet Dr. Joseph O'Dea, a friend of his, into the ring. The horse was alive but not moving. When a horse falls and is hurt, he thrashes, his instinct telling him to get to his feet. A horse unable to stand sparks dread in a horseman. There is no more frightening or disheartening sight than twelve hundred pounds of horseflesh down on the ground, unable to rise. Harry crouched near the horse's head, watching as Dr. O'Dea checked him over in silence. The gelding was perfectly still, moving nothing but his dark brown eyes.

Up in the stands, you could hear a pin drop. The crowd sat in sickening, horrified silence. Someone in management dimmed the lights to the ring. The minutes ticked on, the dark quiet punctuated by the sounds of muffled movement.

Dr. O'Dea, who would later be the chief Olympic equestrian vet, worked over the horse. But there was no hope. The valiant old horse had broken his neck. He would not stand up or walk out of that ring.

In the darkness, as the riders of the equestrian team shed silent tears, Dr. O'Dea put down the old horse. Trail Guide, who had carried the flag of his country, who had campaigned on three continents, the last horse of the American cavalry, did not leave the ring at Madison Square Garden that night with a cooler pulled up over his ears or a blanket of roses over his shoulders. He left in the back of a cart, heaved there by a posse of fifteen strong men, motionless and silent.

Eventually, the lights came back up and the show went on. But the buoyant spirit of festivities had leaked away.

Down in the stables that night, Harry took extra good care of Snowman. He vowed to himself that he would never push his old horse too hard, this animal who had already brought his family untold blessings. Harry gave the horse a scratch on the withers and the old teddy bear rewarded him with a smile. They were survivors. Both of them.

On the long ride back to Long Island, the front seat, as always, was littered with the prizes Snowman had won. There was the blue from the first fault-and-out class, and a few more reds and yellows. In his third year out, Snowman had not brought home the grand prize, but Harry cheered up the children by promising hamburgers for everyone.

Our horse is already a champion, he said, and nobody can take that away from him. And best yet, he's in the trailer and he's on the way home.

24

Branglebrink Farms

St. James, Long Island, 1960–1969

Driving down Moriches Road on the way to the Knox School every day, Harry passed the old Butler place. It was a rambling dairy farm, more than forty acres, with a big cattle barn and plenty of pasture all around. Up on the hill, overlooking the green fields, stood a rambling white farmhouse with green shutters and lots of bedrooms that looked perfect for raising a large family.

Countless times, driving down that road, Harry had pointed to the property and said to Johanna, "Someday, that farm is going to belong to me." The dairy farm had belonged to Charles Butler, a descendant of the original Smith family, after whom Smithtown was named. The farm made its own cream and butter, and its rich ice cream was a popular local favorite in the summer. But Charles Butler had died a couple of years earlier and the farm was no longer a moneymaking business.

It was perfect for the de Leyer family—just a mile up the road from Knox, with plenty of room for a large stable and even a place to build the big indoor ring Harry had always wanted. Snowman's fame had brought business to Harry in abundance and his riding establishment was thriving. Sure, the Butler farm was run-down and its cattle barns would need to be converted, but Harry had never been afraid of hard work. Harry and Johanna schemed and plotted, trying to figure out how to make it happen. Then, just when they seemed to be on the brink of a deal, there was bad news: they could have the land, but there was another bidder

Johanna holding Snowman in the Knox School courtyard. Right to left: Chef, Harriet, Marty, Billy, and Harry junior.

for the rambling farmhouse. Knox wanted to buy the house for their president to live in. Johanna was firm but diplomatic. No farm without the house, she insisted, and in the end, the Butlers relented. All up and down Moriches Road, more and more developments filled with little cookie-cutter houses were springing up, part of the postwar building boom. The de Leyers promised to keep the land as farmland and use it for their horses, and in the end, the family won the day. The old Branglebrink dairy was sold to the de Leyers.

As Harry and Johanna surveyed the new farm, they saw much work to be done, but there would be plenty of room for their horses and growing family, and a big pasture for Snowman to walk around in, just a short hack from the beach. After years of toil, the de Leyer family was living the dream Harry and Johanna had carried with them on the passage from Holland, along with their crate and meager savings: a good-sized piece of ground that belonged to them. Once again, they christened the farm Hollandia, with the colors of yellow and green.

The big pasture with the pine trees became Snowman's new home.

In the late afternoon, near feeding time, the gentle gray sometimes jumped over the pasture fence to return to the barn, but he never gave a sign that he wanted to run away. As Harry had said, "He was too smart for that. He knew where he belonged."

July 1962: in living color, Snowman's homely face peered over the Dutch door of his stall at the new Hollandia Farms, his face surrounded by scores of blue, red, yellow, and tricolor championship ribbons. Another story about the champion, "An Old Jumper's Jackpot," appeared in *Life* magazine, reveling in the fact that the old horse's "legend lived on." There was a picture of the whole family, Harry on Snowman, Johanna on Lady Gray, and the six children, all saddled up and on horseback, including the littlest, only two years old, riding proudly on a Shetland pony.

All aboard: the de Leyer family saddled up near Branglebrink Farms. Left to right: Harry riding Snowman, Johanna on Lady Gray, Chef, Harriet, Marty, Billy, Harry junior, and Andre.

There was also a picture of Snowman out for a swim with three de Leyer children astride bareback, up to their waists in the waves. Though he had continued to show, winning ribbons in 1961 and 1962, he was entered in fewer competitions these days. Harry had decided that Snowman had done enough.

Here, in the grassy pasture under the pine trees, Snowman would live out his days. It took a lot of work to convert the old cattle barns into proper stables, but when it was finished, the Cinderella horse was given a place of honor, right near the barn's entrance. They etched his footprints and name in the concrete in front of his stall door. The Miller Harness Company even came out and laid complimentary carpet on the floor of the stall—a fitting home for the champion.

That fall, two children's books were published about Harry and his famous horse, one a picture book and the other for older readers. Harry toured Snowman all around the country to give exhibitions and do "signings." Harriet and Chef were enlisted as Harry's assistants, often holding Lady Gray when Snowman leapt over her, repeating his best-known trick. After the exhibitions, the enterprising brother and sister would varnish Snowman's hooves with hoof oil and sell his hoofprint "autograph" at twenty-five cents a pop. Harry and Johanna encouraged the kids' entrepreneurial spirit. The de Leyers got used to finding fan letters in their mailbox addressed to Snowman.

One day, Harry took Snowman down to the bookstore in the small neighboring town of Stony Brook. Harry autographed the books and the visiting children got to pet the horse and pluck a single strand from his mane. The Knox School girls had formed a fan club. Each girl got a signed book and a copy of the club membership certificate. Snowman still carried the timid girls around for lessons now and then, but as he got older he spent most of his time just resting at home.

The day the brand-new indoor arena was finished, the de Leyers threw a big party and invited all of the neighbors, the Knox students, and the other riding students. There was a long blue satin ribbon tied across a large entryway. Somebody had the idea that Snowman should be the first to enter the new arena. One of the kids ran to get a bridle and saddle, and Harry swung aboard, cantering toward the ribbon, planning to let Snowman break through. But at the last minute, the horse gathered up his knees and soared—clearing the ribbon by at least a foot. Everyone at the party clapped and cheered at the sight of the sweet old horse flying through the air.

Snowman had the run of the pasture, and he liked to go and stand under the pine trees down in the corner. He was always eager to carry one, two, or three of the kids around, and happy to head to the beach for a

Snowman at a book signing in Stony Brook, New York.

swim. Sometimes Harry still let one of the children take the horse over a big jump. Harriet still remembers the feeling of being nine years old and jumping Snowman over a five-and-a-half-foot fence—the same height as in the open jumper classes—her head so high in the air that she thought she might bang it against the top of the indoor arena. Harry and Johanna had come to expect that local children would come around and ask after him—the books were in constant circulation at the local library, and Snowman kept on winning new sets of younger fans. It was a good life for a horse, a life he'd earned. Sometimes people asked about what was going on with the movie, but Harry had no idea. Apparently, the people in Hollywood had been fighting too much, because the movie never got made.

In 1969, Harry got a phone call from Snowman's old friend Marie Lafrenz. She was now chief publicist for the National Horse Show, and she had an idea. The National Horse Show had moved into the new Madison Square Garden, a cavernous venue built as a modern sports arena. Unlike the house that Tex built, it had big stadium seats and unobstructed sight lines for basketball. But in spite of its vast modern interior, the new Garden was a difficult place for the horse show. It was hard to fill the huge stadium with horse show fans and the new building lacked the charming boxes and promenade that had long characterized the show. Besides, the times they were a-changing, and this kind of spectacle, with women in evening gowns and men in top hats, in what was now the Woodstock era, had lost its appeal.

People still wanted to come to the horse show to ride, but labor disputes with the housekeeping staff meant that the competition could not run in the leisurely, gentlemanly fashion it always had. The program needed to be wrapped by eleven sharp or the horse show committee would have to start paying overtime to the union staff. The demands of television had further changed the nature of the event. It was not enough to thrill the people in the stands; now the show needed to look good on newly colorized home screens, and the networks complained about things like the color of the dirt, which needed to be pale to serve as a more telegenic background for the horses. Plus, there was competitive pressure from other sports. Other activities generated much better box office than the horse show, and their promoters would be happy to take over the National's prime election-week spot. After more than eighty years, Garden magic seemed to be losing its luster.

Marie Lafrenz's main job was to see that the maximum number of tickets got sold. Without box office, the venerable institution could turn into an anachronism that would not survive.

Marie knew just the draw to bring in loyal fans, one of the most beloved horses in Garden history: the Cinderella horse. Harry got a phone call. Would he like to officially retire Snowman in the Garden?

Out in the pasture, now used only as a lesson horse, Snowman had already been off the circuit for half a decade. But Harry knew that his horse had always enjoyed the spectacle and the crowds, and besides, two more children had been added to the de Leyer clan since the horse had stood in the center of the ring. This time, the whole family could come along. With a local boy enlisted as groom, the de Leyers bustled about getting the old gentleman ready for his grand farewell appearance. Johanna picked out matching outfits for the family. Chef and Marty were so tall now that they towered over their father, and Harriet had turned into a beautiful young lady. And finally another girl, Anna-Marie, had been added to the family, a cherubic beauty with a halo of blond curls. The girls and Johanna wore pink dresses, and the boys were handsome in jackets and ties. Harry looked proud in his riding clothes—an elegant navy blue hunt coat and white breeches.

All these years, Harry had kept Snowman's show bridle cleaned and at the ready in a place of honor in the tackroom. His students knew to keep it clean, and never to move it. If Harry came into the tackroom and it wasn't clean and hanging on its hook, he would holler until it was returned.

The de Leyer family gathered in the huge modern arena of the new Garden and Snowman wore his bridle one last time. The big white gates swung open and Harry de Leyer walked into arena under the blazing luminescence of stadium lights. All cleaned up for the occasion, Snow-

Harry leading Snowman around the arena at Madison Square Garden during his retirement ceremony. Snowman's cooler is yellow and green, the colors of Hollandia Farms, and reads "The Cinderella Horse."

man followed willingly behind. Behind him came Johanna and the children, lined up in order of height, all the way down to little Anna-Marie. The lights were dimmed and the horse's coat gleamed under the blazing spotlights. Music played over the giant loudspeakers, and men and women wearing evening finery came out, bearing a red-and-white blanket of roses. Folded up in their arms was a cooler in Hollandia's colors, green and yellow.

Snowman was startled as the show people started to put the cooler and the blanket of roses on him from the wrong side—a horseman always approaches a horse on the "near," or left side, never from the right. But Harry steadied the horse with a gentle hand and a whispered word, and Snowman stood still, allowing the soft green cooler to be placed over his shoulders, followed by the brilliant red-and-white blanket of roses. Snowman and Harry circled the spotlit arena. The roar of the crowd thundered through the giant hall as though it would last forever. The lights flashed on, then dimmed, then came up bright, but the crowd kept clapping and cheering, rising to a standing ovation.

As Harry walked around the ring, leading his beloved horse, he remembered every step along the way, each image of Snowman: arriving at the chicken farm, his haunches covered in snow; finding the horse inside the paddock dragging a rubber tire and a bit of fence behind him; his first few stumbling tries over the cavaletti poles; and, of course, the moment when he won the national championship in '58. But the strongest image was from that first moment on the slaughter truck, when something in the horse's expression had caught his eye. A man could hardly be blamed for blinking back a tear on this night. Harry himself had almost missed this horse's gift, but somehow, the horse had always given him another chance. On the side of Snowman's cooler, in bold yellow letters, was his nickname:

The Cinderella horse.

And this horse truly was.

On the way out of the Garden, the paparazzi waited to catch a glimpse of the equine celebrity. Flashbulbs popped and the big gray champion was caught for the last time—his picture was splashed huge across the back page of the *New York Post* under the headline "SNOWMAN RETIRES." The New York hero had given his last performance.

25

The Cinderella Horse

St. James, Long Island, 1969–1974

Life at Hollandia went on. Schoolteachers brought busloads of children to the farm, eager to see the horse they had read about in their book. In the morning, Snowman wandered out to the pasture on his own. In the evening, he went back to his stall, sometimes jumping the paddock fences to follow in the broodmares. Even now, as they were getting older and turning into teenagers, the de Leyer children still liked to spend time with their pet horse. Like her older brothers and sisters, Anna-Marie learned to ride astride the gentle gray.

In the evenings, after the lessons, when Harry gathered his students around to talk over the day's work, he had a habit of standing next to Snowman's stall. As he talked, he would pat the horse or scratch Snowy's favorite spot on the withers.

Harry had brought along many horses now. He had made other finds and passed them along. Chef and Harriet were starting to show horses, too, and now there was regularly more than one de Leyer name in the horse show results.

Life went on.

But one day, in the fall of 1974, when Harry went down to the barn, he did not see Snowman's familiar face hanging over the stall door, ever at-

Busloads of schoolchildren used to come to Hollandia Farms to visit Snowman.

tentive to Harry's footsteps. He felt a flutter of worry. Every morning for as long as they'd been together, he'd heard the three sharp whinnies from the gray horse greet him in the morning. Today's silence in the barn was eerie.

Harry approached the old horse's stall and peered inside, afraid that maybe the horse was down—always an ominous sign. Snowman stood with his back to Harry, just managing to turn his head at the sound of Harry's voice. Something was not right.

Harry scanned the old horse, and saw that Snowman's legs were swollen up like an elephant's. His giant head hung down, and the look in his eye, though friendly, was listless. He was getting old, twenty-six now, but until today, Snowman had been healthy. Harry grabbed the barn phone and called the vet, asking him to come out as soon as he could.

Harry and Dick Fredericks were friends, and he trusted his judgment, but he paced nervously as the vet examined the horse.

Dr. Fredericks came out of the stall shaking his head. Harry saw the quiet sadness etched on his face.

"It's the kidneys," he said. "He's an old horse. He's lived a good life."

"What can I do?"

"Just keep him comfortable . . . if he's suffering too much you may need to think about putting him down." That was not the answer Harry wanted to hear.

For the next two days, Harry tended to the horse night and day, but as he watched him, he knew the truth. The old horse was ailing. He was in too much pain to eat or to move around much.

Harry stood next to him, whispering to him, trying to coax him to eat something. But looking deep into the horse's eyes, he saw the truth. Years ago, on that winter day in New Holland, Harry had looked into Snowy's eyes and what he had seen was a desire to live, to go on, to be free, and that look couldn't be ignored. In a life filled with death and destruction tapped out to the sound of the goose-stepping marches of the Nazi invasion, Harry had learned young how powerful the will to live really was.

Now, as he stood next to his horse, he also saw the undeniable truth in his eyes. He was a good horse and he had lived a good life. He was ready to go.

It was all he could do to give the nod to the vet. They would lead Snowman out to the part of the pasture under the pine trees where he had loved to stand.

Harry was not a weak man. He had seen plenty of suffering in his life, taken care of enough horses who were hurt or in pain. But everyone understood that Harry did not want to be there. If it had to happen, then okay, but he did not want to witness it.

But when it came time to lead the horse from the barn, the old horse would not move. He stood there, waiting, as though he had decided long ago that only one man would lead him to his destiny.

Harry knew that it was only fair. They had made a commitment to each other long ago, in a snowy parking lot outside an auction barn. Snowman had followed when Harry had pulled him off the van that first time, and he had followed into the cavernous space of Madison Square Garden under the klieg lights and the deafening sound of applause.

Grasping the horse's lead rope, Harry led the horse out to his beloved pasture, haltingly, step by step.

The vet waited under the pine trees. As the big gray closed his eyes for the last time, Harry was there, stroking him on the neck.

A horse is big and he needs a big hole to be buried in, and Harry and the boys were drenched in sweat when they were done.

After it was over, Harry walked back to the barn and got in his truck.

He drove away and did not come back home for two days.

The Galloping Grandfather

Charlottesville, Virginia, Spring 2005

At the age of seventy-seven, Harry de Leyer didn't think it was un-usual to be sixteen feet up on a loading platform, jerking hay bales into the hayloft of his Virginia farm.

He tossed the fifty-pound hay bales into the loft as though he had been doing it all his life—and he had. Though the setting of the farm was spectacular, in the beautiful horse country north of Charlottesville, Virginia, this was no gentleman's farm. There was work to be done from sunup to sundown, and Harry did the lion's share of it.

Though he had once thought he would live forever at Hollandia Farms, this had not come to pass. After Snowman's passing, over time, things changed for the de Leyer family. Eventually, Harry and Johanna divorced. Johanna still lived on the farm in St. James. Now happily remarried, Harry had settled in Virginia, never having forgotten the beauty of the countryside from his time spent at Mr. Dillard's Homewood Farms.

One thing had never changed: caring for horses was hard work. Harry's body was powerful but compact, and his hands were even more knobby: somewhere along the line he had broken every finger at least once. The hair under his baseball cap was snow-white, and from under its brim, the blue eyes that his students called "mesmerizing" still twinkled with his characteristic good humor.

Harry jerked on the twine and tossed the bales like a man half his age. The platform rocked slightly as he hefted each of the bales into the loft of the barn. What happened next occurred in the blink of an eye. As he jerked one bale up, the twine snapped. Harry tumbled backward, his hands flailing, trying to grasp at thin air. But there was nothing to grab hold of. He fell sixteen feet straight down and landed on his head on the hard-packed dirt.

Harry's first thought was shock. Then came anger. Having spent his life training and jumping horses, he had known his fair share of what he called "spills and thrills" and he was almost impervious to pain.

He lay in the dirt, stunned, for a moment, then shoved himself to a sitting position. How many times had Harry fallen from a horse? But deep down, he knew he had never had a fall like this.

Like a fallen horse, he instinctively wanted to stand. He tried to hoist himself up to his feet with his strong arms, but when he tried to walk, he tumbled to the ground. By then, a stable hand had come around the corner of the barn, spotted him, and called for help.

He was still trying to stand when the paramedics arrived. The EMTs were probably used to dealing with people in stress and pain, but Harry was not cooperating. Though they used hard talk and soft talk, nothing seemed to work. The two burly rescue guys tried to strap him to a board by force. Like a flailing bronco, Harry repaid the favor by punching one of them in the nose.

It was not until he was airlifted to the University of Virginia hospital that everyone realized how serious it was. Harry's back was broken in several places.

Most septuagenarians are worried about walking. They're not worried about never riding a horse again. Of course, Harry was a different breed. After almost fifty years in the show ring, he was known as the Galloping Grandfather. He never, ever planned to quit.

It had been many long years since his triumphs with Snowman— almost half a century. But every morning of Harry's life still started out in the barn, caring for his horses, watching them, talking to them, observing them, showing off that intuitive bond that came from a lifetime of living and working alongside the beautiful beasts.

The family gathered round during the long days that Harry spent in the hospital. At first it was touch and go, and each improvement seemed to bring a setback. Word spread like wildfire through the horse community. The beloved Flying Dutchman was in the hospital. Well-wishers poured through the door, and the phone lines lit up. Everyone wanted to know how the old horseman was doing. Harry's wife worried that she would soon be a widow, but Harry was a fighter. During the long hours and days he spent in the hospital, he thought about Snowman—a horse who had refused to be cast off before his time. Harry had gone through hard times before; years ago, his youngest daughter, Anna-Marie, had been in a riding accident and had gone into a coma before fighting back for a full recovery. He had lived through heartaches with some of his children, and the difficulty of a divorce. And many years earlier he had watched his own father go into hiding. They had survived a cataclysmic war. Yes, Harry had had many lessons in bravery in his life. This time, he was determined to pull through—and not just to pull through, but to ride again.

His injuries were severe: water on the brain, and a spine broken in several places. When Harry de Leyer left the hospital alive, his doctors must have been pleased. He needed a walker, but at his age that was about as good a prognosis as one could hope for.

After the accident, Harry spent more time inside. One room in his house was devoted entirely to Snowman: paintings, photos, the framed woolen cooler that had been placed over his withers when he won the championship at the Garden so many years before. And next to it, Snowman's show bridle, with the soft rubber snaffle bit, still cleaned and oiled, hanging in a place of honor.

Harry was sitting in this room when the phone rang. The PetSmart Charities, which donated money for the care and feeding of unwanted horses, wished to honor Snowman by making a model Breyer horse in his image.

At first Harry hesitated. He explained that the horse had done so much for him, and that he never wanted to exploit his memory or do anything that might tarnish his image. But the company reassured him that the proceeds would go toward the care of rescued horses. Harry's only request was that he receive a Snowman model for each of his grandchildren.

Finally, six months after Harry's accident, the model horse was ready for release. The Snowman model, crafted by the artists at Breyer from photographs of the gelding, quickly became a collector's item. Completed, it managed to capture the characteristic that Snowman was so known for: the look in his eye. The back of the box featured a picture of Harry and Snowman clearing an enormous white fence, seeming to soar into the clouds. But the model itself shows Snowman galloping free, the horse who came home to Harry with no saddle and no bridle, with nothing but his heart and the force of his will.

In October 2008, it was time for the Washington International Horse Show, and the Galloping Grandfather was back in the saddle. If there was a bit of stiffness in his back from the steel rods the doctors had placed there, it was hard to see. As the hunters entered the arena in front of a throng of spectators, many old-timers in the stands probably recognized Harry de Leyer. But even for those who didn't know him or remember the story of Snowman, there was no mistaking the smile on his face when he and his teammates galloped back into the ring to receive the yellow third-place rosette.

Harry doffed his velvet cap, tossing it high into the air in his trademark move. His white hair stood on end as he waved to the crowd and beamed. Snowman had taught him this lesson so many years ago. No obstacle is too great to overcome for a man with a dream.

The Galloping Grandfather was back in the saddle. He was not beaten yet.

If you want to visit Snowman's gravestone, it still lies in the big field under the pine trees where the horse liked to stand, next to the fence along Moriches Road that leads down toward the beach. From time to time, people still come and knock on the farmhouse door to ask if they can see it.

The big gray is long gone, but living on is the memory of the horse who was yoked to a plow yet wanted to soar. Snowman and Harry showed the world how extraordinary the most ordinary among us can be. Never give up, even when the obstacles seem sky-high. There is something extraordinary in all of us.

Acknowledgments

To retell the story of *The Eighty-Dollar Champion*, I depended on the time, insights, and generosity of a great many people. First and foremost, this book could never have been written without the kindness and support of Harry and Joan de Leyer. They welcomed me and my family to their beautiful Nederland Farms in Virginia and shared their memories, photographs, and hospitality on countless occasions. Getting to know them was the greatest gift I can imagine.

I owe great thanks to my incomparable editor, Susanna Porter, who was passionate, insightful, and unflagging in her dedication, and to her assistant, Priyanka Krishnan, who helped me through the complicated task of putting a book together with patience and good grace. I am also deeply grateful to the entire incredible team at Ballantine: Libby McGuire and Kim Hovey in the publisher's office, Benjamin Dreyer, Steve Messina, and Mark Maguire in managing editorial and production; cover designers Paolo Pepe and Victoria Allen; book designer Virginia Norey; Quinne Rogers and Kristin Fassler in marketing; and Cindy Murray and Susan Corcoran in publicity. Many thanks for the terrific work of the entire sales team in Westminster, Maryland, especially Cheryl Kelly, whose deep affection for this story was evident. I could not have asked for a more enthusiastic, hardworking, or talented group of people to have on my side.

I am extremely indebted to Jeff Kleinman at Folio Literary Management, whose absolute dedication, creativity, and belief in Snowman's story were instrumental every step of the way. I also want to thank

Edith "Pete" Verloop and Corinne Kleinman for their love of horses and excellent hospitality, and for sharing their family history of life in war-time Holland.

Thanks to the National Sporting Library in Middleburg, Virginia, which awarded me a John H. Daniels Fellowship to support the writing of this book and gave me access to the library's superb equestrian collection. I'd especially like to thank Liz Tobey and Lisa Campbell for their help. Thanks also to Kathy Ball of the Smithtown Library for sharing the rich resources of its local history room, and George Allison of the Knox School for giving me access to the school and grounds, as well as delighting me with his wealth of knowledge about the institution and its history. I also appreciated Lucinda Dyer's incredible hard work and passionate love for big gray horses.

I relied on many people to share their insights with me, especially Bonnie Cornelius Spitzmiller, Phebe Phillips Byrne, Wendy Thomas, Harriet de Leyer, Bernie Traurig, Frank Guadagno, David Elliottt, Marie Debany, Chris Hickey, Sarah Hochsteder, Kathy Kusner, and Kathleen Fallon. Thanks to Noelle King and Diane de Franceaux Grod for their terrific work in bringing the horse community together online. Thanks to William Zinsser for sharing his description of writing for the *New York Herald Tribune*.

Thanks Tasha Alexander, Jon Clinch, Melanie Benjamin, and Betsy Wilmerding for unflagging help and support.

Thanks to Ginger Letts for getting up at five A.M., hitching up the trailer, reminding me to remember my boots and britches, and driving me to horse shows, and also for telling me countless stories about life in an all-girls boarding school in the 1950s. I am indebted to Nora Alalou for her artistic acumen and cheerful unpaid tech support.

Great gratitude to Joey, Nora, Hannah, Willis, and Ali for being the most supportive, enthusiastic, fun, creative, and funny family a writer could ever have.

Last, I'd like to thank my own two-legged teachers, Donna Naylor, Pam Nelson, Hilda Gurney, Rob Gage, and Judy Martin, and my four-legged teachers, Foxy, Jack, Kim, Fuzzy, Princess, Norman, Mary, Ned, Boy, and Conrad Russell. Thanks to them, I know what it feels like to fly.

A Note About Sources

The seed for this book was planted in my mind when I came across a picture of Snowman jumping over another horse. Having grown up around horses in California, I knew plenty of old cowboys and Hollywood stunt riders and I had seen many tricks performed on horses, but I had never seen a horse jumping over another horse. Drawn in by the picture, I did a little research and found that the story behind this horse and his rider was even more intriguing than the picture. I remembered reading a tale, during my horse-crazy girlhood, of a rescued plow horse who became a champion—the story had stayed with me. Now I realized that the story I remembered was the story of Snowman. I tracked down an address for Harry and sent him a letter. A few days later he called me. The first time I spoke to Harry de Leyer, I knew that this was a story I could retell.

Harry retained vivid and detailed memories of his early days in the United States, of his days as a teacher at the Knox School, and of his experiences riding Snowman. He was incredibly generous with his time. I interviewed him for many hours, for the first time in October 2008, right up until the final copyedits were finished. Some of those interviews were conducted over the phone, and some were conducted in person at his farm in Virginia. Harry also shared old home movies of Snowman and some of his competitors. The personal recollections—details about the people, the places, the atmosphere, and, most of all, what it felt like to be riding those daunting courses—were gleaned from those interviews. Where the recollections are based on the observations of others, they are noted. Several other people were extremely generous with their time. Bonnie Cornelius Spitzmiller not only shared her personal memories of her time at Knox but also her old yearbooks and the diary she kept during the time she was a student of Harry's at Knox. Phebe Phillips Byrne, Harry's former student and a former riding director at Knox, shared her detailed personal memories, and also her vast store of knowledge about Knox and its lore. Harry's daughter Harriet de Leyer–Strumpf was also extremely generous in sharing her personal recollections of what it was like growing up in the de Leyer family and riding Snowman. Some of the things Harry told me are based on his experiences alone, and I am grateful for his sharp memory and his patience in answering my questions and checking with family members whenever his own memory failed him on a detail.

In addition to the interviews, I conducted extensive research in periodicals of the time, but a few books were so indispensable that I would like to mention them specifically: *The Fifties*, by David Halberstam, gave me a panoramic overview of the time when this story takes place. *The National Horse Show: A Centennial History*, by Kurth Sprague, was published privately for the centennial of the National Horse Show; I relied heavily on this book for my descriptions of the history of the National Horse Show, the social milieu, and the physical setup. *Snowman*, by Rutherford Montgomery, a children's book published in 1962, was, according to Harry, based on a tape-recorded interview conducted in 1959. This book took liberties with the order of events, collapsing two years into one, but it was helpful for picking up bits of detail and for its descriptions of the young de Leyer family. I am also grateful for two excellent scholarly works about the history of the workhorse in America, *Horses at Work* by Ann Norton Greene and *The Horse in the City* by Clay McShane and Joel A. Tarr.

I was also very fortunate to spend a month as a fellow at the National Sporting Library in Middleburg, Virginia, which graciously shared with me the scrapbooks of Margaret L. Smith, a horse show reporter who collected articles about horse shows from 1953 to the early 1960s. Some of these newspaper clippings were not fully identified. I chose not to cite them specifically, selecting other sources where the citations were complete, but reading the articles and looking at newspaper pictures was helpful to me in setting up the general ambience. Also, the remarkable photo collection of Marshall Hawkins, also in the National Sporting Library, helped me with descriptions of people and the atmosphere of horse shows during that time period. Most important to my research were the library's archives of the horse-related periodical the *Chronicle of the Horse*, which included first-person reports and results from all of the shows mentioned in this book.

Notes

Prologue: A Night in the Spotlight

xiv **Outside of Hollywood:** for an excellent description of the atmosphere at the horse show in the 1950s, see Kurth Sprague, *The National Horse Show: A Centennial History, 1883–1983* (New York: National Horse Show Foundation, 1983).

xiv **Once, a ragtag band of competitors:** John Corry, "Showing Horses on a Shoestring: Many Exhibitors Do Own Stable Work to Save Money," *New York Times,* Nov. 11, 1958.

Chapter 1: The Kills

3 **The largest horse auction:** Rutherford Montgomery, *Snowman* (New York: Duell, Sloan, and Pearce, 1962). Montgomery describes the atmosphere at the auction in the mid-1950s. Also interview with Phebe Phillips Byrne.

4 **For all of their size and strength:** M. A. Stoneridge, "How to Evaluate a Horse for Soundness," in *Practical Horsekeeping* (New York: Doubleday, 1983).

5 **A bunch of horses:** Lawrence Scanlan, *Secretariat: The Horse That God Built* (New York: Thomas Dunne Books, 2007), p. 72.

5 **A rough man:** Montgomery, *Snowman,* p. 10.

5 **It was a cold day:** Montgomery, *Snowman,* p. 3.

6 **The horse was thin:** "Horse That Jumps: From the Slaughterhouse to the Motion Picture Screen," *Fitchburg Sentinel,* December 30, 1959; Harry is quoted as saying that Snowman "was not as undernourished as most horses headed to the slaughterhouse."

Chapter 2: On the Way Home

10   **Now a modern highway:** Ann Norton Greene, *Horses at Work: Harnessing ower in Industrial America* (Cambridge, Mass.: Harvard University Press, 2008), p. 51.

10   **The venerable Packard automobile company:** "Business: Help for Studebaker-Packard," *Time,* Apr. 23, 1956.

10   **Detroit was poised:** "National Affairs: Recession in Detroit," *Time,* Apr. 14, 1958.

10   **After making his way:** David Halberstam, *The Fifties* (New York: Random House, 1993), pp. 134–37.

11   **The area around St. James:** See Geoffrey Fleming, *Images of America: St. James* (Charleston: Arcadia Publishing, 2002), for a good overall description of the history of the Smithtown–St. James area.

11   **It was snowing hard:** Paul Aurandt, "Snow Man," in *Paul Harvey's The Rest of the Story* (New York: Doubleday, 1977), p. 177.

11   **Sure, it was a:** Bradley Harris, "Snowman, the Cinderella Horse of Hollandia Farms," *Smithtown News,* July 10, 2008, p. 12.

13   **"Look, Daddy":** Harriet de Leyer–Strumpf phone interview.

13   **Joseph, whose nickname:** "$80 Wonder Horse Worth $25,000: Snowman, the Equine Phenomenon, Stars at Children's Services Horse Show, May 15–17," *Hartford Courant,* May 10, 1959.

14   **As best Harry could tell:** Virginia Lucey, "Saddle and Spur," *Hartford Courant,* Oct. 5, 1958.

15   **For most horses:** M. A. Stoneridge, *A Horse of Your Own* (Garden City, N.Y.: Doubleday, 1963) p. 270.

17   **Every morning, as soon as:** "Snowman Has a Rival, and She's in His Own Stable," *Port Washington News,* Nov. 5, 1959.

Chapter 3: Land of Clover

19   **Built for a United States senator:** Bradley Harris, "The Knox School Finds a Home in Nissequogue," *Smithtown News,* Sept. 25, 2008, p. 10.

19   **and its outbuildings including:** Preview sales brochure, courtesy of Old Long Island, http://www.oldlongisland.com.

19   **Even in an economy:** Harris, "Knox School."

19   **The gray-shingled stable:** Phebe Phillips Byrne phone interview. (The stable doors are now painted red and white, but during Harry's era, they were green and white.)

19   **When he cracked the whip:** Phebe Phillips Byrne interview.

19   **The horseshoe-shaped stable:** George Allison interview.

20   **Around the turn of the twentieth century:** Fleming, *Images of America.*

21   **Constructed during boom times:** Ibid.

Chapter 4: An Ordinary Farm Chunk

22   **In 1950, there were still:** Joseph Mischka, *The Percheron Horse in America* (Whitewater, Wisc.: Heart Prairie Press, 1991), p. 100.

22   **The reduction of the equine population:** Greene, *Horses at Work*. The chapter "From Horse Powered to Horseless," pp. 244–75, provides an excellent description of the factors that influenced the decline of the horse population in the early twentieth century.

23   **In 1900, the value:** Ben K. Green, *Horse Tradin'* (New York: Alfred A. Knopf, 1963), p. v.

23   **States in the Mississippi:** Ibid. The introduction to veterinarian Green's reminiscences about his life working the horse trade in the early twentieth century provides a good overview of the west-to-east horse and mule trade in the United States.

23   **"Great big broad-hipped":** Ibid., p. 175.

23   **"In the fall":** "Horses for Sale at Auction," *Horse Magazine,* April 1956.

23   **In the 1970s:** American Horse Council, http://www.horsecouncil.org.

24   **On opening day:** *The Official Report of the Organizing Committee for the XIV Olympiad* (London: The Organizing Committee for the XIV Olympiad, 1948), p. 222.

25   **But the American Jockey Club:** Phil Livingston and Ed Roberts, *War Horse: Mounting the Cavalry with America's Finest Horses* (Albany, Tex.: Bright Sky Press, 2003), p. 10, and Elizabeth Tobey, personal communication.

25   **Despite the declining:** Livingston and Roberts, *War Horse,* pp. 10–15.

25   **Prior to the First World War:** Greene, *Horses at Work,* p. 227.

26   **Wartime consumption:** Major-General Sir John Moore, *Our Servant the Horse: An Appreciation of the Part Played by Animals During the War, 1914–1918* (London: H & W Brown, 1931), p. 12.

26   **To address the concern:** "Horses to Be Improved; Federal Authorities, Through Remount Program, to Aid Breeders," *New York Times,* June 8, 1919.

26   **The program selected:** Livington and Roberts, *War Horse,* p. 16.

26   **Appropriate for riding:** Ibid.

26   **In the 1920s:** Ibid.

27   **But the Second World War:** Ibid. For an overview of the end of the army's Remount Program, during and after World War II, see pp. 147–222.

28   **Once a horse:** Lynne Ames, "At Work: Where Do the Amish Train Their Horses?" *New York Times,* Oct. 18, 2003, provides an explanation of how Amish horses are trained to pull a wagon or plow.

28   **The traditional American workhorse's:** Clay McShane and Joel A. Tarr, *The Horse in the City: Living Machines in the Nineteenth Century* (Baltimore: Johns Hopkins University Press, 2007), pp. 28–35.

28   **As the horse illustrator:** Thomas Meagher, *The Gigantic Book of Horse Wisdom* (New York: Skyhorse, 2007), p. 327.

29   **Horses were generally sold in teams:** McShane and Tarr, *Horse in the City*, pp. 25–26.

29   **Photographs of urban street scenes:** Ibid., p. 46.

29   **In a midcentury veterinary:** E. T. Baker, *The Home Veterinarian's Handbook: A Guide for Handling Emergencies in Farm Animals and Poultry* (New York: Macmillan, 1944), p. 49.

29   **A graphic picture:** "Horse Meat: War Has Created Demand for This Unrationed Commodity," *Life*, June 1943, pp. 65–68.

29   **More often, horsemeat:** McShane and Tarr, *Horse in the City*, pp. 27–30.

30   **When English author Anna Sewell:** Susan Chitty, *The Woman Who Wrote "Black Beauty"* (London: Hodder & Stoughton, 1971), p. 187.

30   **The sentimental and:** Greene, *Horses at Work*, pp. 200–20.

30   **This point of view dovetailed:** McShane and Tarr, *Horse in the City*, pp. 36–57.

31   **The original mission:** Ibid., p. 87.

31   **Born in 1811, Bergh:** Unitarian Universalist Association, "Henry Bergh," www.uua.org/uua/uuhs/duub/articles/henrybergh.html.

31   **The ASPCA adopted:** McShane and Tarr, *Horse in the City*, p. 47.

31   **The MSPCA passed out:** Ibid., *Horse in the City*, p. 202.

32   **Though the role of the workhorse:** Ibid., *Horse in the City*, pp. 165–77.

Chapter 5: A School for Young Ladies

34   **The 1950s was:** I am indebted to Bonnie Cornelius Spitzmiller, Phebe Phillips Byrne, and Wendy Plumb Thomas for sharing their reminiscences of the Knox School.

35   **In the early 1900s:** *Who's Who in America*, vol. 6 (Chicago: A. N. Marquis, 1910), p. 2234.

35   **Mary Alice Knox envisioned:** "Knox @ 100: A Centennial History of the Knox School," Knox School website: www.knoxschool.org.

35   **But Miss Knox would:** Ibid.

36   **First, in 1912:** Ibid.

36   **Among the board's criteria:** George Allison phone interview.

36   **In 1954:** "Knox @ 100."

36   **Every moment of a Knox:** Phebe Phillips Byrne phone interview.

38   **While many of the girls:** Bonnie Cornelius Spitzmiller phone interview.

38   **"It was like being in jail:** Ibid.

38   **While some Knox:** Phebe Phillips Byrne interview.

38   **Girls flouted the rules:** Bonnie Cornelius Spitzmiller interview, George Allison interview.

39   **Bonnie Cornelius grew up:** Bonnie Cornelius Spitzmiller interview.

40   **Mrs. Phinney was:** Ibid.

41   **Even Sundays were:** Ibid.

41   **The five-day girls:** Knox School yearbook, 1957.

41   **Charlotte Haxall Noland:** Mary Custis Lee De Butts and Rosalie Noland Woodland, eds., *Charlotte Haxall Noland, 1883–1969* (Middleburg, Va.: Foxcroft, 1971).

41   **M. Carey Thomas:** "History of the Bryn Mawr School," http://www.brynmawr.pvt.k12.md.us/about/history.aspx.

41   **In the nineteenth century:** Jane Hunter, *How Young Ladies Became Girls* (New Haven: Yale University Press, 2003), provides an excellent overview of the growth of girls' education.

43   **Swinging lightly onto:** Bonnie Cornelius Spitzmiller interview.

45   **Now, as a riding instructor:** Ibid.

46   **"Rode Chief":** Bonnie Cornelius Spitzmiller diary entry.

47   **The next day at the barn:** Harriet de Leyer–Strumpf interview.

48   **The Meadowbrook Hunt:** A. Henry Higginson and Julian Ingersoll Chamberlain, *The Hunts of the United States and Canada: Their Masters, Hounds and Histories* (Boston: Frank L. Wiles, 1908), pp. 72–78 and pp. 168–69.

48   **Many feared that:** Bradley Harris, "Still Tracking Foxes in the Smithtown Hunt," *Smithtown News,* Aug. 21, 2008, p. 10.

48   **Originally, the sport of foxhunting:** Ibid.

48   **At that time, the master:** Ibid.

49   **The dress code required:** Lisa Mancuso, "Thrill of the Hunt: Equestrian Honored with Club Lifetime Achievement Award," *Smithtown News,* Apr. 1, 2010.

49   **One day, Harry and the girls:** Bonnie Cornelius Spitzmiller interview.

50   **With the truck idling:** Bonnie Cornelius Spitzmiller interview and Phebe Phillips Byrne interview.

50   **Bonnie remembers a hunt breakfast:** Bonnie Cornelius Spitzmiller interview.

51   **Knox girls, boarders:** Phebe Phillips Byrne interview.

51   **At the end of one day's hunt:** Bonnie Cornelius Spitzmiller diary entry.

Chapter 6: Hollandia Farms

54   **The fastest way to sell a horse:** Frankie Guadagno, blacksmith apprenticed to Milton Potter as a teen, phone interview.

55   **Johanna kept a neat ledger:** Montgomery, *Snowman,* p. 36.

Chapter 7: How to Make a Living at Horses

57   **Out of about two million:** U.S. Census documentation, http://www.census.gov/population/www/documentation/twps0029/twps0029.html.

59   **As the demand for farm labor:** "Operation Wetback," *The Handbook of Texas Online,* http://www.tshaonline.org/handbook/online/articles/OO/pq01.html.

66   **Between 1950 and 1955:** "Mickey Walsh, Horse Trainer, 86," *New York Times,* Aug. 19, 1983.

66   **Now at the very top of his game:** Matthew Parker, "Stoneybrook and Walsh, for the Love of the Race," North Carolina Visitors Bureau, http://www.ncvisitorcenter.com/Stoneybrook_and_Walsh.html.

68   **Bill McCormick was a drinker:** Bradley Harris, "Snowman, the Cinderella Horse of Hollandia Farms," p. 12.

Chapter 8: The Stable Boy

72   **From the long, tree-lined lane:** Sharon Trautwein phone interview.

73   **Ten-year-old Sharon:** Ibid.

Chapter 9: Where the Heart Is

76   **In the months since:** Ed Corrigan, "Snowman Returns for Final Accolade," *New York Times,* Nov. 9, 1969.

79   **Horses are born:** For a discussion of horses and jumping, see Vladimir S. Littauer, *Common Sense Horsemanship* (New York: Van Nostrand, 1951).

79   **The tradition moved to England:** Roger Longrigg, *The Complete History of Fox Hunting* (New York: Clarkson Potter, 1975), pp. 87–89.

80   **Snowman had always had an intelligent:** "Horse That Jumps," *Fitchburg Sentinel.*

81   **"I've got your horse":** Montgomery, *Snowman,* p. 41.

82   **"You sold me a jumper":** Ibid.

Chapter 10: The Horse Can Jump

87   **Like other mammals:** M. A. Stoneridge, *A Horse of Your Own,* p. 266.

88   **All horses have some ability:** Vladimir S. Littauer, *Jumping the Horse* (New York: Derrydale, 1931), pp. 32–41.

88   **Until 1878:** McShane and Tarr, *Horse in the City,* pp. 204–06.

88   **But when a horse jumps:** Littauer, *Jumping the Horse,* pp. 57–66.

89   **The first step:** William Steinkraus, *Riding and Jumping* (Garden City, N.Y.: Doubleday, 1961), pp. 74–76.

89   **One of the hardest things:** Littauer, *Jumping the Horse,* pp. 41–50.

90   **A "bad rider will disturb":** Ibid., p. 41.

90   **Styles of riding have evolved:** Ibid., pp. 1–13.

92   **As Prince Philip:** Meagher, *The Gigantic Book of Horse Wisdom,* p. 578.

92   *Snowman?:* Bonnie Cornelius Spitzmiller interview.

93   He'd decided to put his gutsiest rider: Ibid.
96   Some jumping competitions: Sprague, The National Horse Show; see pp. 45–47 for a discussion of reactions to the high jumping competitions during the early years of the National Horse Show.

Chapter 11: A Grim Business

98   Called "David Harums": Appleton's Cyclopedia of American Biography, vol. 7 (New York: Appleton, 1901), p. 279.
98   As the popular newspaper columnist: John Gould, "Hoss Trading: A Lesson for Diplomats," New York Times Magazine, Nov. 16, 1947.
98   A horse trader was skilled: McShane and Tarr, Horse in the City, pp. 19–22.
98   In 1897, the Chicago: Ibid.
99   Many Depression-era farmers: Mischka, The Percheron Horse in America, pp. 100–08.
99   "When I get him": "Horse Showing Is a Grim Business," Palm Beach Post, Nov. 17, 1962.
99   Out on eastern: Frankie Guadagno interview.
99   People called them: Ibid.
100   The other traders: Ibid.
100   When the U.S. Army cavalry: "FBI Rangers View G.I. Horse Trading," New York Times, May 14, 1946.
100   Riding apparel was sold: "More Children Saddle Up Each Year Despite Cost," New York Times, Nov. 5, 1957.
104   As Jack Frohm: "Horse Showing Is a Grim Business."

Chapter 12: Horses, Owners, and Riders

106   Writers in horse-oriented: "Conversation Piece," Chronicle of the Horse, Aug. 29, 1958.
106   That the amateurs: Marie C. Lafrenz, "Professional Versus Amateur," New York Herald Tribune, Apr. 19, 1960.
107   Teenage boys collected: Dave Elliot, former student of Harry's, phone interview.
107   The de Leyers didn't ask: Ibid.
115   It was no surprise: "Mann Horses Pace Show," New York Times, Sept. 5, 1957.

Chapter 13: Sinjon

120   The well-known equestrian writer: M. A. Stoneridge, A Horse of Your Own, p. 270.
120   In The Complete Book of Show Jumping: Judy Crago, "Selection, Train-

ing, and Care," in William Steinkraus and Michael Clayton, eds., *The Complete Book of Show Jumping* (New York: Crown, 1975), p. 45.

121 **But at Sands Point:** "De Leyer, Maker of Champions, Dreams of His Greatest One," *New York Times*, Mar. 7, 1965.

122 **only the top twelve horses:** See Richard Rust, *Renegade Champion: The Unlikely Rise of Fitzrada* (Lanham, Md.: Taylor Trade, 2008), pp. 139–43, for a discussion of the show schedules and elimination rounds.

123 **Several of the top British:** Dean McGowan, "Pat Smythe, Ace Woman Rider, Takes U.S. Officials Over Jumps," *New York Times*, Nov. 5, 1957.

123 **Meanwhile, back at the Garden:** "65th National Horse Show to Begin an Eight-Day Run at Garden on Tuesday," *New York Times*, Nov. 1, 1953.

123 **The National Horse Show social rituals:** Sprague, *The National Horse Show*, pp. 80–86.

123 **"The prettiest sight":** *The Philadelphia Story*, film, Metro-Goldwyn-Mayer, 1940.

123 **A New York social columnist:** Russell Edwards, "National Horse Show Here Has a 76-Year History of Strange and Wondrous Things," *New York Times*, Nov. 1, 1959.

123 **The annual spectacle:** John Rendel, "8-Day Horse Show Opens Here Today; Jumping Teams Will Parade Around the Garden Ring in Formal Ceremony," *New York Times*, Nov. 5, 1957.

124 **One of the greatest international:** Sprague, *The National Horse Show*, pp. 80–86.

126 **The footing was soft:** Judy Schachter, personal communication.

129 **The closing ceremony:** "Horse Show Ends with Many Fetes," *New York Times*, Nov. 13, 1957.

Chapter 14: The Circuit

133 **The wealthiest Americans:** Paul Fussell, *Class: A Guide Through the American Status System* (New York: Touchstone, 1992), p. 30.

133 **Called "coupon clippers":** Andrew Beveridge, "The Idle Rich," *Gotham Gazette*, Nov. 2006.

133 **These all-white, all-Protestant:** Fussell, *Class*, pp. 28–30.

133 **A mix of amateurs and professionals:** Rust, *Renegade Champion*, p. 142.

134 **The professionals relied on:** "Horse Showing Is a Grim Business," *Palm Beach Post*, Nov. 17, 1962.

134 **In an era when:** Halberstam, *The Fifties*, pp. 692–98 and 623–25.

134 **A contemporary article:** Milton Bracker, "Philadelphia Society, Changing but Changeless," *New York Times*, Jan. 14, 1957.

134 **Devon's show grounds:** "History," Devon Horse Show, http://www.thedevonhorseshow.org/about-history.php.

135 **The *Times* revealed:** Bracker, "Philadelphia Society."

135 **straw boaters:** Susan Wilmerding, personal communication, Nov. 16, 2010.

135 **Back in St. James:** "$80 Wonder Horse," *Hartford Courant*, May 10, 1959.

135 **And Snowman, too:** Phebe Phillips Byrne interview.

136 **The only taste:** "Devon," *The Chronicle of the Horse*, June 14, 1958.

137 **The first quarter of 1958:** "The Recession of 1958," www.Time.com, Oct. 15, 2008.

138 **The Kentucky Derby:** http://en.wikipedia.org/wiki/Kentucky_Derby.

138 **Pioneers in a variety of sports:** Halberstam, *The Fifties*, pp. 691–97.

139 **Then in January:** "Roy Campanella Continues to Gain; Injured Catcher Gets Some Feeling Back in Body, but Legs Still Paralyzed," *New York Times*, Jan. 31, 1958.

139 **In front of Andante's stall:** Montgomery, *Snowman*, p. 72.

140 **Everyone knew the owner:** "Business," *Time*, Dec. 30, 1957.

140 **Andante's rider:** "Dave T. Kelley," National Show Jumping Hall of Fame, http://www.showjumpinghalloffame.net/.

140 **Most people thought he:** "Green Is Injured in Horse Show Test," *New York Times*, Sept. 16, 1955.

140 **At the big shows:** "Horse Showing Is a Grim Business," *Palm Beach Post*, Nov. 17, 1962.

140 **The de Leyers did everything:** Montgomery, *Snowman*, p. 16.

141 **Part of a generation:** Harriet de Leyer–Strumpf phone interview.

141 **When all of the barn:** Montgomery, *Snowman*, p. 56.

141 **Harry had brought four:** "Sands Point," *Chronicle of the Horse*, June 22, 1958.

142 **The show, founded:** Harry V. Forgeron, "Town Puts Heart in Its Horse Show, Port Washington Lions Find Willing Hands for Event That Built Ballfield," *New York Times*, May 15, 1960.

144 **Historians surmise:** Littauer, *Jumping the Horse*, p. 3.

144 **An old English proverb:** Meagher, *The Gigantic Book of Horse Wisdom*, p. 414.

144 **The crowd at Sands Point:** Forgeron, "Town Puts Heart."

144 **Andante, a touchy mare:** Alice Higgins, "Exit Jumping: Andante, an Aged Prima Donna, Begins Her Last Season with a Flamboyant Win at Devon," *Sports Illustrated*, June 20, 1960.

145 **After a few more rounds:** Video footage reviewed courtesy of the private collection of Harry de Leyer.

145 **Later, the children swore:** Montgomery, *Snowman*, p. 61.

146 **Dave Kelley smiled:** Ibid.

147 **Marie Lafrenz, in charge:** Obituary, Marie C. Lafrenz, *US Eventing News*, May 18, 2007.

147 **Harness racing, long a popular:** Charles Leerhson, *Crazy Good: The True Story of Dan Patch, the Most Famous Horse in America* (New York: Simon & Schuster, 2009), pp. 120–21.

147 **Even an *I Love Lucy*:** "Lucy Wins a Race Horse," *I Love Lucy*, Feb. 3, 1958.

147 **In 1956, when:** "Junk Wagon Horse Takes a Fling at Broadway Chase," *New York Times*, Apr. 17, 1956.

148 **The pioneering sports promoter:** George Vecsey, "Raceway Era: When Dog Days Became Trotter Nights," *New York Times*, July 22, 1988.

148 **It was a tough time:** See Richard Kluger, *The Paper: The Life and Death of the "New York Herald Tribune"* (New York: Alfred A. Knopf, 1986), for an overview of the newspaper business in New York in the late 1950s.

148 **Marie believed that:** Marie C. Lafrenz, "Horse Show Publicity," *The Whole Horse Catalogue*, ed. Steven D. Price (New York: Fireside, 1998), pp. 252–53.

149 **Marie had discovered:** Ibid.

149 **As one of the very few:** Obituary, Marie C. Lafrenz, *US Eventing News*, May 18, 2007.

149 **"Phones rang incessantly":** William Zinsser, "The Daily Miracle: Life with the Mavericks and Oddballs at the *Herald Tribune*," *American Scholar*, vol. 77, no. 1 (Winter 2008).

151 **He gently probed:** Montgomery, *Snowman*, p. 64.

151 **"What are you going to do?":** Ibid.

154 **In the first go-through:** Forgeron, "Town Puts Heart."

154 **The jump crew:** Ibid.

154 **Chef and Harriet:** Montgomery, *Snowman*, p. 61.

157 **"stoically keep muddling":** Bill Stott, "Anthem of 1950s America," http://www.billstott.blogspot.com/search/label/American%20cultural%20history.

Chapter 15: New Challenges

158 **The vast television audience:** Robert Lyon, *On Any Given Sunday: A Life of Bert Bell* (Philadelphia: Temple University Press, 2010), pp. 290–92.

161 **The rain had deterred:** "Fairfield County Hunt," *Chronicle of the Horse*, July 11, 1958, p. 20.

161 **While the footing:** Ibid.

162 **On the last day:** Ibid.

163 **Right from the start:** Ibid.

164 **There was still another:** Ibid.

166 **After Fairfield, horse show:** Montgomery, *Snowman*, p. 84.

Chapter 16: The Things That Really Matter

169 **That morning, Harry put:** "Smithtown," *Chronicle of the Horse*, Sept. 12, 1958, p. 19.

172 **Calling long-distance:** Montgomery, *Snowman*, p. 96.

Chapter 17: Piping Rock

174   **the country's "elegantsia":** John Lahr, "King Cole," *New Yorker,* July 12, 2004, http://www.newyorker.com/archive/2004/07/12/040712crat_atlarge.

174   **It was in the woods:** Ibid.

174   **Lida Fleitmann:** "Miss Lida Fleitmann, Horsewoman, to Wed," *New York Times,* Feb. 1, 1922.

175   **Designed in 1913, the club:** "Piping Rock's Millionaire's Colony Opens New Club," *New York Times,* May 26, 1912.

175   **The horse show's jumping contests:** "Society Aids at Piping Rock Club," *New York Times,* Oct. 5, 1912.

176   **known as "Locust Valley lockjaw":** William Safire, "Locust Valley Lockjaw," *New York Times Magazine,* Jan. 18, 1987.

176   **"her voice was full of money":** F. Scott Fitzgerald, *The Great Gatsby* (1925; reprint, New York: Scribner, 1999), p. 120.

176   **Eleo Sears posed:** "Piping Rock Horse Show," photograph with caption, *Chronicle of the Horse,* Oct. 3, 1958.

176   **Eleo Sears was one of:** Peggy Miller Franck, *Prides Crossing: The Unbridled Life and Impatient Times of Eleo Sears* (Beverly, Mass.: Commonwealth Editions, 2009), provides excellent background to the life and times of Eleonora Sears.

176   **Once, in the middle:** "Miss Sears Turns Runaway, Swerves Animal from Bolting Among Spectators at Lawn Tennis Match," *New York Times,* Sept. 28, 1911.

176   **Miss Sears was so well known:** "Miss Sears' Skating Outfit; She Prefers Cap and Muff of Knitted Wool for Cold Days," *New York Times,* Feb. 19, 1912.

176   **She had popularized:** Franck, *Prides Crossing,* pp. 145–46.

177   **"Any professionals seen":** "Society Amateurs in the Saddle: Piping Rock Horse Show Attracts Hunting Set to Locust Valley Grounds," *New York Times,* Oct. 4, 1913.

178   **Her two horses:** Bill Bryan, "U.S. Team Success," *Chronicle of the Horse,* Aug. 15, 1958, p. 30.

178   **In 1958, the press:** "Steinkraus Wins at London Show," *New York Times,* July 21, 1958.

178   **On July 18, 1958:** Bryan, "U.S. Team Success," p. 30.

178   **For both of these horse-and-rider:** "National's Diamond Jubilee," *Chronicle of the Horse,* Sept. 12, 1958, p. 30.

179   **Miss Sears was one:** Bill Bryan, "History of the United States Equestrian Team," *Chronicle of the Horse,* Oct. 31, 1958, pp. 15–18.

182   **Transatlantic horse travel:** "Fly Your Bloodstock," advertisement, *Chronicle of the Horse,* Oct. 31, 1958.

182   **Bred in the United:** William Steinkraus, *Great Horses of the United States Equestrian Team* (New York: Dodd, Mead & Company, 1977), p. 53.

182   **Steinkraus was an elegant:** Alice Higgins, "Thinker on Horseback," *Sports Illustrated*, Dec. 15, 1958.

182   **The horse had already:** Bryan, "U.S. Team Success," p. 30.

182   **The press had been impressed:** Ibid.

184   **At Piping Rock, it was:** Kathleen Fallon phone interview.

184   **Schooling jumps were set:** Marie Debany phone interview.

184   **All of the fences:** Ibid.

189   **Harry grinned again at the children:** Montgomery, *Snowman*, p. 118.

190   **Wendy Plumb, one of Harry's pupils:** Wendy Plumb Thomas, personal communication.

191   **The crowd paused in silence:** "Snow Man First in Jumping Event; Beats Diamant for Title in Piping Rock Horse Show," *New York Times*, Sept. 15, 1958.

191   **He was happy to answer:** Montgomery, *Snowman*, p. 121.

196   **But before it had actually:** "Snow Man First in Jumping Event."

Chapter 18: The Indoor Circuit

199   **"Grab the mane!":** Phebe Phillips Byrne interview.

200   **Johanna had started a scrapbook:** Harriet de Leyer–Strumpf interview.

200   **Harry let Bonnie:** Bonnie Cornelius Spitzmiller interview.

202   **The show opened:** "German Rider Clinches Laurels in Washington Show," *New York Times*, Oct. 15, 1958, and Toni Brewer, "Washington International," *Chronicle of the Horse*, Oct. 24, 1958.

202   **But people hoping to see:** Brewer, "Washington International."

203   **On October 15, the show's:** "German Rider Clinches Laurels."

203   **Next in line:** Brewer, "Washington International."

203   **That night in front of the president:** Alice Higgins, "Deutschland über Alles: At Brand-New Washington Show, Germans Collected Everything but the Tickets," *Sports Illustrated*, Oct. 27, 1958.

204   **The culminating event:** Brewer, "Washington International."

Chapter 19: The Diamond Jubilee

206   **The National truly was:** Sprague, *The National Horse Show*, p. 82.

207   **Some of the big barns:** Corry, "Showing Horses on a Shoestring."

207   **To the press and the public:** Sprague, *The National Horse Show*, p. xvi.

210   **Among the stodgy denizens:** Ibid., pp. 28–33.

210   **Until 1925:** Ibid., p. 29.

210   **Around the arena:** Russell Edwards, "National Horse Show Here Has a 76-Year History of Strange and Wondrous Things," *New York Times*, Nov. 1, 1959.

210   **In 1928, the horse show:** Sprague, *The National Horse Show*, p. 80.

211   **Grooms from the Mexican team:** Ibid., p. 82.

211   **"patterned himself on":** Ibid., p. v.

211   **There was a series of articles:** Milton Bracker, "Philadelphia Society."

212   "every decent stable": Sprague, *The National Horse Show*, p. 82.

212   A series of photographs: "Attendant Saddling Horse Backstage," photographs, *Life*, Nov. 1960.

213   Until the early 1950s: Sprague, *National Horse Show*, p. 84.

214   the *World-Telegran and Sun* had run: Willard Mullin cartoon, *New York World-Telegram and Sun*, Nov. 4, 1958, p. 18.

217   The entrance to the Garden: Sprague, *The National Horse Show*, p. 87.

217   "melton and mink": Ibid., p. 87.

217   The first tier of seats: Ibid., p. 88.

218   Families clutching programs: Ibid., p. 89.

218   In addition to the competitions: Ibid., pp. 170–212 and "National Horse Show Begins Run," *Schenectady Gazette*, Nov. 4, 1958.

219   With all of the dazzle: "National Horse Show," *Chronicle of the Horse*, Nov. 21, 1958.

219   The Cuban team paraded: "Five Cubans Stage Protest of Countrymen in Show," *New York Times*, Nov. 5, 1958.

219   Some in the crowd hooted and heckled: "Sidelights of the National," *Chronicle of the Horse*, Nov. 21, 1958.

220   "The crowd seemed to have inherited": Virginia Lucey, "Saddle and Spur," *Hartford Courant*, Nov. 16, 1958.

220   They were noisy: Montgomery, *Snowman*, p. 116.

221   There was an open spot: Sprague, *The National Horse Show*, p. 98.

221   The ringmaster, Honey Craven: Ibid., p. 94.

223   The trainer Cappy Smith: Ibid., p. 91.

223   Riders looked for opportunities: Ibid., p. 90.

224   The gatekeeper, who worked for Eleo Sears: Ibid., p. 92.

229   One competitor referred: Ibid., p. xvi.

Chapter 20: "Deutschland über Alles"

231   Knowing that, as: Lafrenz, "Horse Show Publicity," p. 252.

231   If it wasn't too far: Corry, "Showing Horses on a Shoestring."

231   Snowman ambled along: Montgomery, *Snowman*, p. 124.

233   "Keep your clothes nice": Ibid., p. 124.

233   Alice Higgins of: "Deutschland über Alles."

233   The nighttime performance: Alice Higgins, "German Cliffhanger," *Sports Illustrated*, Nov. 24, 1958.

235   Nobody at the show: Phebe Phillips Byrne interview.

236   When Snowman soared: Higgins, "German Cliffhanger."

Chapter 21: Famous!

240   The businessman was not only: "Genuine Risk Dies; Filly Won Kentucky Derby," *New York Times*, Aug. 18, 2008.

240   **"sad-eyed horse":** "Doomed Horse Leaps from Kill Pen to Fame," *Chicago Daily Tribune,* Nov. 8, 1958.

240   **"Snowman paws the ground":** "Snowman Has Rival."

242   **One was an actor:** A. H. Weiler, "Movie to Relate Story of a Horse; Bob Hope May Play Role of Snowman's Rescuer," *New York Times,* Sept. 25, 1961 and "By Way of Report: John Huston's Full Slate—La John Dolce Vita Is Acquired—Snowman Saga," *New York Times,* Jan. 22, 1961.

243   **Harry's mother was suffering:** Harriet de Leyer–Strumpf interview.

246   **And there were also several pages:** "Old Nag's Long Jump from Plow Horse; Discarded Farm Horse Finds Unexpected Fame," *Life,* Nov. 9, 1959, pp. 63–66.

247   **"We have no sentimental attachment":** "Jumper Windsor Castle Is Sold in $50,000 Deal," *New York Times,* Nov. 6, 1959.

248   **Harry was invited:** "In the Country," *Chronicle of the Horse,* Dec.1, 1959.

Chapter 22: The Wind of Change

249   **Harriet, a daring rider:** Harriet de Leyer–Strumpf interview.

250   **When a new teenager:** Dave Elliot interview.

251   **But during a preshow exhibition:** "Jumping King Snow Man Is Hurt in Fall," *Chicago Daily Tribune,* June 26, 1960.

252   **A *Reader's Digest* article:** Philip B. Kunhardt, "The Farm Horse That Became a Champion," *Animals You Will Never Forget* (Pleasantville, N.Y.: Reader's Digest Books, 1969; condensed from *Farmer's Advocate,* 1960 and reprinted in *Reader's Digest,* Nov. 1960).

252   **"This has been a season of plenty":** Alice Higgins, "The Year of the Jumpers: A Spectacular Open Event in New York Tops a Season of Excellent Performances Around the Country by American and Foreign Horses," *Sports Illustrated,* Nov. 20, 1961.

253   **The exhibition was on:** "Snowman Gives Exhibition Today in Horse Show," *Washington Post,* Sept. 24, 1960.

253   **At home, they had been practicing:** Harriet de Leyer–Strumpf interview.

255   **The Armory looked splendid:** Anne Christmas, "Washington International," *Chronicle of the Horse,* Nov. 18, 1960.

256   **The great grand prix rider:** Bernie Traurig phone interview.

259   **Sitting astride the bay:** Christmas, "Washington International."

Chapter 23: Camelot

261   **Corporate sponsorship had arrived:** Sprague, *The National Horse Show,* pp. 101–28.

261   **The classes had been rearranged:** "Society: She Ain't What She Used to Be," *Time,* Nov. 9, 1962.

262 **In fact, originally, the team:** Joseph O'Dea, *DVM, Olympic Vet* (Geneseo, N.Y.: Castlerea Press, 1996), p. 20.

263 **The brave old horse:** John Rendel, "Stumble Results in a Broken Neck," *New York Times*, Nov. 5, 1960.

263 **The gelding was perfectly:** O'Dea, *Olympic Vet*, p. 20.

264 **Eventually, the lights came back up:** John Rendel, "Stumble Results."

Chapter 24: Branglebrink Farms

265 **Countless times, driving:** Bradley Harris, "Cinderella Horse," p. 12.

265 **The dairy farm had:** Geoffrey Fleming, *Images of America*, p. 93.

266 **Knox wanted to buy the house:** Harris, "Cinderella Horse."

267 **Another story about the champion:** "An Old Jumper's Jackpot," *Life*, July 27, 1962.

268 **Harriet and Chef:** Harriet de Leyer–Strumpf interview.

268 **The Knox School girls had formed:** Phebe Phillips Byrne interview.

268 **There was a long blue satin ribbon:** Dave Elliot interview.

269 **Harriet still remembers:** Harriet de Leyer–Strumpf interview.

270 **The demands of television:** Sprague, *The National Horse Show*, pp. 235–71.

271 **All these years, Harry:** Phebe Phillips Byrne interview.

272 **The roar of the crowd:** Ed Corrigan, "Snowman Returns for Final Accolade."

272 **Flashbulbs popped:** Chris Hickey interview.

Chapter 25: The Cinderella Horse

273 **Schoolteachers brought busloads:** Claire Nicolas White, "Cinderella Horse Stars on L.I.," *New York Times*, Oct. 22, 1972.

273 **Like her older brothers and sisters:** Harris, "Cinderella Horse."

273 **In the evenings:** Phebe Phillips Byrne interview.

275 **But when it came time:** Harriet de Leyer–Strumpf interview.

Epilogue: The Galloping Grandfather

279 **Harry had gone through:** Ed Corrigan, "Serious Fall off Horse Fails to Deter Youngster," *New York Times*, Dec. 11, 1977.

Bibliography

"Advertising: Man in a Hurry." *Time*, Mar. 6, 1950.

"Alice Higgins, Magazine Writer on Equestrian Sports, Is Dead." *New York Times*, Sept. 19, 1974.

Ames, Lynne. "At Work: Where Do the Amish Train Their Horses?" *New York Times*, Oct. 18, 2003.

"And a Bow to the Supporting Cast." *Sports Illustrated*, Jan. 5, 1959.

Aurandt, Paul. "Snow Man." In *Paul Harvey's The Rest of the Story*. Edited and compiled by Lynne Harvey. New York: Doubleday, 1977.

Aurichio, Andrea. "And Thereby Hang Some Tails." *New York Times*, July 20, 1980.

Austin, Dale. "Snowman Wins Jump-off in Show, Two Mounts Unseat Riders, Hurdles Fall." *Washington Post*, Oct. 28, 1960.

Baker, E. T. *The Home Veterinarian's Handbook: A Guide for Handling Emergencies in Farm Animals and Poultry*. New York: Macmillan, 1944.

"Black Atom Takes Horse Show Lead." *Washington Post*, Oct. 26, 1960.

Bracker, Milton. "Philadelphia Society, Changing but Changeless." *New York Times*, Jan. 14, 1957.

Brewer, Toni. "Washington International." *Chronicle of the Horse*, Oct. 24, 1958.

Bryan, Bill. "History of the United States Equestrian Team." *Chronicle of the Horse*, Oct. 31, 1958.

———. "U.S. Team Success." *Chronicle of the Horse*, Aug. 15, 1958.

"Business." *Time*, Dec. 30, 1957.

"*By Way of Re*port: John Huston's Full Slate—La John Dolce Vita Is Acquired—Snowman Saga." *New York Times*, Jan. 22, 1961.

"Chapot, U.S., Wins Jump-off in Show; Beats Germany's Winkler by 1 Second—President Sees Washington Event." *New York Times*, Oct. 16, 1958.

"Children's Services." *Chronicle of the Horse*, June 12, 1959.

Christmas, Anne. "Washington International." *Chronicle of the Horse*, Nov. 18, 1960.

"Classy Jumpers to Battle at Ox Ridge." *Sunday Bridgeport Herald*, May 29, 1960.

"Conversation Piece." *Chronicle of the Horse,* Aug. 29, 1958.

Corrigan, Ed. "De Leyer's Two Jumpers Help Argentines over Rough Spot." *New York Times,* Nov. 28, 1971.

———. "Doomed Horse Leaps from Kill Pen to Fame." *Chicago Tribune,* Nov. 8, 1958.

———. "Serious Fall off Horse Fails to Deter Youngster." *New York Times,* Dec. 11, 1977.

———. "Snowman Returns for Final Accolade." *New York Times,* Nov. 9, 1969.

Corry, John. "Showing Horses on a Shoestring: Many Exhibitors Do Own Stable Work to Save Money." *New York Times,* Nov. 11, 1958.

Crago, Judy. "Selection, Training, and Care." In William Steinkraus and Michael Clayton, eds., *The Complete Book of Show Jumping.* New York: Crown, 1975.

"Crowd in Furs Sees Piping Rock Horse Show." *New York Times,* Oct. 7, 1909.

"Dappled Gray Scores, Snowman Gets Meyner Prize at Paramus Horse Show." *New York Times,* Oct. 13, 1958.

De Butts, Mary Custis Lee, and Rosalie Noland Woodland, eds. *Charlotte Haxall Noland, 1883–1969.* Middleburg, Va.: Foxcroft, 1971.

"De Leyer, Maker of Champions, Dreams of His Greatest One." *New York Times,* Mar. 7, 1965.

"De Leyer Paces Show." *New York Times,* July 21, 1958.

Devereux, Frederick L. *Famous American Horses: 21 Steeplechasers, Trotters, Cowponies, Flat Racers, Show Horses and Battle Mounts That Have Made History.* Old Greenwich, Conn.: Devin-Adair, 1975.

"Devon." *The Chronicle of the Horse,* June 14, 1958.

"Diamant Captures 3d Jump-off, Wins Horse Show Prize." *New York Times,* Sept. 12, 1958.

"Diamant Registers Horse Show Victory." *New York Times,* Sept. 16, 1958.

Dioguardi, Ralph. "The Horse Nobody Wanted." *Smithtown Sunday Digest,* May 20, 1979.

"Doomed Horse Leaps from Kill Pen to Fame." *Chicago Daily Tribune,* Nov. 8, 1958.

"Douglaston Wins Horse Show Title." *New York Times,* May 5, 1958.

Edwards, Russell. "National Horse Show—Good-by to the Garden." *New York Times,* Oct. 8, 1967.

———. "National Horse Show Here Has a 76-Year History of Strange and Wondrous Things." *New York Times,* Nov. 1, 1958.

"$80 Wonder Horse Worth $25,000: Snowman, the Equine Phenomenon, Stars at Children's Services Horse Show, May 15–17." *Hartford Courant,* May 10, 1959.

"Equestrian Team Will Be Assisted at Fete in Darien." *New York Times,* June 11, 1961.

"Fairfield County Hunt." *Chronicle of the Horse,* July 11, 1958.

"FBI Rangers View G.I. Horse Trading." *New York Times,* May 14, 1946.

Fitzgerald, F. Scott. *The Great Gatsby.* 1925. Reprint, New York: Scribner, 1999.

"Five Cubans Stage Protest of Countrymen in Show." *New York Times,* Nov. 5, 1958.

Fleming, Geoffrey. *Images of America: St. James.* Charleston: Arcadia Publishing, 2002.

"Fly Your Bloodstock." Advertisement. *Chronicle of the Horse,* Oct. 31, 1958.

Forgeron, Harry V. "Town Puts Heart in Its Horse Show: Port Washington Lions Find Willing Hands for Event That Built Ballfield." *New York Times,* May 15, 1960.

Franck, Peggy Miller. *Prides Crossing: The Unbridled Life and Impatient Times of Eleo Sears.* Beverly, Mass.: Commonwealtrh Editions, 2009.

Fussell, Paul. *Class: A Guide Through the American Status System.* New York: Touchstone, 1992.

Gava, Adrienne E. *Dark Horse: A Life of Anna Sewell.* Thrupp, U.K.: Sutton, 2004.

"Gayford, Canada, First in Jumping." *New York Times,* Nov. 4, 1960.

"Genuine Risk Dies; Filly Won Kentucky Derby." *New York Times,* Aug. 18, 2008.

"German Rider Clinches Laurels in Washington Show." *New York Times,* Oct. 15, 1958.

Gish, Noel J. *Looking Back Through the Lens.* Smithtown, N.Y.: Smithtown Historical Society, 1996.

Goldstein, Andrew. "Joe Goldstein, Dogged New York Sports Promoter, Dies at 81." *New York Times,* Feb. 15, 2009.

Gould, John. "Hoss Trading: A Lesson for Diplomats." *New York Times Magazine,* Nov. 16, 1947.

Green, Ben K. *Horse Tradin'.* New York: Alfred A. Knopf, 1963.

"Green Is Injured in Horse Show Test." *New York Times,* Sept. 16, 1955.

Greene, Ann Norton. *Horses at Work: Harnessing Power in Industrial America.* Cambridge, Mass.: Harvard University Press, 2008.

"Grim Reaper at National." *Chronicle of the Horse,* Nov. 21, 1958.

Halberstam, David. *The Fifties.* New York: Random House, 1993.

"Harold S. Vanderbilt and Miss Sears." *New York Times,* Aug. 23, 1911.

Harris, Bradley. "The Early Beginnings of the Smithtown Hunt." *Smithtown News,* July 31, 2008.

————. "Growing Up on the La Rosa Estate in Nissequogue." *Smithtown News,* Sept. 18, 2008.

————. "James Clinch Smith Brings Polo to Smithtown." *Smithtown News,* Dec. 4, 2008.

————. "The Knox School Finds a Home in Nissequogue." *Smithtown News,* Sept. 25, 2008.

————. "Lathrop Brown Estate, a Southern Colonial Mansion," *Smithtown News,* Aug. 28, 2008.

————. "Ponies Once Pranced at St. James Driving Park." *Smithtown News,* Nov. 27, 2008.

———. "The Smithtown Horse Show." *Smithtown News,* Jan. 8, 2009.

———. "The Smithtown Polo Club." *Smithtown News,* Jan. 1, 2009.

———. "Snowman, the Cinderella Horse of Hollandia Farms." *Smithtown News,* July 10, 2008.

———. "Still Tracking Foxes in the Smithtown Hunt." *Smithtown News,* Aug. 21, 2008.

Higgins, Alice. "Deutschland über Alles: At Brand-New Washington Show, Germans Collected everything but the Tickets." *Sports Illustrated,* Oct. 27, 1958.

———. "Exit Jumping: Andante, an Aged Prima Donna, Begins Her Last Season with a Flamboyant Win at Devon." *Sports Illustrated,* June 20, 1960.

———. "German Cliffhanger." *Sports Illustrated,* Nov. 24, 1958.

———. "Revival of an Old Ruckus." *Sports Illustrated,* Nov. 14, 1960.

———. "The 67th National Horse Show Had Some Great Horses, Some Thrilling Riders, and Some Unexpected Light Moments." *Sports Illustrated,* Nov. 21, 1955.

———. "Thinker on Horseback." *Sports Illustrated,* Dec. 15, 1958.

———. "The Year of the Jumpers: A Spectacular Open Event in New York Tops a Season of Excellent Performances Around the Country by American and Foreign Horses." *Sports Illustrated,* Nov. 20, 1961.

Higginson, A. Henry, and Julian Ingersoll Chamberlain. *The Hunts of the United States and Canada: Their Masters, Hounds and Histories.* Boston: Frank L. Wiles, 1908.

Hopper, Hedda. "Hollywood," *Hartford Courant,* Nov. 17, 1960.

"Horse Saved from Execution Becomes Champion." *Bridgeport Day,* Nov. 7, 1958.

"Horses for Sale at Auction." *Horse Magazine,* April 1956.

"Horse Show Begins, U.S. Riders Featured." *Spokesman-Review,* Nov. 1, 1959.

"Horse Show Ends with Many Fetes." *New York Times,* Nov. 13, 1957.

"Horse Showing Is a Grim Business." *Palm Beach Post,* Nov. 17, 1962.

"Horse-Show Jumping Taken by Uncle Max." *New York Times,* Oct. 21, 1962.

"Horses to Be Improved; Federal Authorities, Through Remount Program, to Aid Breeders." *New York Times,* June 8, 1919.

"Horse That Jumps: From the Slaughterhouse to the Motion Picture Screen." *Fitchburg Sentinel,* December 30, 1959.

Hunter, Jane. *How Young Ladies Became Girls.* New Haven: Yale University Press, 2003.

"Hunter Tests Led by Paxson Entry." *New York Times,* June 14, 1959.

Igou, Brad. "An Amishman Talks About Horses." *Amish Country News,* Winter 1996.

"In the Country." *Chronicle of the Horse,* Dec. 1, 1959.

"Jumper Windsor Castle Is Sold in $50,000 Deal." *New York Times,* Nov. 6, 1959.

"Jumping King Snow Man Is Hurt in Fall." *Chicago Daily Tribune,* June 26, 1960.

"Junk Wagon Horse Takes a Fling at Broadway Chase." *New York Times,* Apr. 17, 1956.

Kluger, Richard. *The Paper: The Life and Death of the "New York Herald Tribune."* New York: Alfred A. Knopf, 1986.

Kunhardt, Philip B. "The Farm Horse That Became a Champion." *Animals You Will Never Forget.* Pleasantville, N.Y.: Reader's Digest Books, 1969.

Lafrenz, Marie C. "Horse Show Publicity." *The Whole Horse Catalogue.* Edited by Steven D. Price. New York: Fireside, 1998.

———. "Increase in Number of Thoroughbreds." *New York Herald Tribune,* Mar. 6, 1960.

———. "Professional Versus Amateur." *New York Herald Tribune,* Apr. 19, 1960.

"Lakeville." *Chronicle of the Horse,* Aug. 15, 1958.

Langdon, John. *Horses, Oxen, and Technological Innovation.* Cambridge: Cambridge University Press, 1986.

Leerhson, Charles. *Crazy Good: The True Story of Dan Patch, the Most Famous Horse in America.* New York: Simon & Schuster, 2009.

Lipsyte, Robert. "Joey Goldstein." Sports of the Times. *New York Times,* Mar. 18, 1969.

Littauer, Mary Aiken. "Whither Horse Shows." *Chronicle of the Horse,* Sept. 19, 1958.

Littauer, Vladimir S. *Common Sense Horsemanship.* New York: Van Nostrand, 1951.

———. *Jumping the Horse.* New York: Derrydale, 1931.

Livingston, Phil, and Ed Roberts. *War Horse: Mounting the Cavalry with America's Finest Horses.* Albany, Tex.: Bright Sky Press, 2003.

"Local Riders and Mounts Take Part in International Show." *Long Islander,* Nov. 14, 1958.

Longrigg, Roger. *The Complete History of Fox Hunting.* New York: Clarkson Potter, 1975.

Lucey, Virginia. "Afternoon Events Halted by Rain." *Hartford Courant,* Sept. 28, 1958.

———. "Benefit Horse Show Opens with Jumpers." *Hartford Courant,* May 16, 1959.

———. "Saddle and Spur." *Hartford Courant,* Oct. 5, 1958.

———. "Saddle and Spur." *Hartford Courant,* Nov. 16, 1958.

———. "Saddle and Spur." *Hartford Courant,* Sept. 6, 1959.

———. "Saddle and Spur." *Hartford Courant,* Nov. 1, 1959.

———. "Saddle and Spur." *Hartford Courant,* Nov. 11, 1959.

———. "Saddle and Spur." *Hartford Courant,* Nov. 22, 1959.

———. "Saddle and Spur." *Hartford Courant,* July 24, 1960.

———. "Two Jumpers Capture Honors at Horse Show." *Hartford Courant,* May 18, 1959.

Lyon, Robert. *On Any Given Sunday: A Life of Bert Bell.* Philadelphia: Temple University Press, 2010.

Mancuso, Lisa. "Thrill of the Hunt: Equestrian Honored with Club Lifetime Award." *Smithtown News,* Apr. 1, 2010.

"Mann Horses Pace Show." *New York Times*, Sept. 5, 1957.

McCardle, Dorothy. "Jumping Horse Cops Fame, Wealth." *Washington Post*, Sept. 18, 1960.

McGowan, Dean. "Pat Smythe, Ace Woman Rider, Takes U.S. Officials Over Jumps." *New York Times*, Nov. 5, 1957.

———. "Steinkraus Scores for Third U.S. Jumping Triumph at National Horse Show." *New York Times*, Nov. 7, 1958.

———. "West Germany's Thiedemann Scores Twice at Garden." *New York Times*, Nov. 11, 1958.

"McLain Street Wins Open Jumper Title." *New York Times*, Sept. 10, 1961.

McShane, Clay, and Joel A. Tarr. *The Horse in the City: Living Machines in the Nineteenth Century*. Baltimore: Johns Hopkins University Press, 2007.

Meagher, Thomas. *The Gigantic Book of Horse Wisdom*. New York: Skyhorse, 2007.

"Mickey Walsh, Horse Trainer, 86." *New York Times*, Aug. 19, 1983.

Mischka, Joseph. *The Percheron Horse in America*. Whitewater, Wisc.: Heart Prairie Press, 1991.

"Miss Lida Fleitmann, Horsewoman, to Wed." *New York Times*, Feb. 1, 1922.

"Miss Maloney Guides Kitalpha to Pony Crown at Southampton." *New York Times*, Aug. 19, 1962.

"Miss Payne Rides Mare to 4 Blues." *New York Times*, June 22, 1958.

"Miss Sears Guest of Mrs. Belmont." *New York Times*, Aug. 14, 1911.

"Miss Sears Not Engaged; Member of Her Family Denies She Is Betrothed to Harold S. Vanderbilt." *New York Times*, Aug. 11, 1911.

"Miss Sears' Skating Outfit; She Prefers Cap and Muff of Knitted Wool for Cold Days." *New York Times*, Feb. 19, 1912.

"Miss Sears Turns Runaway, Swerves Animal from Bolting Among Spectators at Lawn Tennis Match." *New York Times*, Sept. 28, 1911.

Montgomery, Rutherford. *Snowman*. New York: Duell, Sloan, and Pearce, 1962.

Moore, Major-General Sir John. *Our Servant the Horse: An Appreciation of the Part Played by Animals During the War, 1914–1918*. London: H & W Brown, 1931.

"More Children Saddle Up Each Year Despite Cost." *New York Times*, Nov. 5, 1957.

Morenstern, George. "Minding My Own Business: Let Us Now Praise Famous Horses." *Chicago Tribune*, June 17, 1973.

"National Horse Show." *Chronicle of the Horse*, Nov. 21, 1958.

"National Horse Show Begins Run." *Schenectady Gazette*, Nov. 4, 1958.

"National's Diamond Jubilee." *Chronicle of the Horse*, Sept. 12, 1958.

"Naute Mia Heads Working Hunters." *New York Times*, Sept. 7, 1958.

"New Country Club Piping Rock Will Be Devoted to Sports Chiefly with Horses." *New York Times*, Oct. 9, 1911.

"New Look at the Capitol Armory." *Lewiston Daily Sun*, Jan. 12, 1961.

"The 1958 PHA Trophy." Photograph with caption. *Chronicle of the Horse*, Oct. 10, 1958.

"Nosing Around." *St. James Times*, July 22, 1993.

"The Not-So-Grave Tale of the Cinderella Horse." *St. James Times-Beacon,* Mar. 14, 1991.

Obituary, Marie C. Lafrenz. *US Eventing News,* May 18, 2007.

O'Dea, Joseph. *DVM, Olympic Vet.* Geneseo, N.Y.: Castlerea Press, 1996.

The Official Report of the Organizing Committee for the XIV Olympiad. London: The Organizing Committee for the XIV Olympiad, 1948.

"Old Nag's Long Jump from Plow Horse; Discarded Farm Horse Finds Unexpected Fame," *Life,* Nov. 9, 1959.

"Open Jumping Goes to Windsor Castle." *New York Times,* Aug. 12, 1960.

Parker, Betsy Burke. "Living Legends: Harry De Leyer Riding into the Future in the Saddle of His Past." *In and Around Horse Country,* Feb.–Mar. 2009.

"Paxson's Gelding Takes Third Blue; Flying Curlew Sets Pace in Piping Rock Fixture; Snowman Triumphs." *New York Times,* Sept. 17, 1960.

"Peter Gunn Scores in Fairfield Show." *New York Times,* Jun. 25, 1961.

"Petersen Gelding Wins Hunter Prize." *New York Times,* Aug. 20, 1962.

"Petersen Horse Captures Trophy." *New York Times,* Aug. 7, 1960.

"Piping Rock Horse Show." Photograph with caption. *Chronicle of the Horse,* Oct. 3, 1958.

"Piping Rock's Millionaire's Colony Opens New Club." *New York Times,* May 26, 1912.

"Presentation of the 1958 PHA Award." Photograph with caption. *Chronicle of the Horse,* Nov. 21, 1958.

"Promissory Notes of the Past Screen Season." *New York Times,* Dec. 31, 1961.

Rendel, John. "8-Day Horse Show Opens Here Today; Jumping Teams Will Parade Around the Garden Ring in Formal Ceremony." *New York Times,* Nov. 5, 1957.

———. "German Riders Score in Horse Show; 24-Fault Effort Wins Nations Cup." *New York Times,* 1958.

———. "Irish Rider Takes a First and a Second as National Horse Show Opens Here." *New York Times,* Nov. 1, 1961.

———. "Irish Team Wins Good Will Challenge Trophy in Horse Show at Garden." *New York Times,* Nov. 4, 1961.

———. "Stumble Results in a Broken Neck." *New York Times,* Nov. 5, 1960.

———. "United States Team Retires Special Challenge Trophy at Show in Garden." *New York Times,* Nov. 5, 1958.

———. "Wiley Is Winner Second Straight Year." *New York Times,* Nov. 5, 1958.

Rodenas, Paula. *The de Nemethy Years: One Man's Influence on American Riding.* New York: Arco, 1983.

"Roy Campanella Continues to Gain; Injured Catcher Gets Some Feeling Back in Body, but Legs Still Paralyzed." *New York Times,* Jan. 31, 1958.

Rule Book. American Horse Shows Association, 1958.

Rust, Richard. *Renegade Champion: The Unlikely Rise of Fitzrada.* Lanham, Md.: Taylor Trade, 2008.

Safire, William. "Locust Valley Lockjaw." On Language. *New York Times Magazine,* Jan. 18, 1987.

"Sands Point." *Chronicle of the Horse,* June 22, 1958.

Scanlan, Lawrence. *Secretariat: The Horse That God Built.* New York: Thomas Dunne Books, 2007.

Self, Margaret Cabell. *The Horseman's Encyclopedia.* New York: A. S. Barnes, 1946.

"Sidelights of the National." *Chronicle of the Horse,* Nov. 21, 1958.

"65th National Horse Show to Begin an Eight-Day Run at Garden on Tuesday." *New York Times,* Nov. 1, 1953.

Smith, Margaret L. "National Horse Show." *Chronicle of the Horse,* Nov. 21, 1958.

———. "Penna National Horse Show." *Chronicle of the Horse,* Nov. 7, 1958.

———. Scrapbooks. In the collection of the National Sporting Library, Middleburg, Virginia.

"Smithtown." *Chronicle of the Horse,* Sept. 12, 1958.

"Snowman and Pedro Capture Jumper Crowns in Connecticut." *New York Times,* June 27, 1960.

"Snowman Captures Horse Show Honors." *New York Times,* May 22, 1961.

"Snowman Featured in Benefit Next Week." *New York Observer,* June 16, 1963.

"Snowman First in Jumper Class, Windsor Castle Second in 1959 Ranking." *New York Times,* Jan. 3, 1960.

"Snow Man First in Jumping Event; Beats Diamant for Title in Piping Rock Horse Show." *New York Times,* Sept. 15, 1958.

"Snow Man Gains Jumper Laurels." *New York Times,* May 8, 1961.

"Snowman Gives Exhibition Today in Horse Show." *Washington Post,* Sept. 24, 1960.

"Snowman Has a Rival, and She's in His Own Stable." *Port Washington News,* Nov. 5, 1959.

"Snow Man Injured in Jump." *New York Times,* June 26, 1960.

"Snowman Leaves Memories in Hearts of Horsemen." *Smithtown Messenger,* Oct. 3, 1974.

"Snowman, Legendary Jumper, Retired to St. James Pasture." *Smithtown Messenger,* Nov. 20, 1969.

"Snow Man Scores in L.I. Horse Show," *New York Times,* June 9, 1958.

"Snowman Takes Jumper Honors; De Leyer's Gelding Defeats High Tore for Open Title in North Shore Show." *New York Times,* Sept. 13, 1959.

"Snowman Tops at Ox Ridge." *Bridgeport Post,* June 20, 1960.

"Snowman Triumphs in Second Jump-off." *New York Times,* June 24, 1960.

"Snowman Winning Honors in National Horse Show." *Smithtown Messenger,* Nov. 2, 1961.

"Society Aids at Piping Rock Club." *New York Times,* Oct. 5, 1912.

"Society Amateurs in the Saddle: Piping Rock Horse Show Attracts Hunting Set to Locust Valley Grounds." *New York Times,* Oct. 4, 1913.

"Society: She Ain't What She Used to Be." *Time,* Nov. 9, 1962.

"Sport: Back in the Saddle." *Time,* Nov. 13, 1950.

"Sport: Grand Old Girl." *Time,* Dec. 25, 1939.

"The Sporting Calendar." *Chronicle of the Horse*, Aug. 29, 1958.

Sprague, Kurth. *The National Horse Show: A Centennial History, 1883–1983*. New York: National Horse Show Foundation, 1983.

Steinkraus, William. *Great Horses of the United States Equestrian Team*. New York: Dodd, Mead & Company, 1977.

———. *Riding and Jumping*. Garden City, N.Y.: Doubleday, 1961.

"Steinkraus Captures Jumping Event: Course Cleared in 32.39 Seconds." *New York Times*, Nov. 10, 1969.

"Steinkraus Wins at London Show." *New York Times*, July 21, 1958.

Stoneridge, M. A. *A Horse of Your Own*. Garden City, N.Y.: Doubleday, 1963.

———. "How to Evaluate a Horse for Soundness." In *Practical Horsekeeping*. New York: Doubleday, 1983.

Stott, Bill. "Anthem of 1950s America." http://billstott.blogspot.com/search/label/American%20cultural%20history.

Tantalo, Victor. "Horse Show Promotion." *Chronicle of the Horse*, May 8, 1959.

"Thomas School Team Champions at Knox School Horse Show." *Long Islander*, May 1, 1958.

"Three Blues Won by Mann Entries; Fiore Rides Riviera Wonder and Topper to Victories at Stony Brook Show." *New York Times*, Sept. 6, 1957.

"3 De Leyer Horses Win at Stony Brook." *New York Times*, Sept. 5, 1958.

"Towson Man Wins London Horse Show." *Washington Post*, July 24, 1958.

"U.S. Riders Take Second, Third in Irish Show." *Washington Post*, Aug. 6, 1958.

Van Liew, Barbara F., and Elizabeth Shepherd, eds. *Head of the Harbor: A Journey Through Time*. Laurel, N.Y.: Main Road Books, 2005.

Vecsey, George. "Raceway Era: When Dog Days Became Trotter Nights." *New York Times*, July 22, 1988.

"Walsh's Girls Help Him over Belmont Hurdles; Trainer's Daughters Exercise Horses 6 Days a Week." *New York Times*, May 27, 1958.

Weiler, A. H. "Movie to Relate Story of a Horse; Bob Hope May Play Role of Snowman's Rescuer." *New York Times*, Sept. 25, 1961.

———. "Promissory Notes of the Past Screen Season." *New York Times*, Dec. 31, 1961.

Weiner, Tim. "Robert Lantz, Agent to the Stars, Dies." *New York Times*, Oct. 20, 2007.

White, Claire Nicolas. "Cinderella Horse Stars on L.I." *New York Times*, Oct. 22, 1972.

"Wiley Is Winner Second Straight Year, U.S. Rider Takes West Point Trophy Again at Garden." *New York Times*, Nov. 5, 1958.

"Wiley Triumphs After Jump-off." *New York Times*, Nov. 8, 1959.

"Windsor Castle Takes Jumping Title at Armory." *Washington Post*, Oct. 31, 1960.

"Woman Rider Hurt in Jumping Contest." *New York Times*, Oct. 2, 1915.

Zinsser, William. "The Daily Miracle: Life with the Mavericks and Oddballs at the *Herald Tribune*," *American Scholar*, vol. 77, no. 1 (Winter 2008).

Index

(Page numbers in *italic* refer to illustrations.)

Illustration Credits

Pages iv–v: Photograph by George Silk. Time-Life Pictures/ Getty Images.

Page 14: From the personal collection of Harry de Leyer.

Page 16: From *Rose Leaves*, the Knox School yearbook, 1957, courtesy of Bonnie Cornelius Spitzmiller. Used with the permission of the Knox School.

Page 20: From *Rose Leaves*, the Knox School yearbook, 1957, courtesy of Bonnie Cornelius Spitzmiller. Used with the permission of the Knox School.

Page 37: From *Rose Leaves*, the Knox School yearbook, 1959, courtesy of Bonnie Cornelius Spitzmiller. Used with the permission of the Knox School.

Page 39: From *Rose Leaves*, the Knox School yearbook, 1957, courtesy of Bonnie Cornelius Spitzmiller. Used with the permission of the Knox School.

Page 43: From *Rose Leaves*, the Knox School yearbook, 1959, courtesy of Bonnie Cornelius Spitzmiller. Used with the permission of the Knox School.

Page 50: From *Rose Leaves*, the Knox School yearbook, 1957, courtesy of Bonnie Cornelius Spitzmiller. Used with the permission of the Knox School.

Page 59: From the personal collection of Harry de Leyer.

Page 61: From the personal collection of Harry de Leyer.

Page 62: From the personal collection of Harry de Leyer.

Page 63: From the personal collection of Harry de Leyer.

Page 84: Photograph by George Silk. Time-Life Pictures/Getty Images.

Page 95: Photograph by George Silk. Time-Life Pictures/Getty Images.

Page 110: Photograph by Marshall Hawkins. Distributed by Robert McClanahan.

Page 113: From the personal collection of Harry de Leyer.

Page 131: Photograph by George Silk. Time-Life Pictures/Getty Images.

Page 143: Photograph by George Silk. Time-Life Pictures/Getty Images.

Page 151: © David Stekert of Budd Studios.

Page 155: © David Stekert of Budd Studios.

Page 162: From the personal collection of Harry de Leyer.

Page 165: From the personal collection of Harry de Leyer.

Page 175: From the National Sporting Library & Museum Archives.

Page 179: From the National Sporting Library & Museum Archives.

Page 181: From the National Sporting Library & Museum Archives.

Page 213: Photograph by Stan Wayman. Time-Life Pictures/Getty Images.

Page 214: Photograph by Stan Wayman. Time-Life Pictures/Getty Images.

Page 216: Photograph by Goya Mili. Time-Life Pictures/Getty Images.

Page 245: Photograph by George Silk. Time-Life Pictures/Getty Images.

Page 251: © Bill Ray.

About the Author

ELIZABETH LETTS is the award-winning author of two novels, *Quality of Care* and *Family Planning,* and one children's book, *The Butter Man. Quality of Care* was a Literary Guild, Double-day Book Club, and Books-A-Million Book Club selection. An equestrian from childhood, Letts represented California as a junior equestrian, and was runner-up in the California Horse and Rider of the Year competition. She currently lives with her husband and four children in Baltimore, Maryland.

About the Type

This book was set in Monotype Dante, a typeface designed by Giovanni Mardersteig (1892–1977). Conceived as a private type for the Officina Bodoni in Verona, Italy, Dante was originally cut only for hand composition by Charles Malin, the famous Parisian punch cutter, between 1946 and 1952. Its first use was in an edition of Boccaccio's *Trattatello in laude di Dante* that appeared in 1954. The Monotype Corporation's version of Dante followed in 1957. Though modeled on the Aldine type used for Pietro Cardinal Bembo's treatise *De Aetna* in 1495, Dante is a thoroughly modern interpretation of that venerable face.